Publisher
Robyn Moore

Color
Brian Miller

abstractstudiocomics.com
mail@abstractstudiocomics.com

ECHO
DESERT RUN

by

Terry Moore

p Phi = 22 {1+ [(2/3) / (F1+F2 Phi) + (1/5) / (F3+F4 Phi)
- (1/7) / (F5+F6 Phi)]- [(2/9) / (F7+F8 Phi) + (1/11) / (F9+F10 Phi)
- (1/13) / (F11+F12 Phi)]+ [(2/15) / (F13+F14 Phi)
+ (1/17) / (F15+F16 Phi) - (1/19) / (F17+F18 Phi)]- … }
= 5.083203692....

The Biwabik Sum by Ed Oberg and Jay A. Johnson

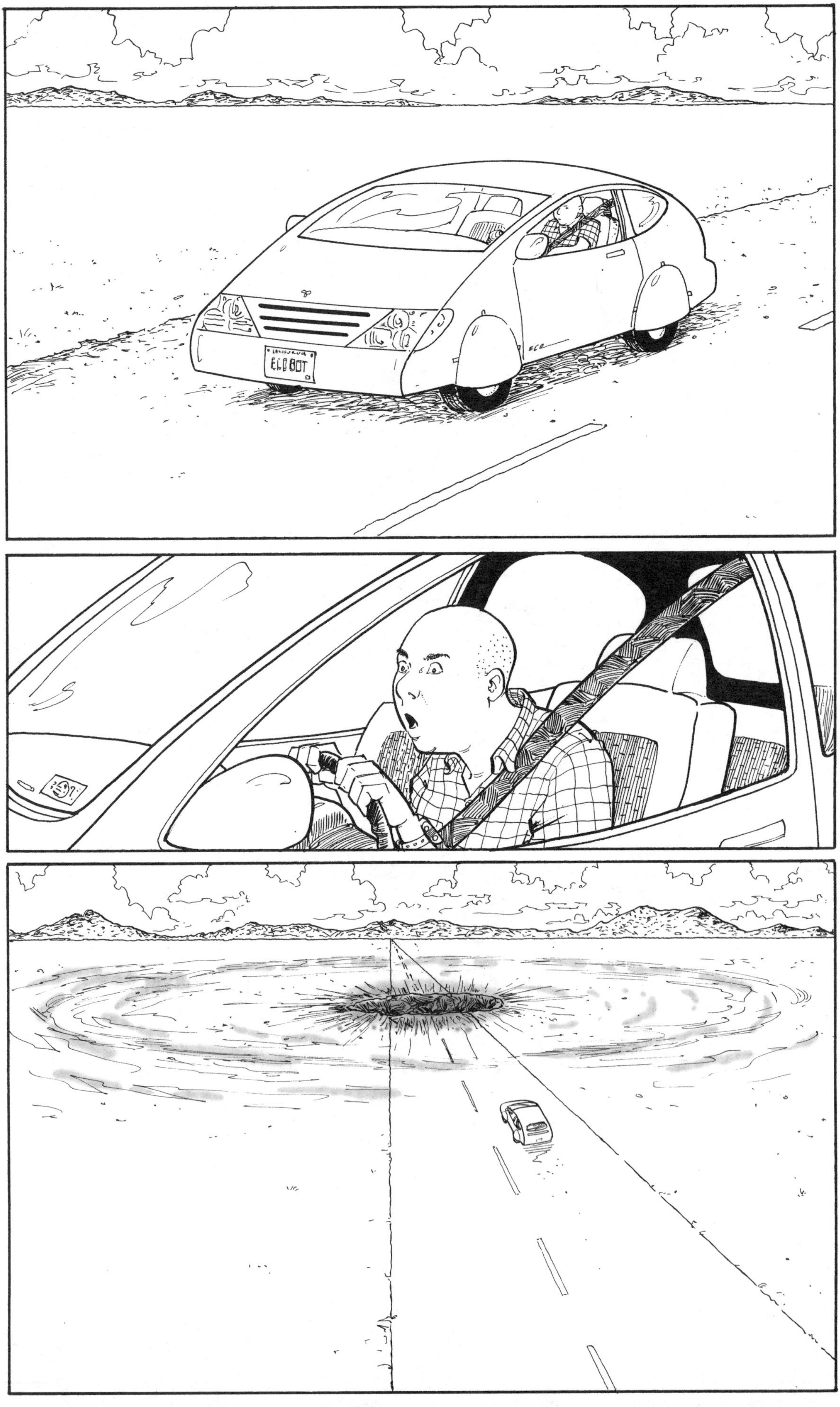
ECOBOT

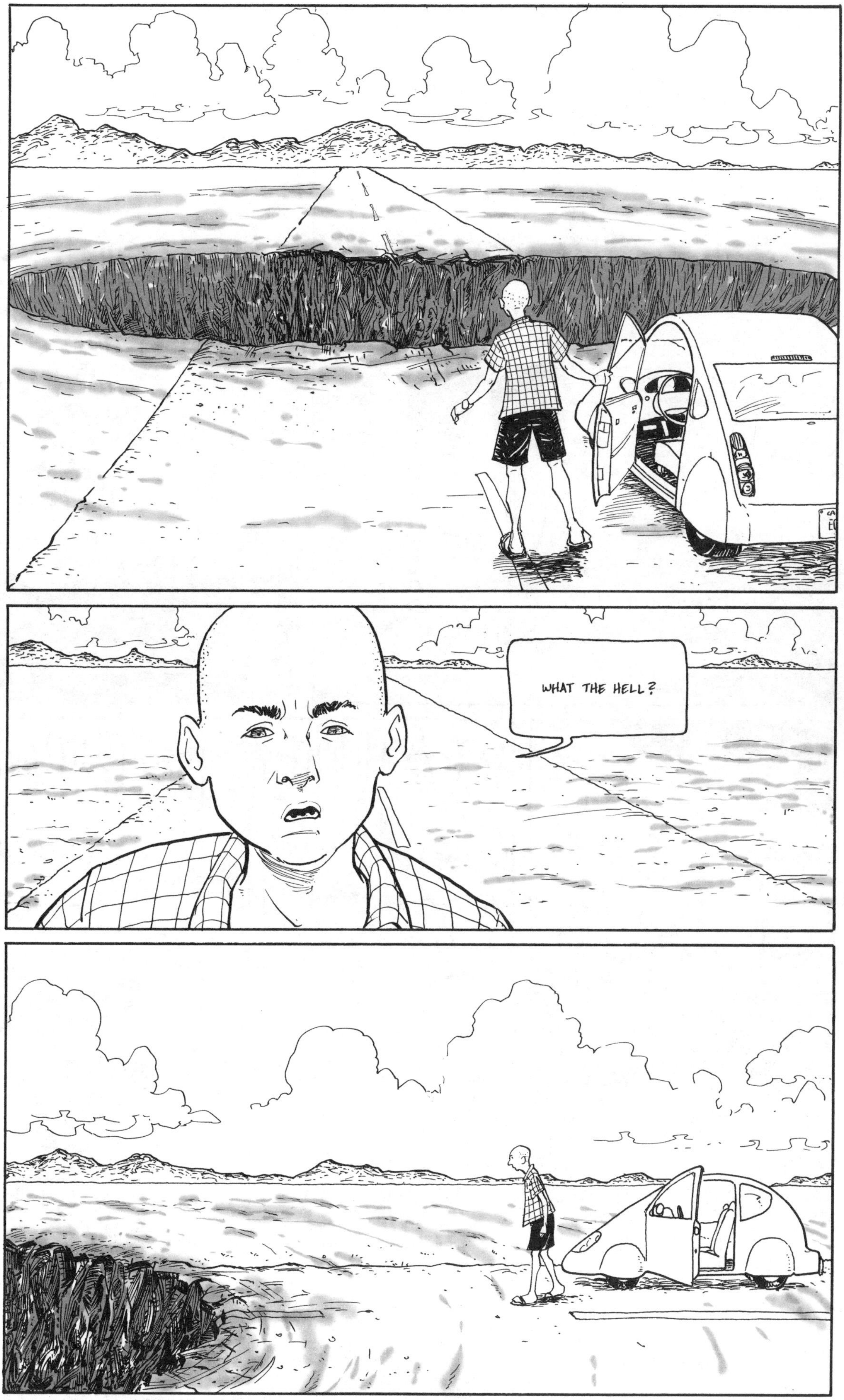
WHAT THE HELL?

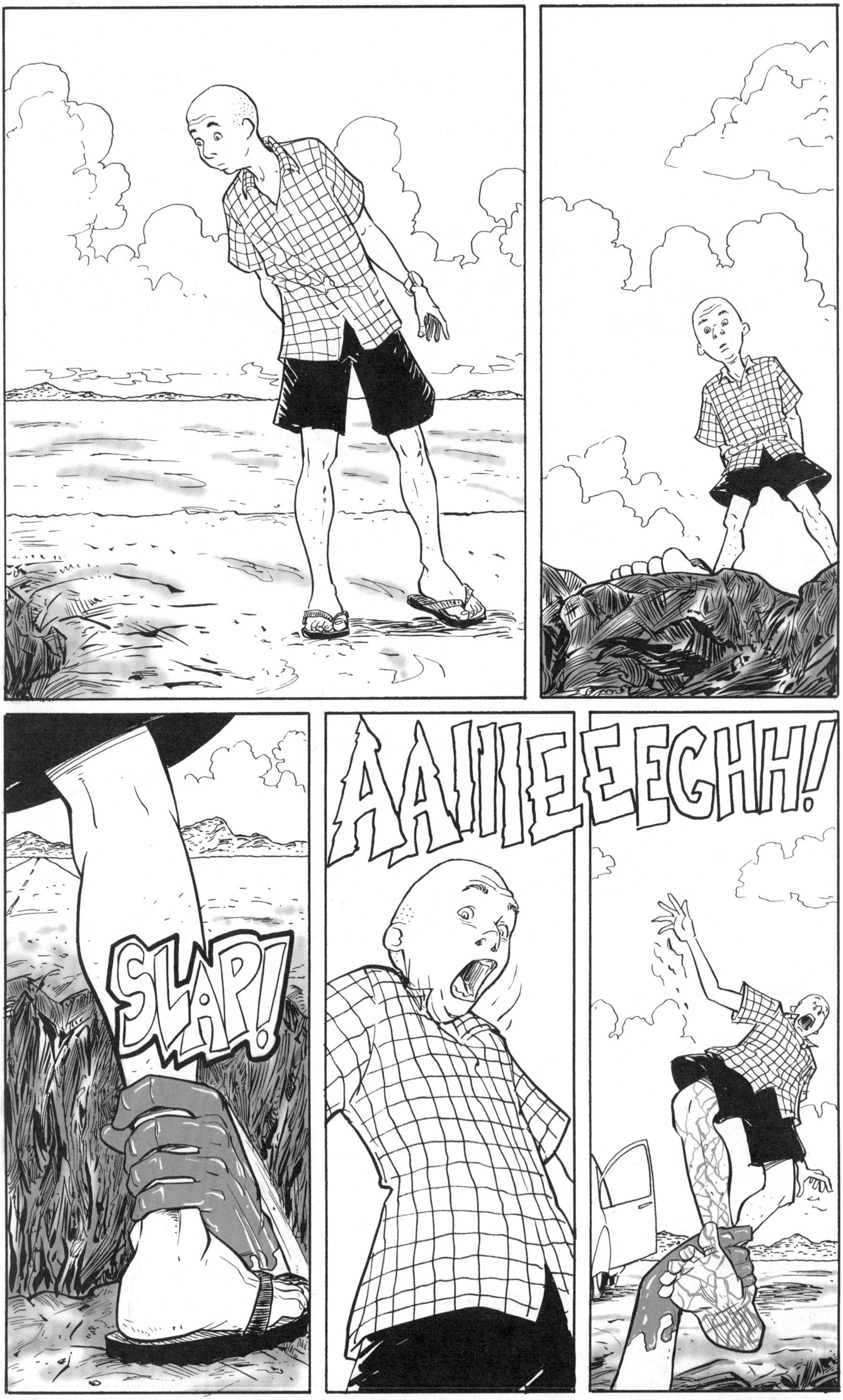
SLAP!
AAIIIEEECHH!

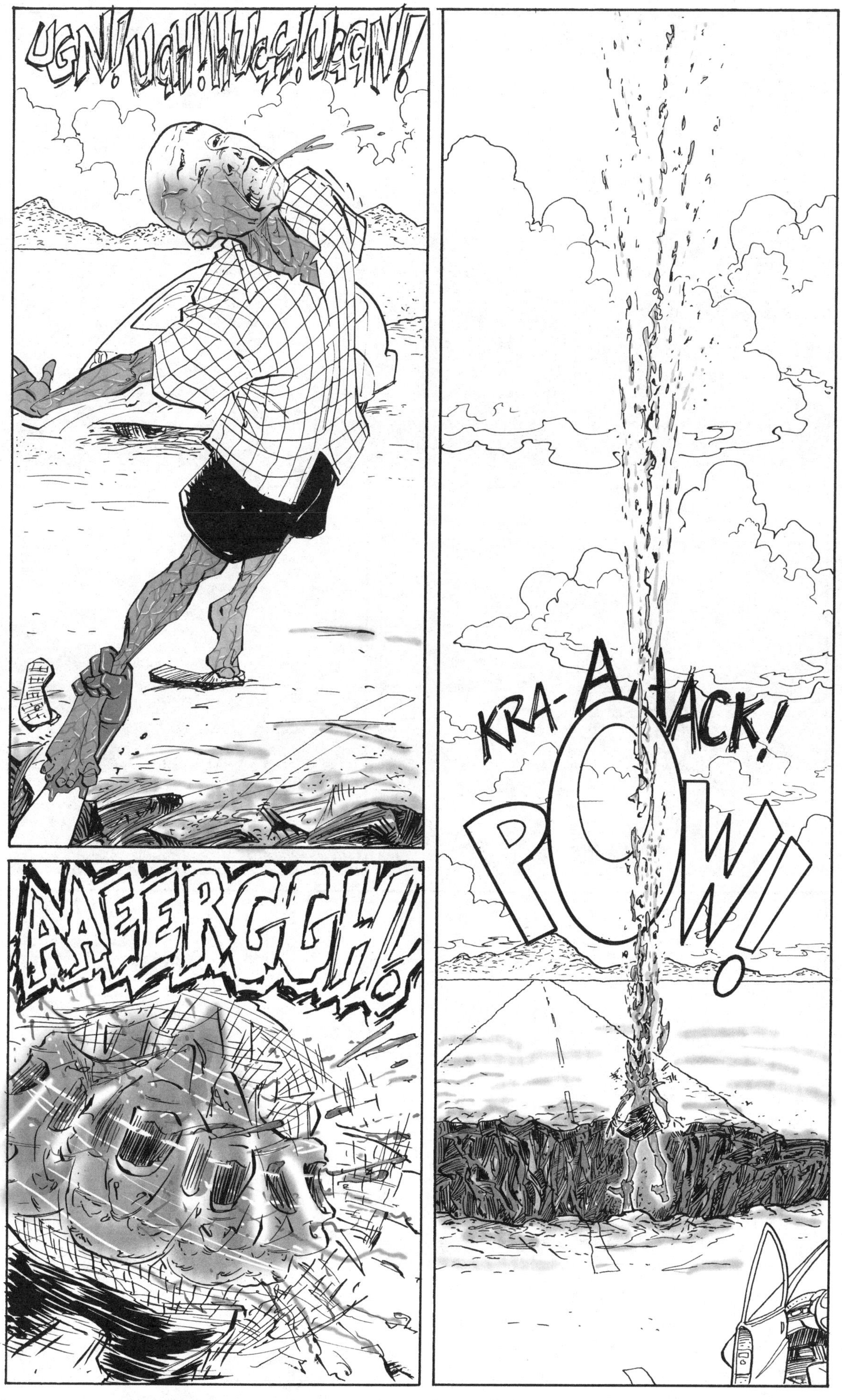
UGN! UGH! HUGG! UGGN!
AAEERGGH!
KRA-ATACK!
POW!

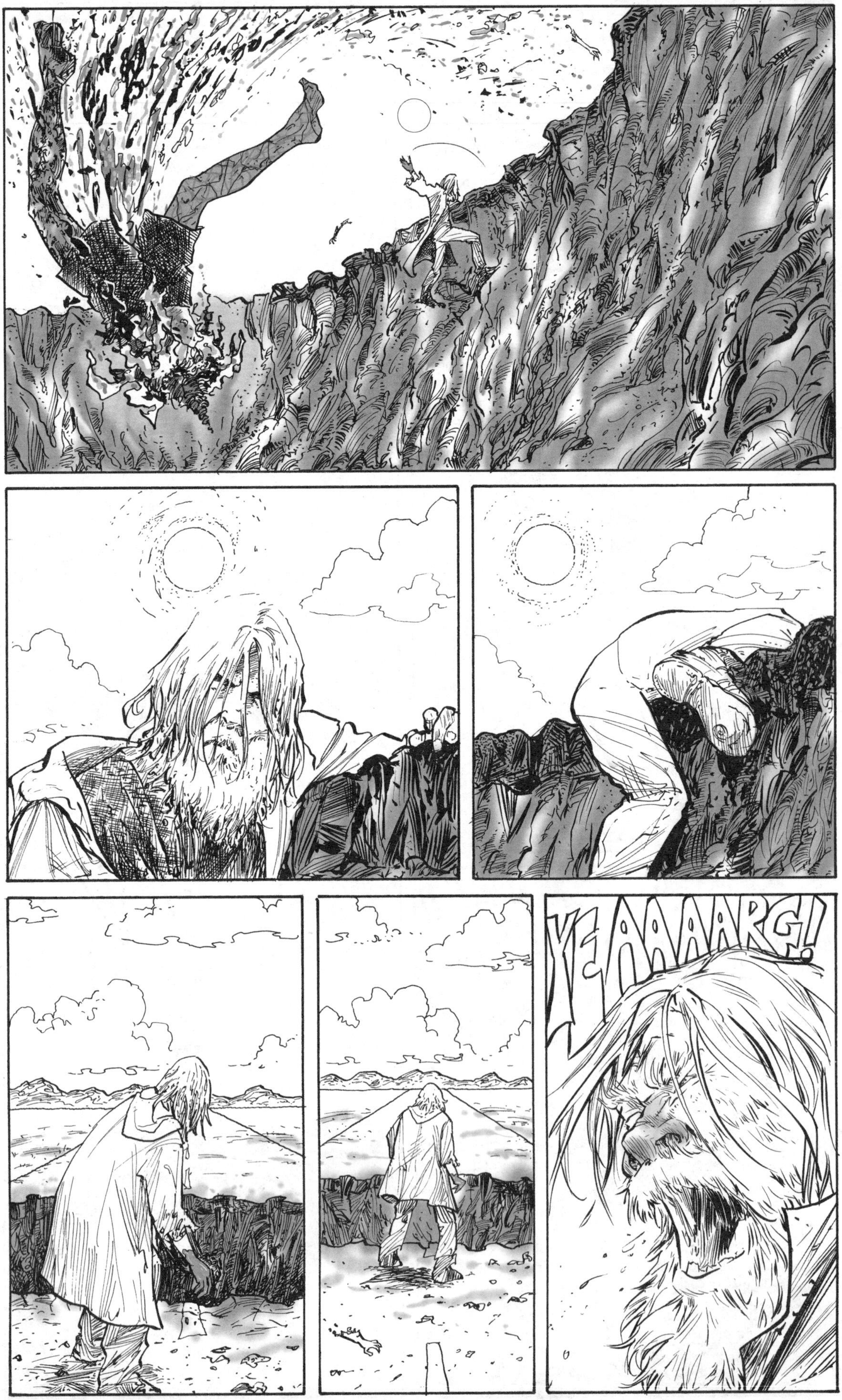
YEAAAARG!

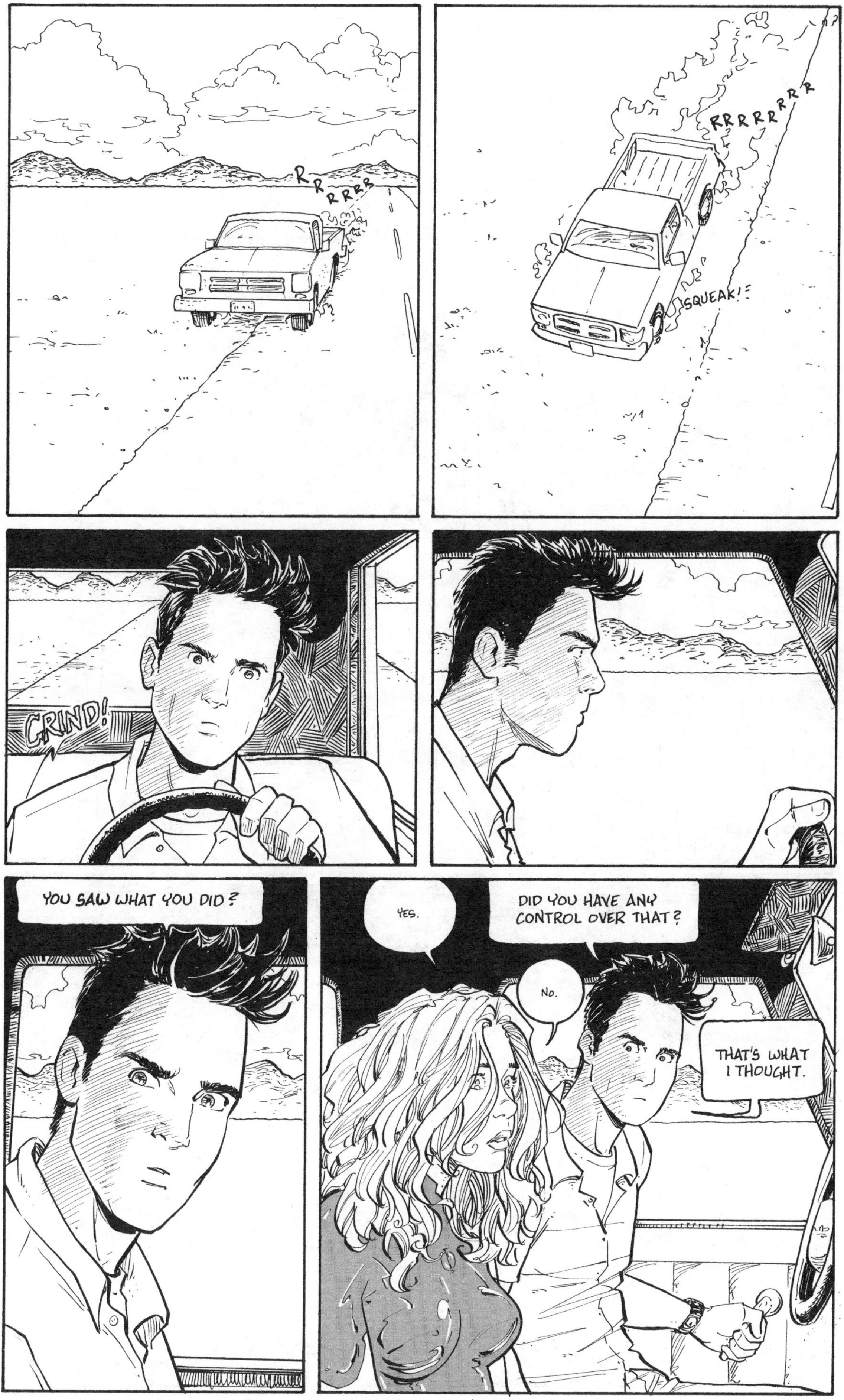
RRRRRR
RRRRRRRRR
SQUEAK!
GRIND!
YOU SAW WHAT YOU DID?
YES.
DID YOU HAVE ANY CONTROL OVER THAT?
NO.
THAT'S WHAT I THOUGHT.

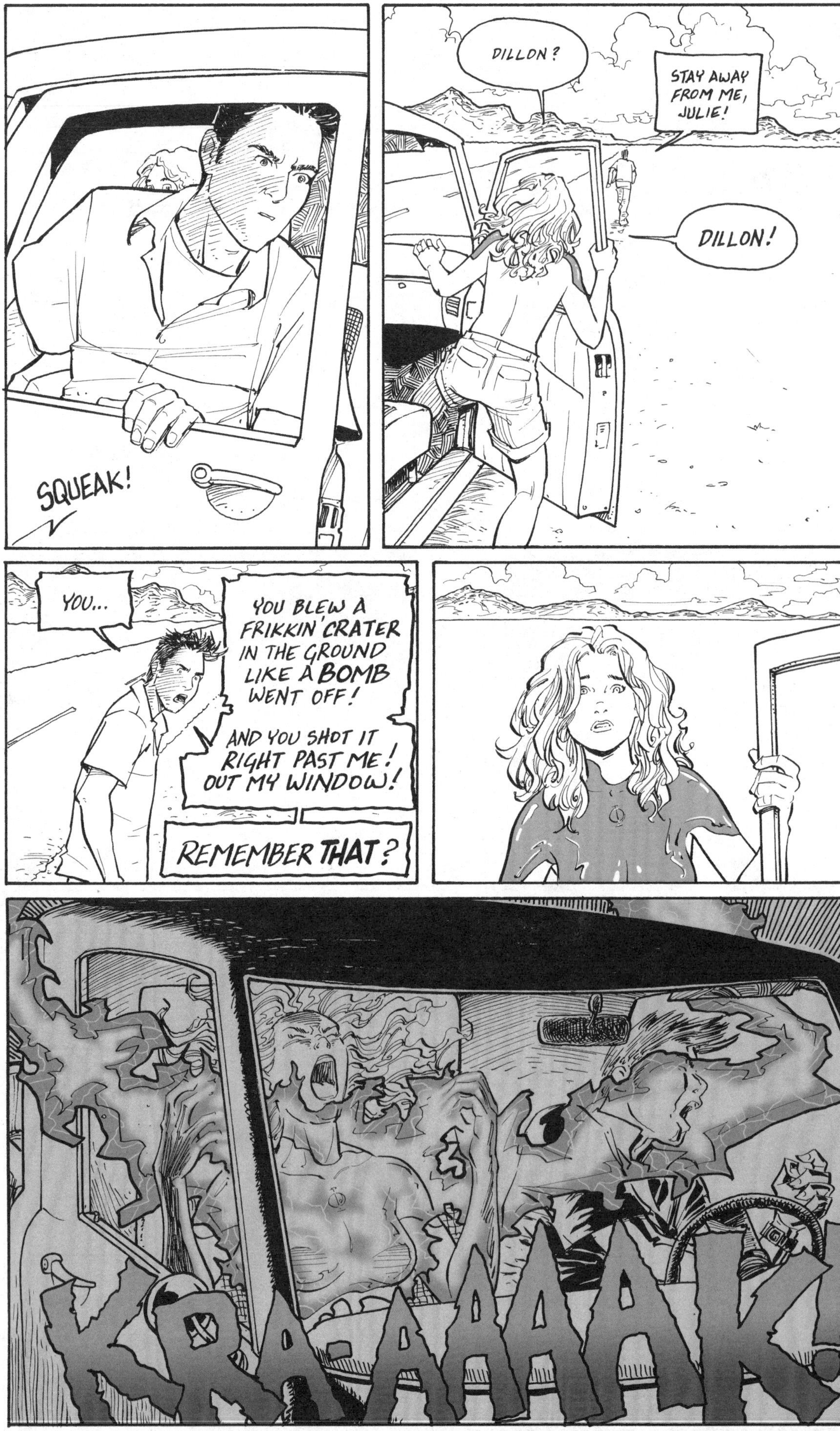
SQUEAK!
DILLON?
STAY AWAY FROM ME, JULIE!
DILLON!
YOU...
YOU BLEW A FRIKKIN' CRATER IN THE GROUND LIKE A BOMB WENT OFF!
AND YOU SHOT IT RIGHT PAST ME! OUT MY WINDOW!
REMEMBER THAT?
KRA-AAAK!

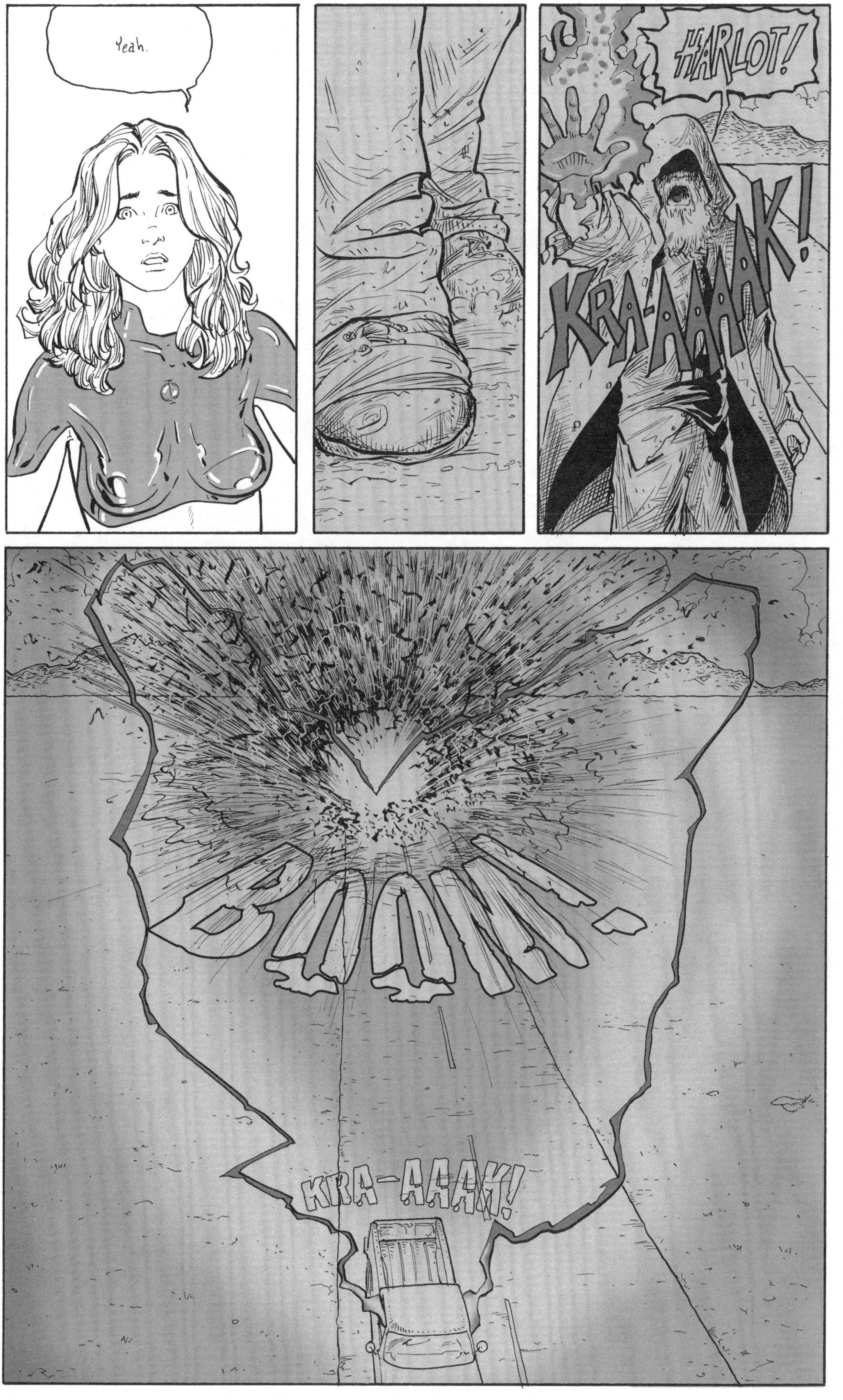
Yeah.
HARLOT!
KRA-AAAAK!
BOOM!
KRA-AAAK!

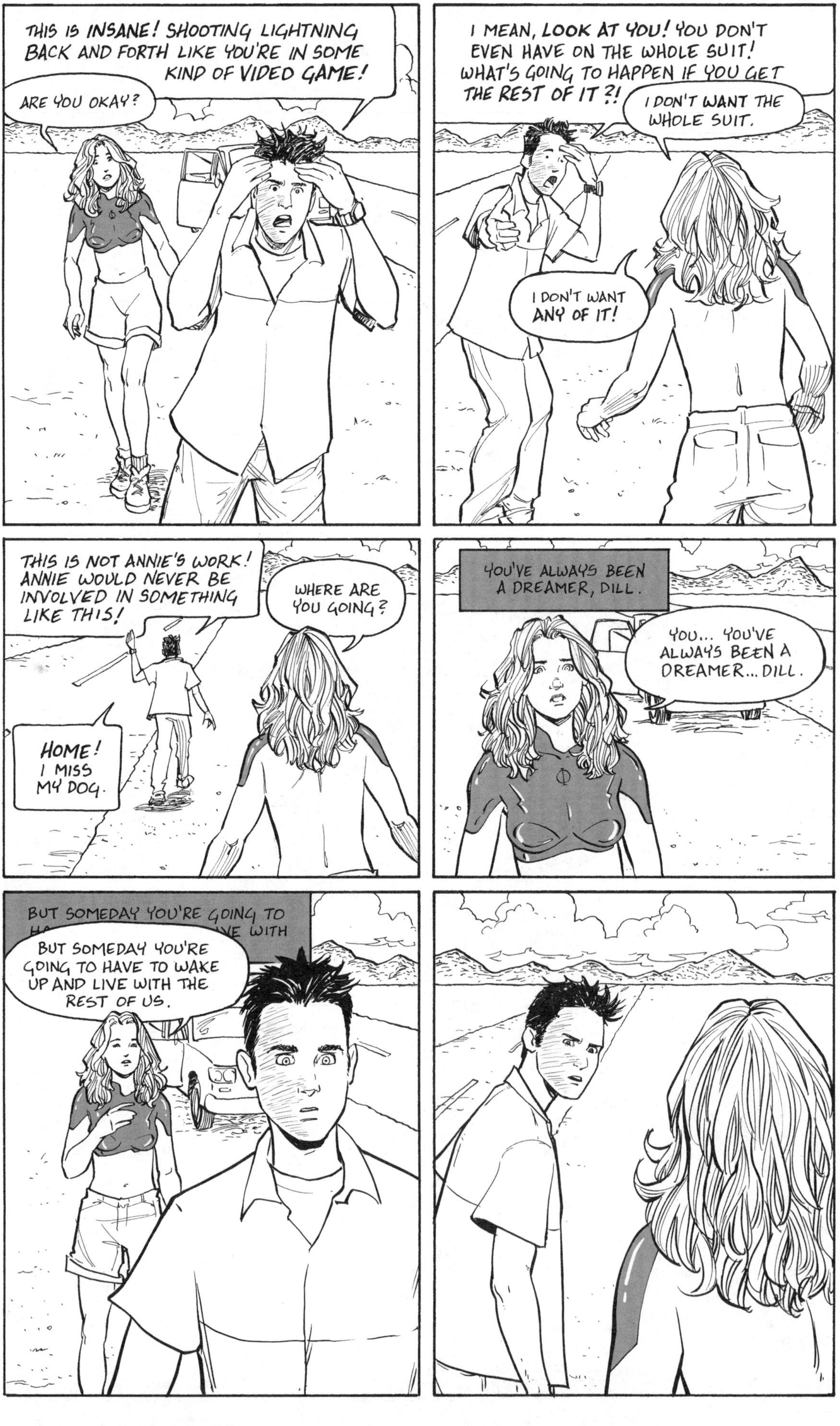
THIS IS INSANE! SHOOTING LIGHTNING BACK AND FORTH LIKE YOU'RE IN SOME KIND OF VIDEO GAME!
ARE YOU OKAY?
I MEAN, LOOK AT YOU! YOU DON'T EVEN HAVE ON THE WHOLE SUIT! WHAT'S GOING TO HAPPEN IF YOU GET THE REST OF IT?!
I DON'T WANT THE WHOLE SUIT.
I DON'T WANT ANY OF IT!
THIS IS NOT ANNIE'S WORK! ANNIE WOULD NEVER BE INVOLVED IN SOMETHING LIKE THIS!
WHERE ARE YOU GOING?
HOME! I MISS MY DOG.
YOU'VE ALWAYS BEEN A DREAMER, DILL.
YOU... YOU'VE ALWAYS BEEN A DREAMER... DILL.
BUT SOMEDAY YOU'RE GOING TO
BUT SOMEDAY YOU'RE GOING TO HAVE TO WAKE UP AND LIVE WITH THE REST OF US.

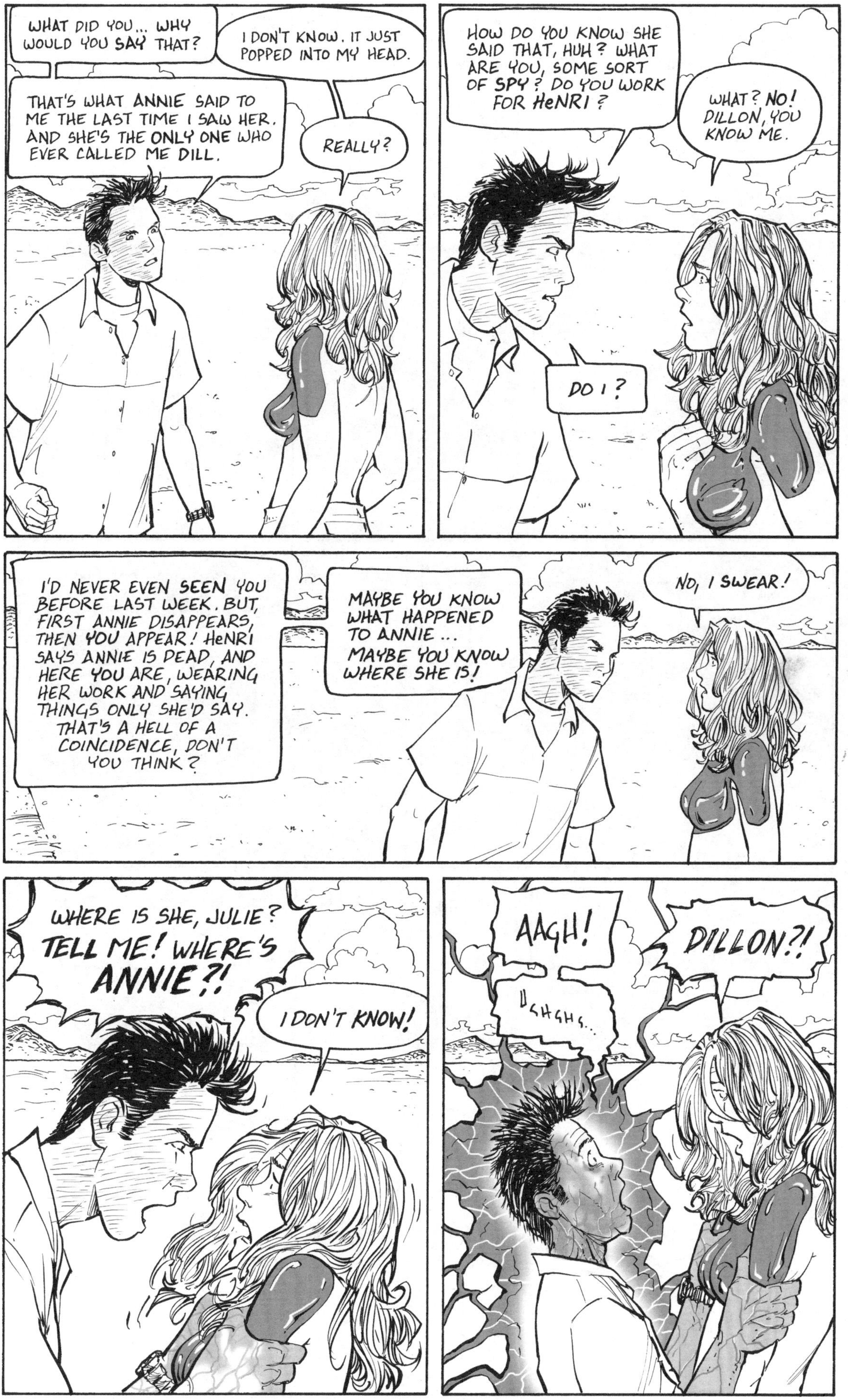
WHAT DID YOU... WHY WOULD YOU SAY THAT?
THAT'S WHAT ANNIE SAID TO ME THE LAST TIME I SAW HER. AND SHE'S THE ONLY ONE WHO EVER CALLED ME DILL.
I DON'T KNOW. IT JUST POPPED INTO MY HEAD.
REALLY?
HOW DO YOU KNOW SHE SAID THAT, HUH? WHAT ARE YOU, SOME SORT OF SPY? DO YOU WORK FOR HeNRI?
DO I?
WHAT? NO! DILLON, YOU KNOW ME.
I'D NEVER EVEN SEEN YOU BEFORE LAST WEEK. BUT, FIRST ANNIE DISAPPEARS, THEN YOU APPEAR! HeNRI SAYS ANNIE IS DEAD, AND HERE YOU ARE, WEARING HER WORK AND SAYING THINGS ONLY SHE'D SAY. THAT'S A HELL OF A COINCIDENCE, DON'T YOU THINK?
MAYBE YOU KNOW WHAT HAPPENED TO ANNIE... MAYBE YOU KNOW WHERE SHE IS!
NO, I SWEAR!
WHERE IS SHE, JULIE? TELL ME! WHERE'S ANNIE?!
I DON'T KNOW!
AAGH!
USHGHS...
DILLON?!

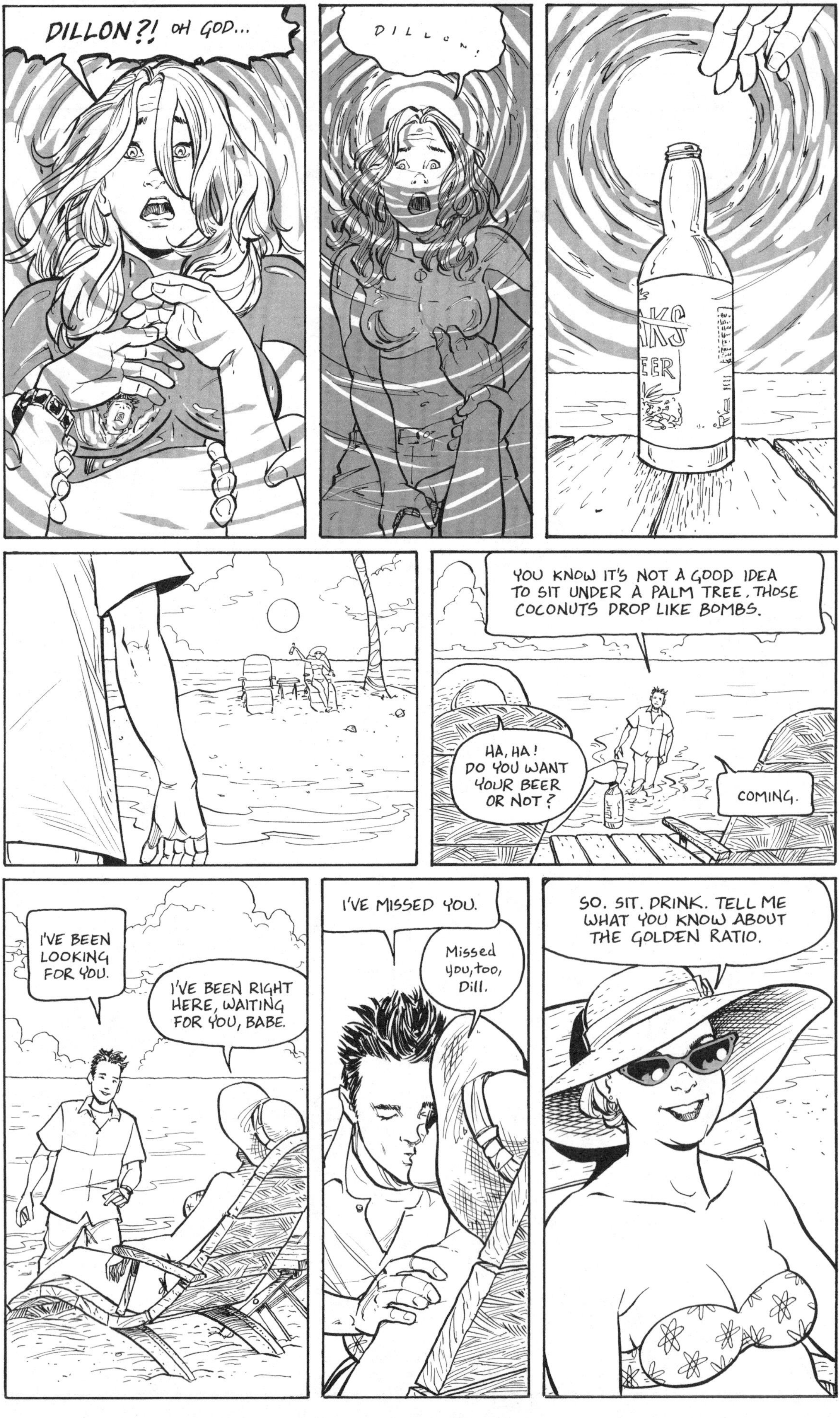
DILLON?! OH GOD...
D I L L O N !
YOU KNOW IT'S NOT A GOOD IDEA TO SIT UNDER A PALM TREE. THOSE COCONUTS DROP LIKE BOMBS.
HA, HA! DO YOU WANT YOUR BEER OR NOT?
COMING.
I'VE BEEN LOOKING FOR YOU.
I'VE BEEN RIGHT HERE, WAITING FOR YOU, BABE.
I'VE MISSED YOU.
Missed you, too, Dill.
SO. SIT. DRINK. TELL ME WHAT YOU KNOW ABOUT THE GOLDEN RATIO.

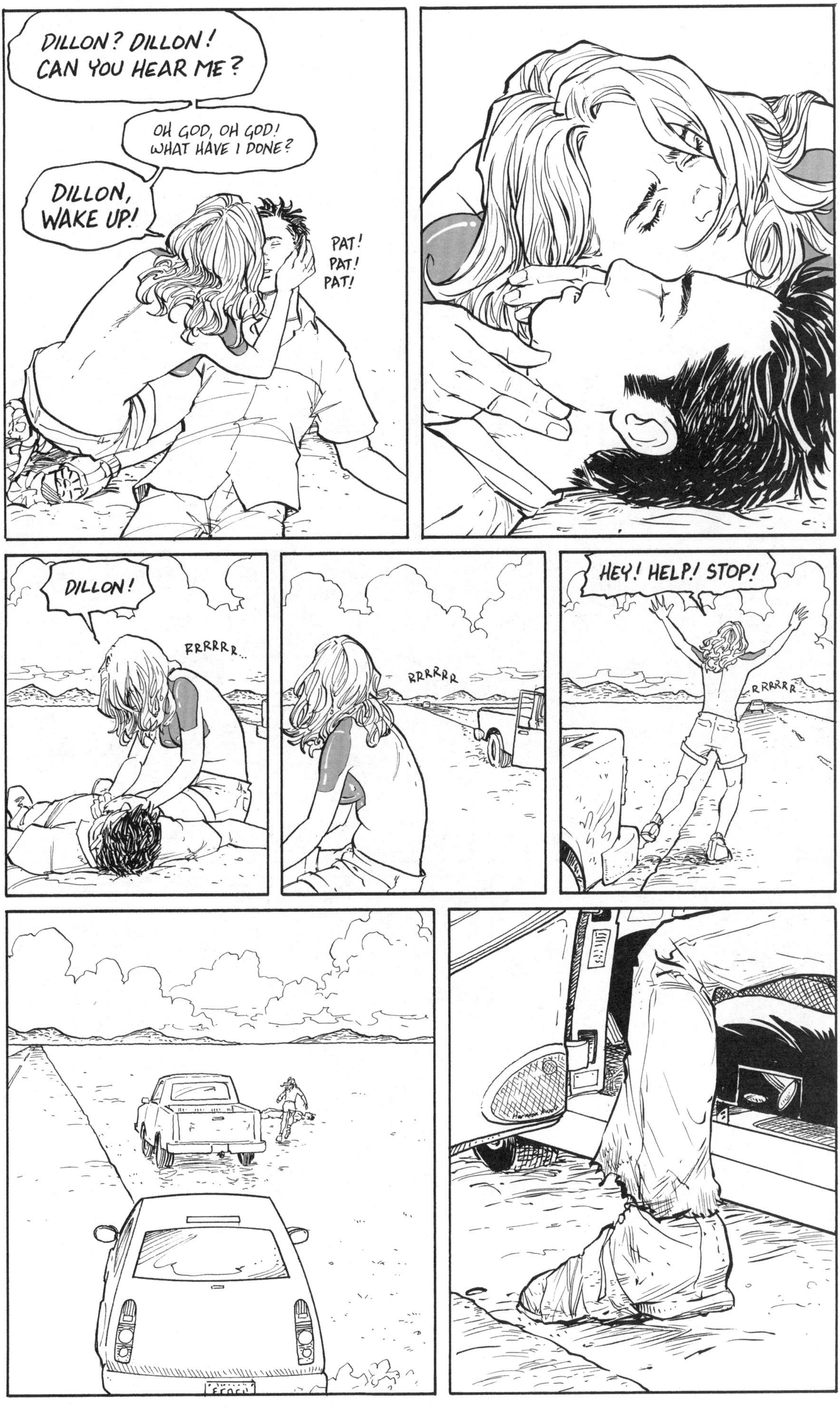
DILLON? DILLON!
CAN YOU HEAR ME?
OH GOD, OH GOD!
WHAT HAVE I DONE?
DILLON,
WAKE UP!
PAT!
PAT!
PAT!
DILLON!
RRRRRR...
RRRRRR
HEY! HELP! STOP!
RRRRRR

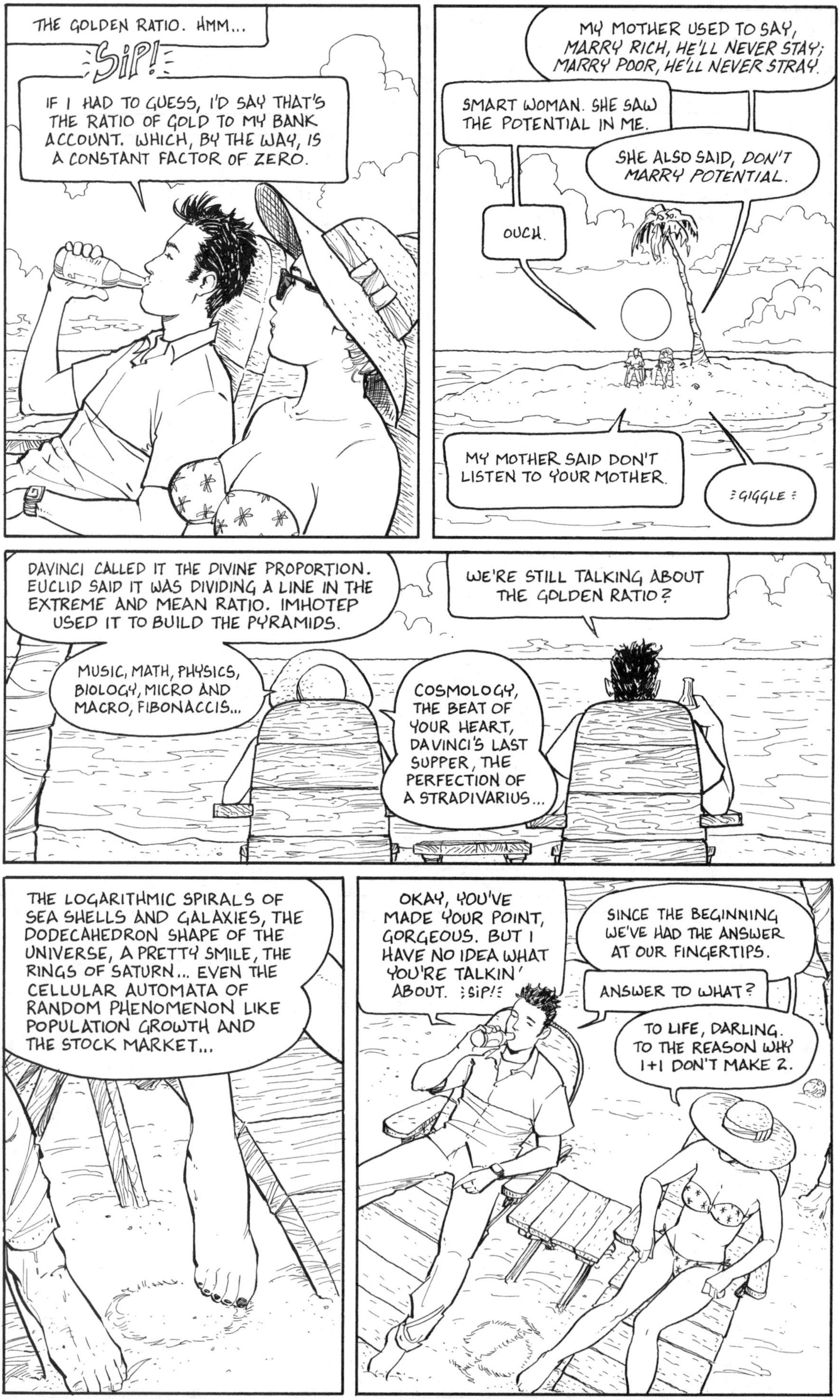
THE GOLDEN RATIO. HMM...
SIP!
IF I HAD TO GUESS, I'D SAY THAT'S THE RATIO OF GOLD TO MY BANK ACCOUNT. WHICH, BY THE WAY, IS A CONSTANT FACTOR OF ZERO.
MY MOTHER USED TO SAY, MARRY RICH, HE'LL NEVER STAY; MARRY POOR, HE'LL NEVER STRAY.
SMART WOMAN. SHE SAW THE POTENTIAL IN ME.
SHE ALSO SAID, DON'T MARRY POTENTIAL.
OUCH.
MY MOTHER SAID DON'T LISTEN TO YOUR MOTHER.
GIGGLE
DAVINCI CALLED IT THE DIVINE PROPORTION. EUCLID SAID IT WAS DIVIDING A LINE IN THE EXTREME AND MEAN RATIO. IMHOTEP USED IT TO BUILD THE PYRAMIDS.
WE'RE STILL TALKING ABOUT THE GOLDEN RATIO?
MUSIC, MATH, PHYSICS, BIOLOGY, MICRO AND MACRO, FIBONACCIS...
COSMOLOGY, THE BEAT OF YOUR HEART, DAVINCI'S LAST SUPPER, THE PERFECTION OF A STRADIVARIUS...
THE LOGARITHMIC SPIRALS OF SEA SHELLS AND GALAXIES, THE DODECAHEDRON SHAPE OF THE UNIVERSE, A PRETTY SMILE, THE RINGS OF SATURN... EVEN THE CELLULAR AUTOMATA OF RANDOM PHENOMENON LIKE POPULATION GROWTH AND THE STOCK MARKET...
OKAY, YOU'VE MADE YOUR POINT, GORGEOUS. BUT I HAVE NO IDEA WHAT YOU'RE TALKIN' ABOUT. SIP!
SINCE THE BEGINNING WE'VE HAD THE ANSWER AT OUR FINGERTIPS.
ANSWER TO WHAT?
TO LIFE, DARLING. TO THE REASON WHY 1+1 DON'T MAKE 2.

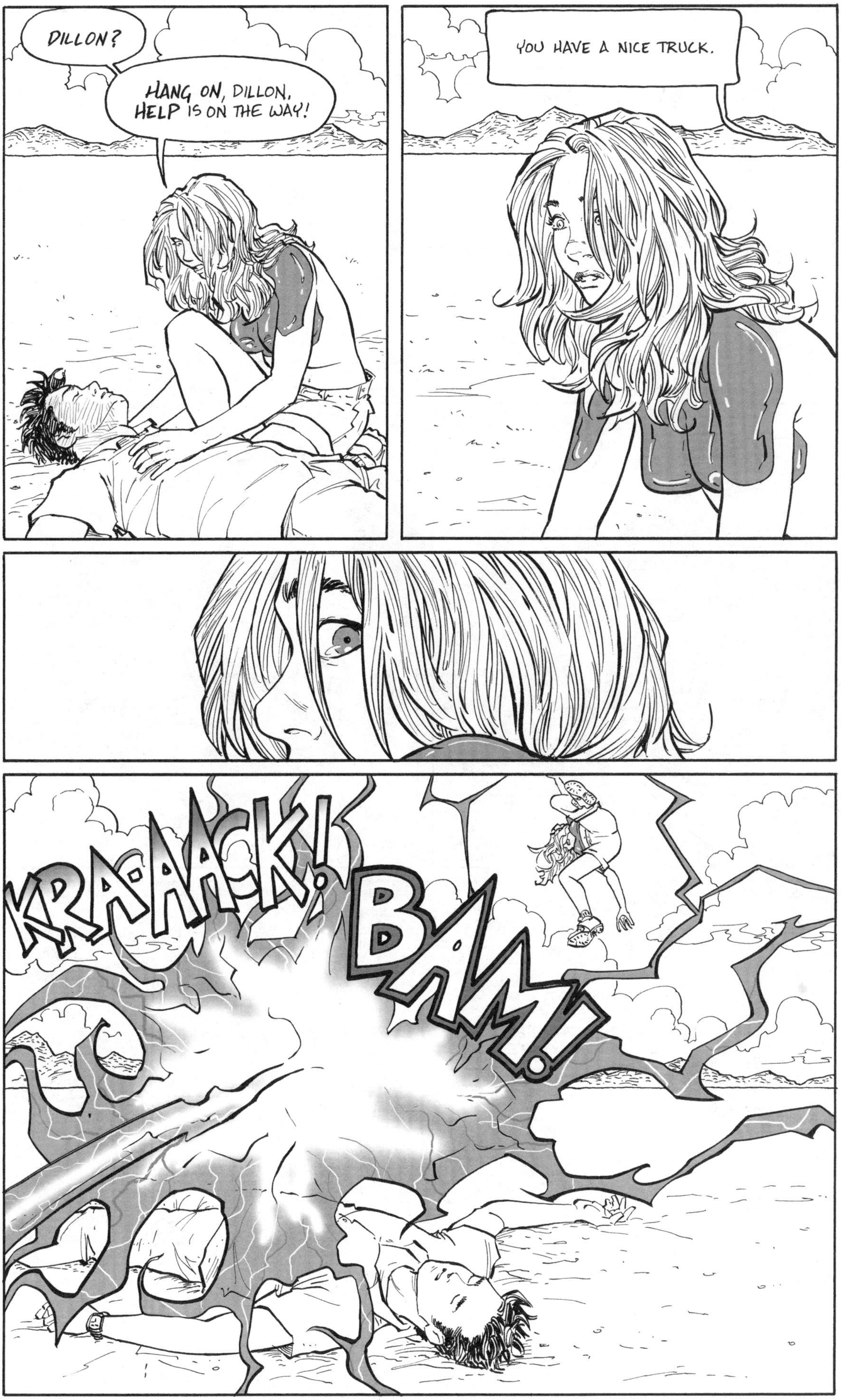
DILLON?
HANG ON, DILLON, HELP IS ON THE WAY!
YOU HAVE A NICE TRUCK.
KRA-AACK!
BAM!

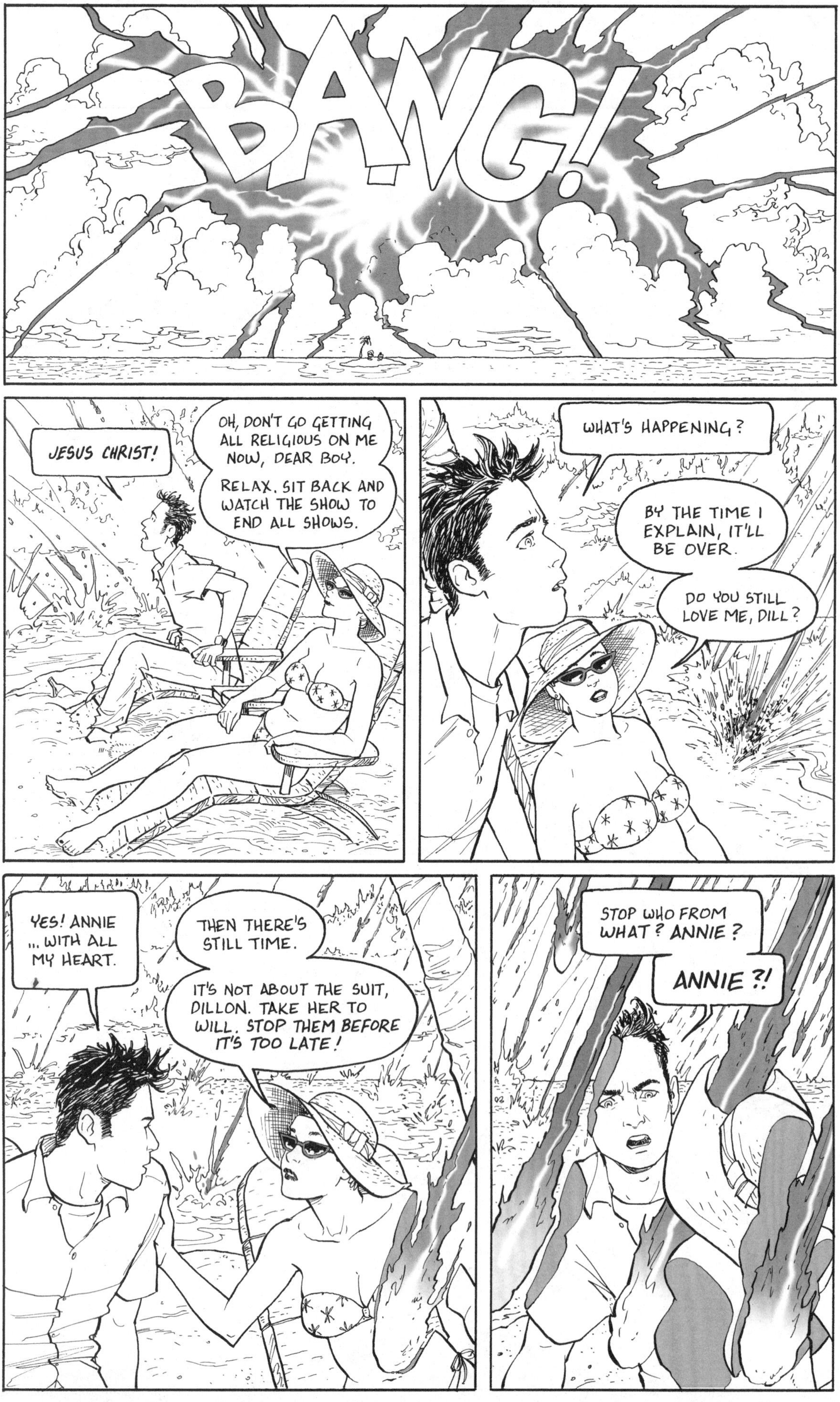
BANG!
JESUS CHRIST!
OH, DON'T GO GETTING ALL RELIGIOUS ON ME NOW, DEAR BOY.
RELAX. SIT BACK AND WATCH THE SHOW TO END ALL SHOWS.
WHAT'S HAPPENING?
BY THE TIME I EXPLAIN, IT'LL BE OVER.
DO YOU STILL LOVE ME, DILL?
YES! ANNIE ... WITH ALL MY HEART.
THEN THERE'S STILL TIME.
IT'S NOT ABOUT THE SUIT, DILLON. TAKE HER TO WILL. STOP THEM BEFORE IT'S TOO LATE!
STOP WHO FROM WHAT? ANNIE?
ANNIE?!

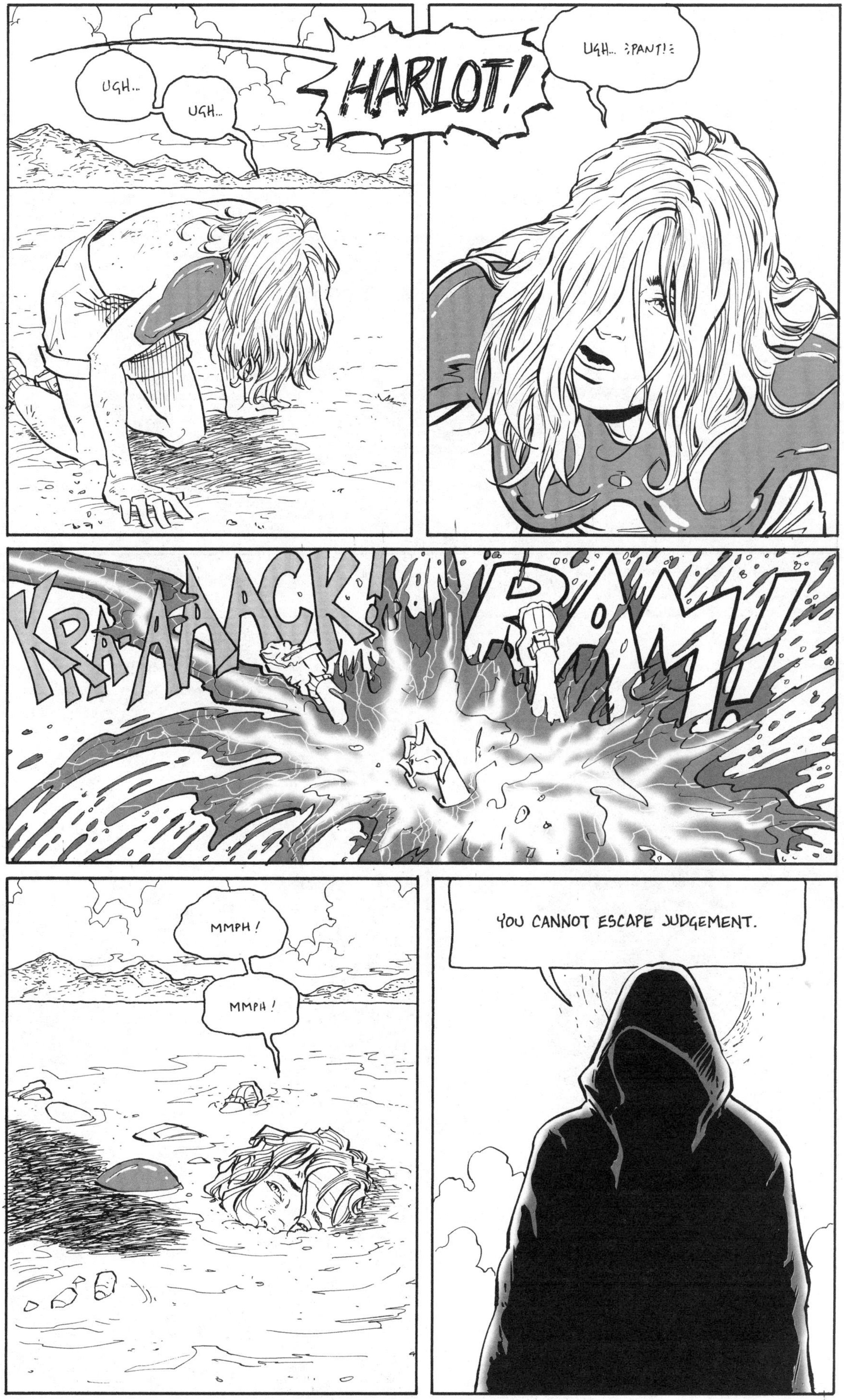
UGH...
UGH...
HARLOT!
UGH... PANT!
KRA-AAACK!
BAM!
MMPH!
MMPH!
YOU CANNOT ESCAPE JUDGEMENT.

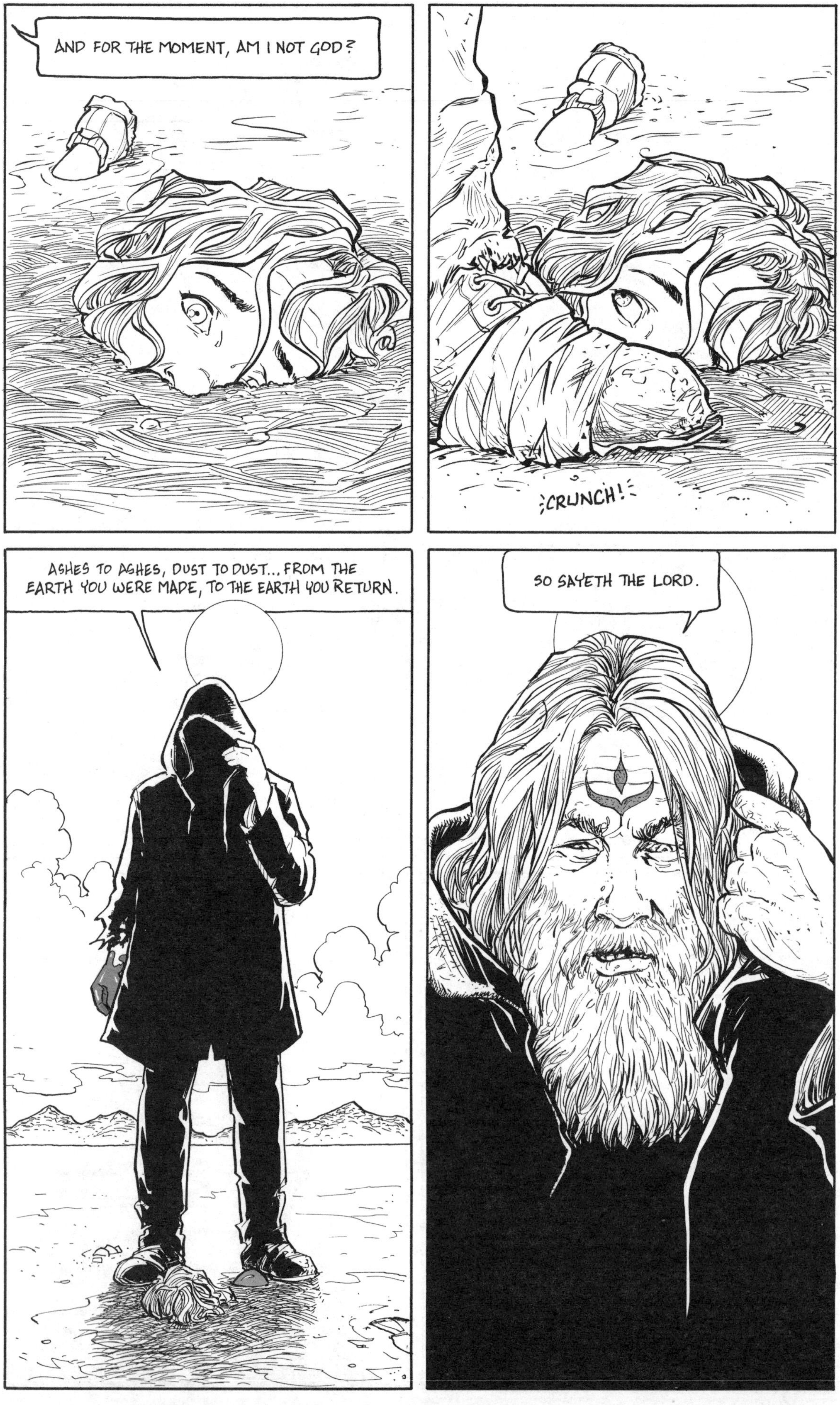
AND FOR THE MOMENT, AM I NOT GOD?
CRUNCH!
ASHES TO ASHES, DUST TO DUST... FROM THE EARTH YOU WERE MADE, TO THE EARTH YOU RETURN.
SO SAYETH THE LORD.

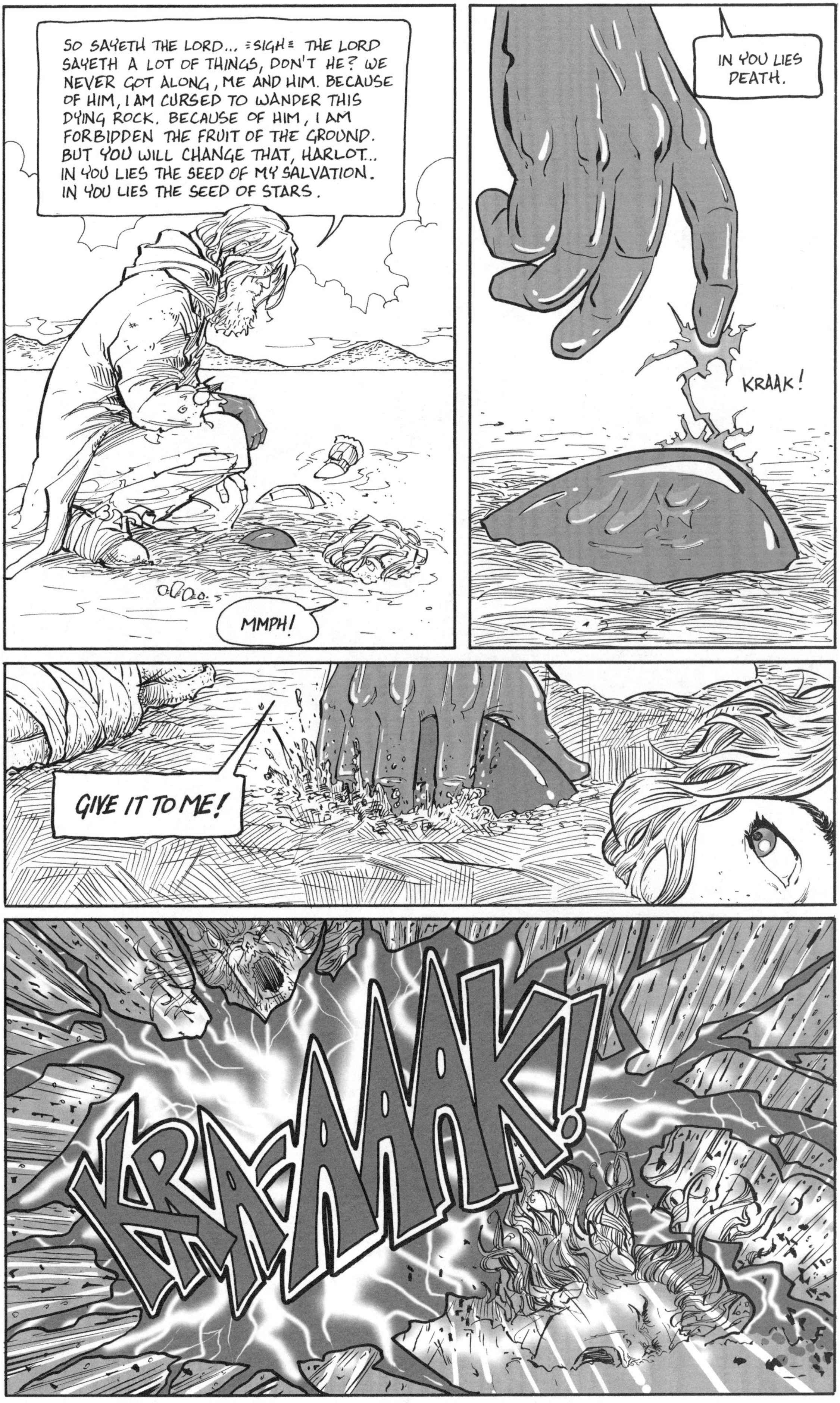
SO SAYETH THE LORD... =SIGH= THE LORD SAYETH A LOT OF THINGS, DON'T HE? WE NEVER GOT ALONG, ME AND HIM. BECAUSE OF HIM, I AM CURSED TO WANDER THIS DYING ROCK. BECAUSE OF HIM, I AM FORBIDDEN THE FRUIT OF THE GROUND. BUT YOU WILL CHANGE THAT, HARLOT... IN YOU LIES THE SEED OF MY SALVATION. IN YOU LIES THE SEED OF STARS.
MMPH!
IN YOU LIES DEATH.
KRAAK!
GIVE IT TO ME!
KRA-AAAK!

I have noticed even people who claim everything
is predestined, and that we can do nothing to
change it, look before they cross the road.
—Stephen Hawking

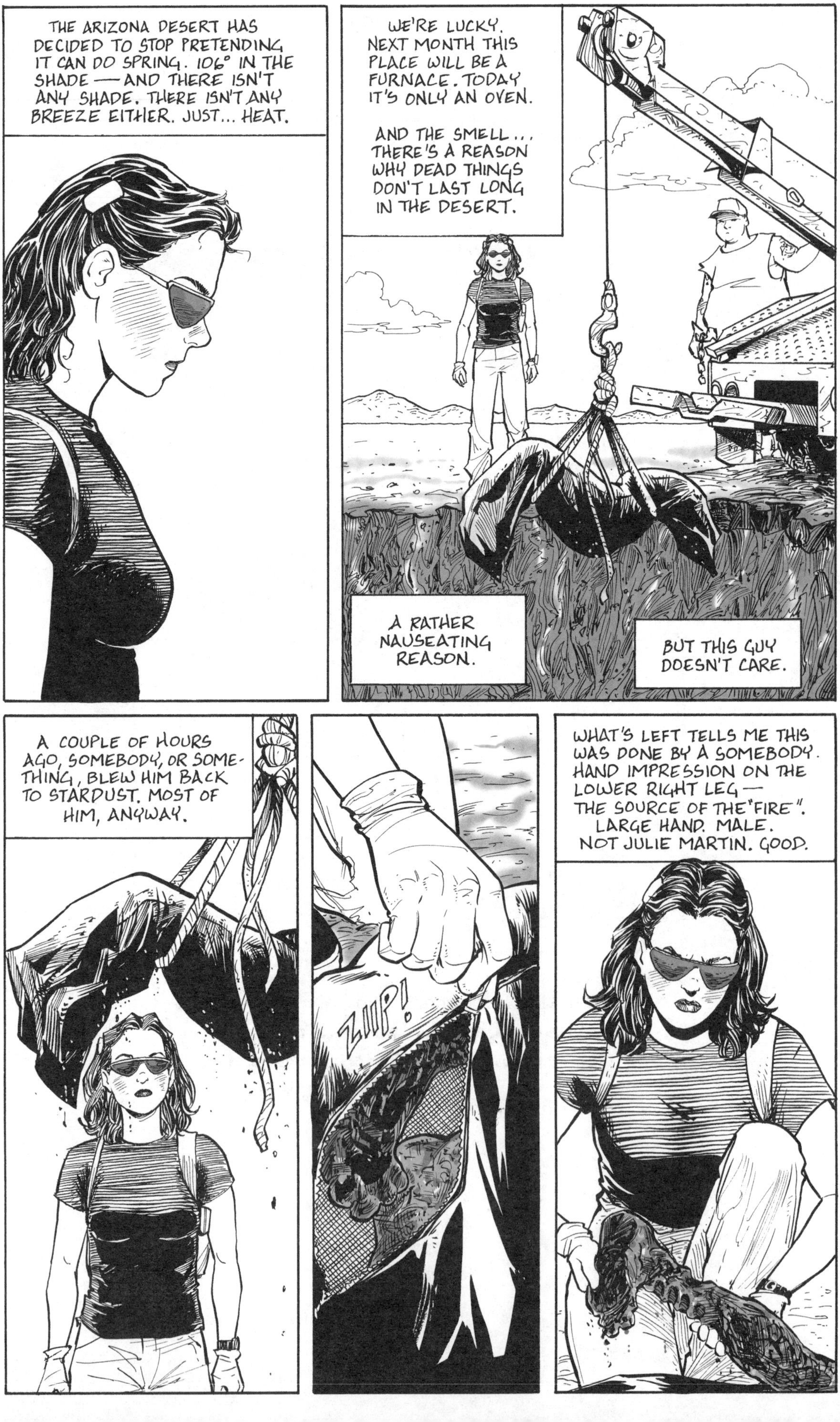
THE ARIZONA DESERT HAS DECIDED TO STOP PRETENDING IT CAN DO SPRING. 106° IN THE SHADE — AND THERE ISN'T ANY SHADE. THERE ISN'T ANY BREEZE EITHER. JUST... HEAT.
WE'RE LUCKY. NEXT MONTH THIS PLACE WILL BE A FURNACE. TODAY IT'S ONLY AN OVEN.
AND THE SMELL... THERE'S A REASON WHY DEAD THINGS DON'T LAST LONG IN THE DESERT.
A RATHER NAUSEATING REASON.
BUT THIS GUY DOESN'T CARE.
A COUPLE OF HOURS AGO, SOMEBODY, OR SOMETHING, BLEW HIM BACK TO STARDUST. MOST OF HIM, ANYWAY.
ZIIP!
WHAT'S LEFT TELLS ME THIS WAS DONE BY A SOMEBODY. HAND IMPRESSION ON THE LOWER RIGHT LEG — THE SOURCE OF THE "FIRE". LARGE HAND. MALE. NOT JULIE MARTIN. GOOD.

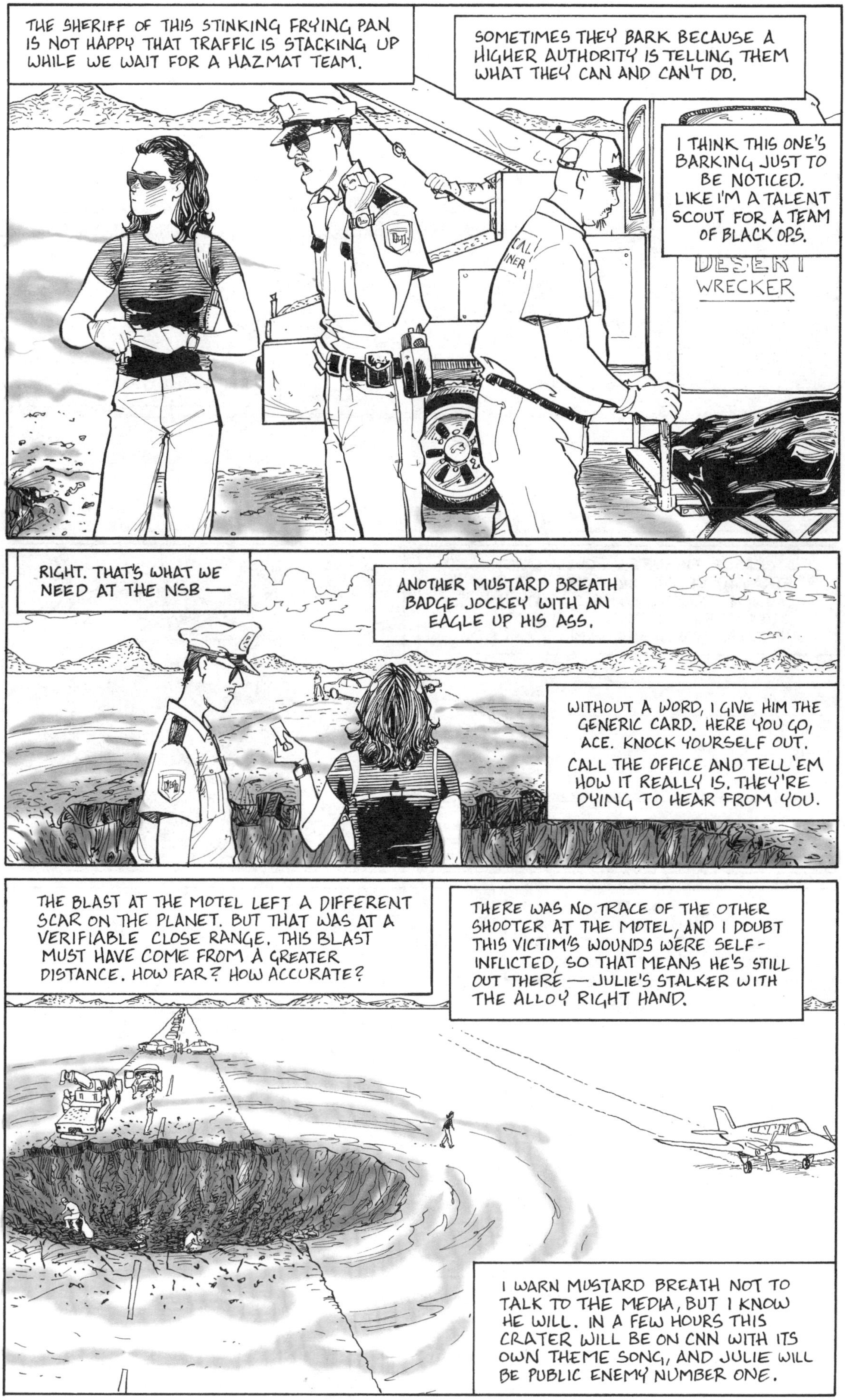
THE SHERIFF OF THIS STINKING FRYING PAN IS NOT HAPPY THAT TRAFFIC IS STACKING UP WHILE WE WAIT FOR A HAZMAT TEAM.
SOMETIMES THEY BARK BECAUSE A HIGHER AUTHORITY IS TELLING THEM WHAT THEY CAN AND CAN'T DO.
I THINK THIS ONE'S BARKING JUST TO BE NOTICED. LIKE I'M A TALENT SCOUT FOR A TEAM OF BLACK OPS.
DESERT WRECKER
RIGHT. THAT'S WHAT WE NEED AT THE NSB —
ANOTHER MUSTARD BREATH BADGE JOCKEY WITH AN EAGLE UP HIS ASS.
WITHOUT A WORD, I GIVE HIM THE GENERIC CARD. HERE YOU GO, ACE. KNOCK YOURSELF OUT.
CALL THE OFFICE AND TELL 'EM HOW IT REALLY IS. THEY'RE DYING TO HEAR FROM YOU.
THE BLAST AT THE MOTEL LEFT A DIFFERENT SCAR ON THE PLANET. BUT THAT WAS AT A VERIFIABLE CLOSE RANGE. THIS BLAST MUST HAVE COME FROM A GREATER DISTANCE. HOW FAR? HOW ACCURATE?
THERE WAS NO TRACE OF THE OTHER SHOOTER AT THE MOTEL, AND I DOUBT THIS VICTIM'S WOUNDS WERE SELF-INFLICTED, SO THAT MEANS HE'S STILL OUT THERE — JULIE'S STALKER WITH THE ALLOY RIGHT HAND.
I WARN MUSTARD BREATH NOT TO TALK TO THE MEDIA, BUT I KNOW HE WILL. IN A FEW HOURS THIS CRATER WILL BE ON CNN WITH ITS OWN THEME SONG, AND JULIE WILL BE PUBLIC ENEMY NUMBER ONE.

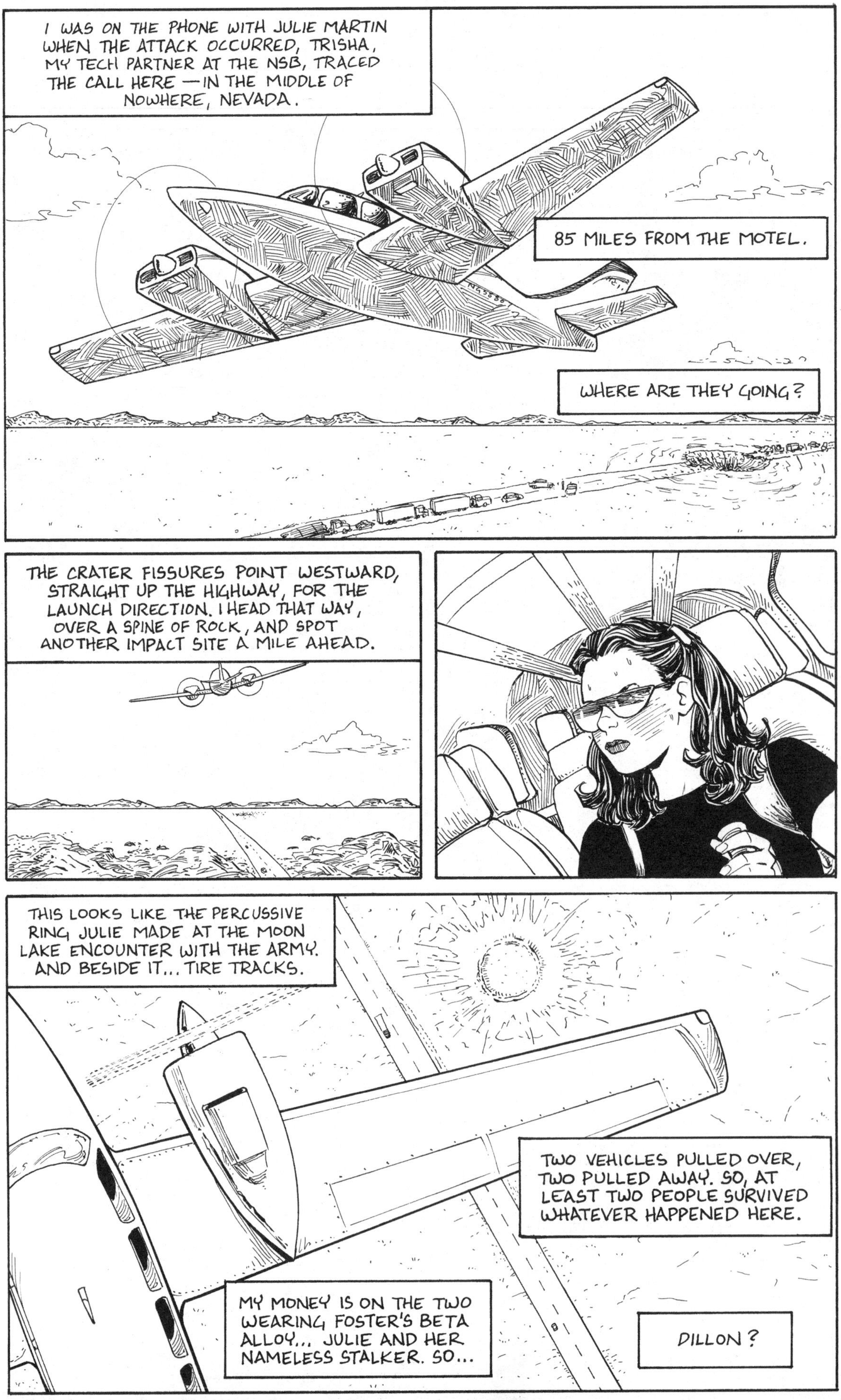
I WAS ON THE PHONE WITH JULIE MARTIN WHEN THE ATTACK OCCURRED, TRISHA, MY TECH PARTNER AT THE NSB, TRACED THE CALL HERE — IN THE MIDDLE OF NOWHERE, NEVADA.
85 MILES FROM THE MOTEL.
WHERE ARE THEY GOING?
THE CRATER FISSURES POINT WESTWARD, STRAIGHT UP THE HIGHWAY, FOR THE LAUNCH DIRECTION. I HEAD THAT WAY, OVER A SPINE OF ROCK, AND SPOT ANOTHER IMPACT SITE A MILE AHEAD.
THIS LOOKS LIKE THE PERCUSSIVE RING JULIE MADE AT THE MOON LAKE ENCOUNTER WITH THE ARMY. AND BESIDE IT... TIRE TRACKS.
TWO VEHICLES PULLED OVER, TWO PULLED AWAY. SO, AT LEAST TWO PEOPLE SURVIVED WHATEVER HAPPENED HERE.
MY MONEY IS ON THE TWO WEARING FOSTER'S BETA ALLOY... JULIE AND HER NAMELESS STALKER. SO...
DILLON?

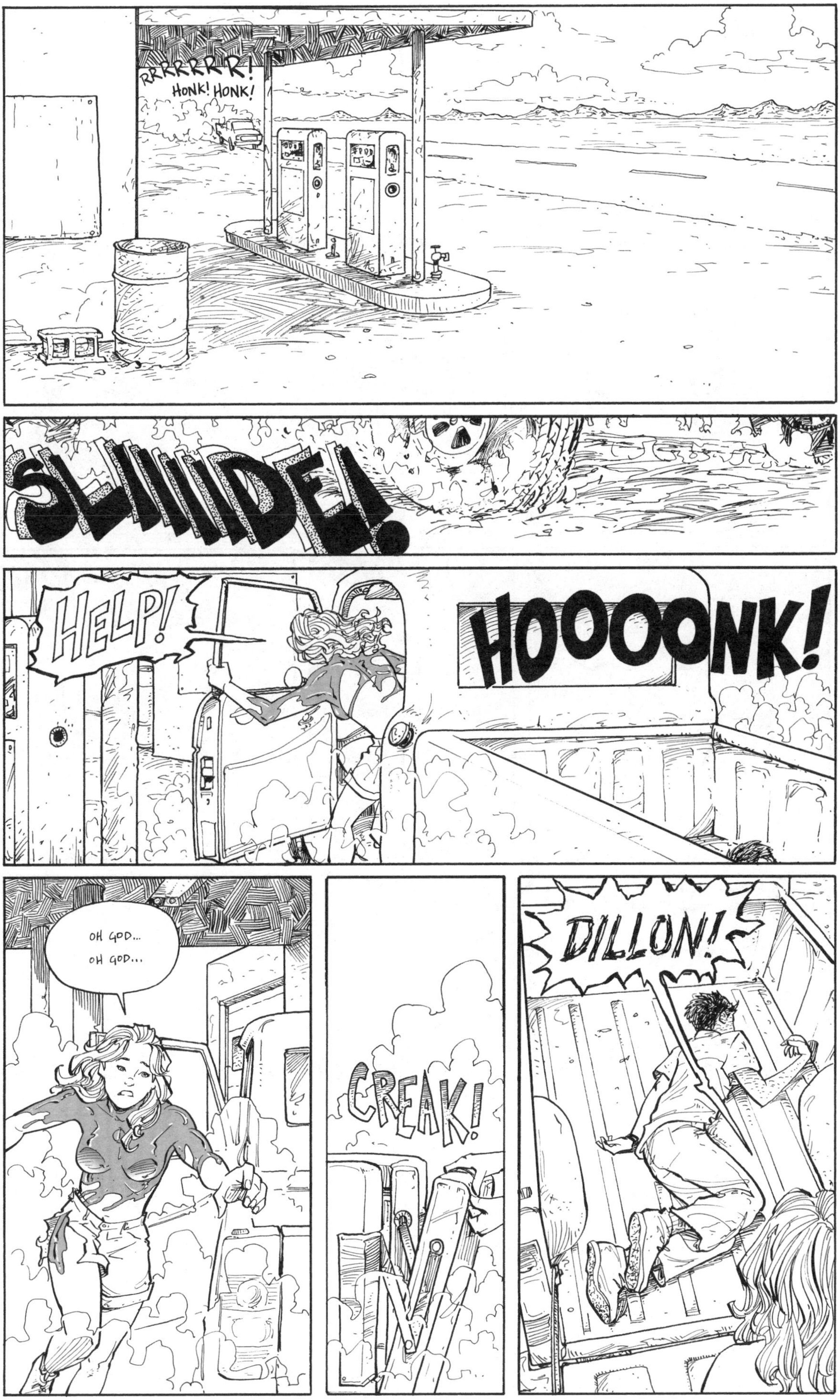
RRRRRRR!
HONK! HONK!
SLIIIIDE!
HELP!
HOOOONK!
OH GOD...
OH GOD...
CREAK!
DILLON!

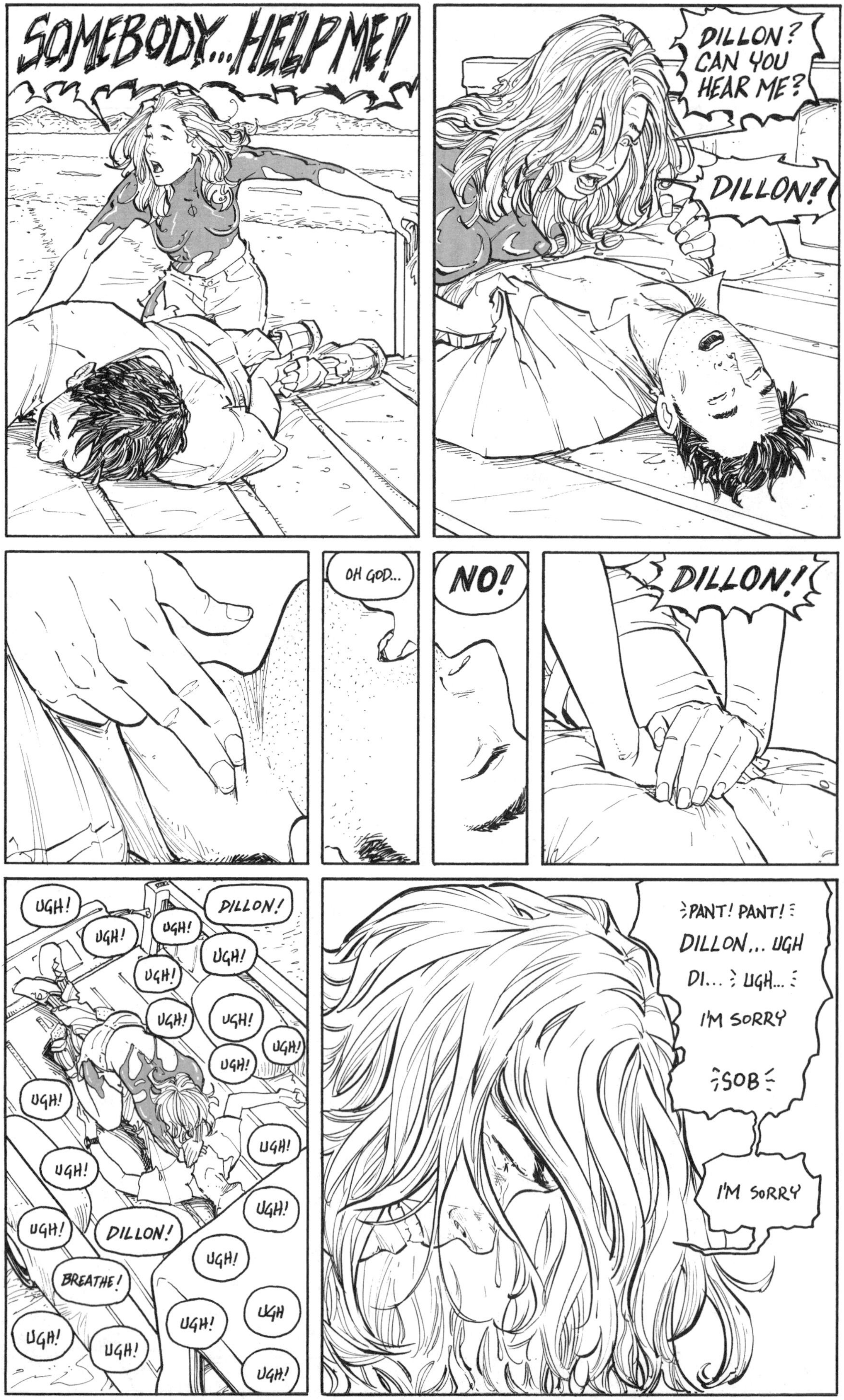
SOMEBODY... HELP ME!
DILLON? CAN YOU HEAR ME?
DILLON!
OH GOD...
NO!
DILLON!
UGH!
DILLON!
UGH!
UGH!
UGH!
UGH!
UGH!
UGH!
UGH!
UGH!
UGH!
UGH!
UGH!
UGH!
DILLON!
UGH!
BREATHE!
UGH!
UGH!
UGH!
UGH
UGH!
UGH!
PANT! PANT!
DILLON... UGH
DI... UGH...
I'M SORRY
SOB
I'M SORRY

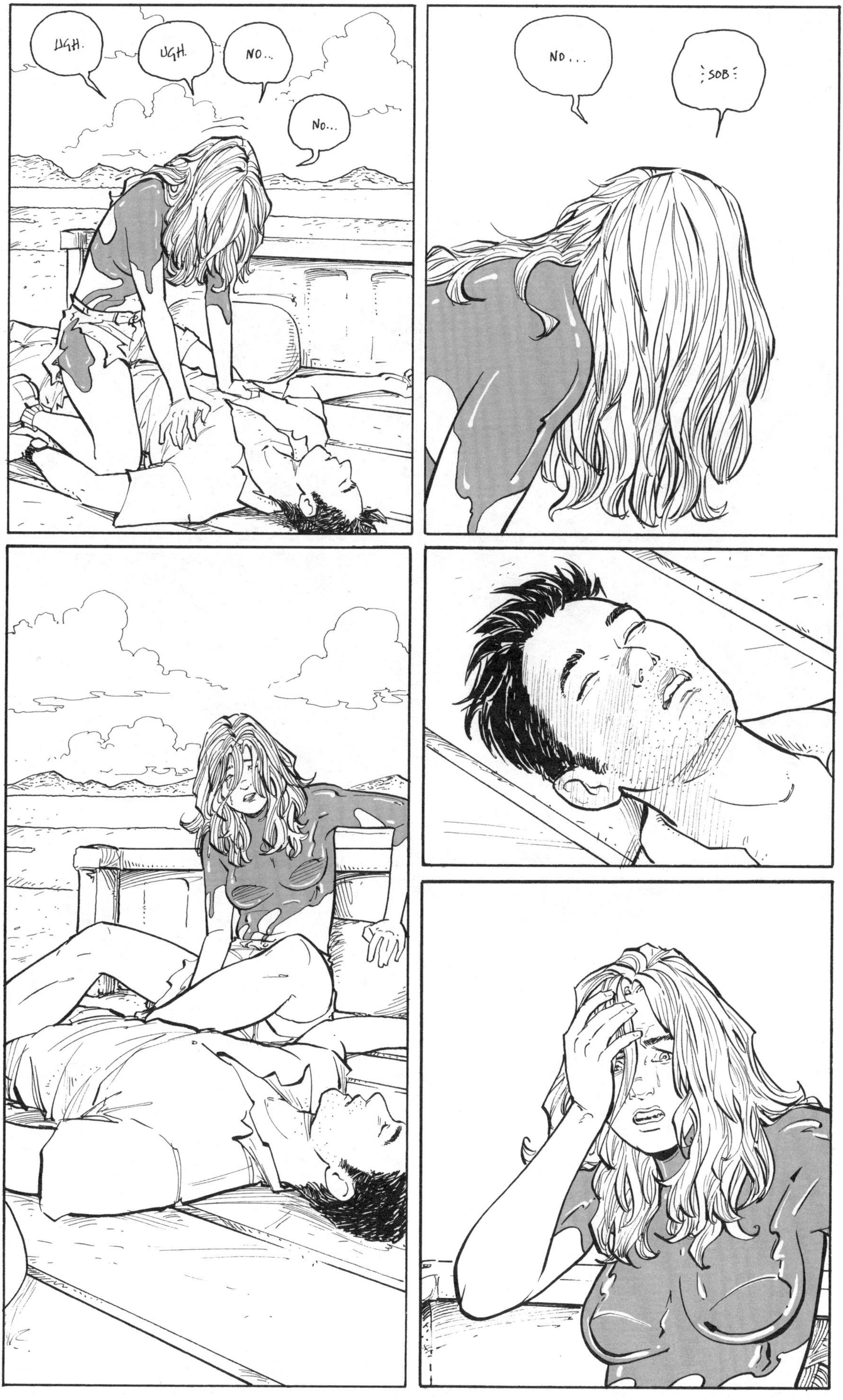
UGH.
UGH.
NO...
NO...
NO...
SOB

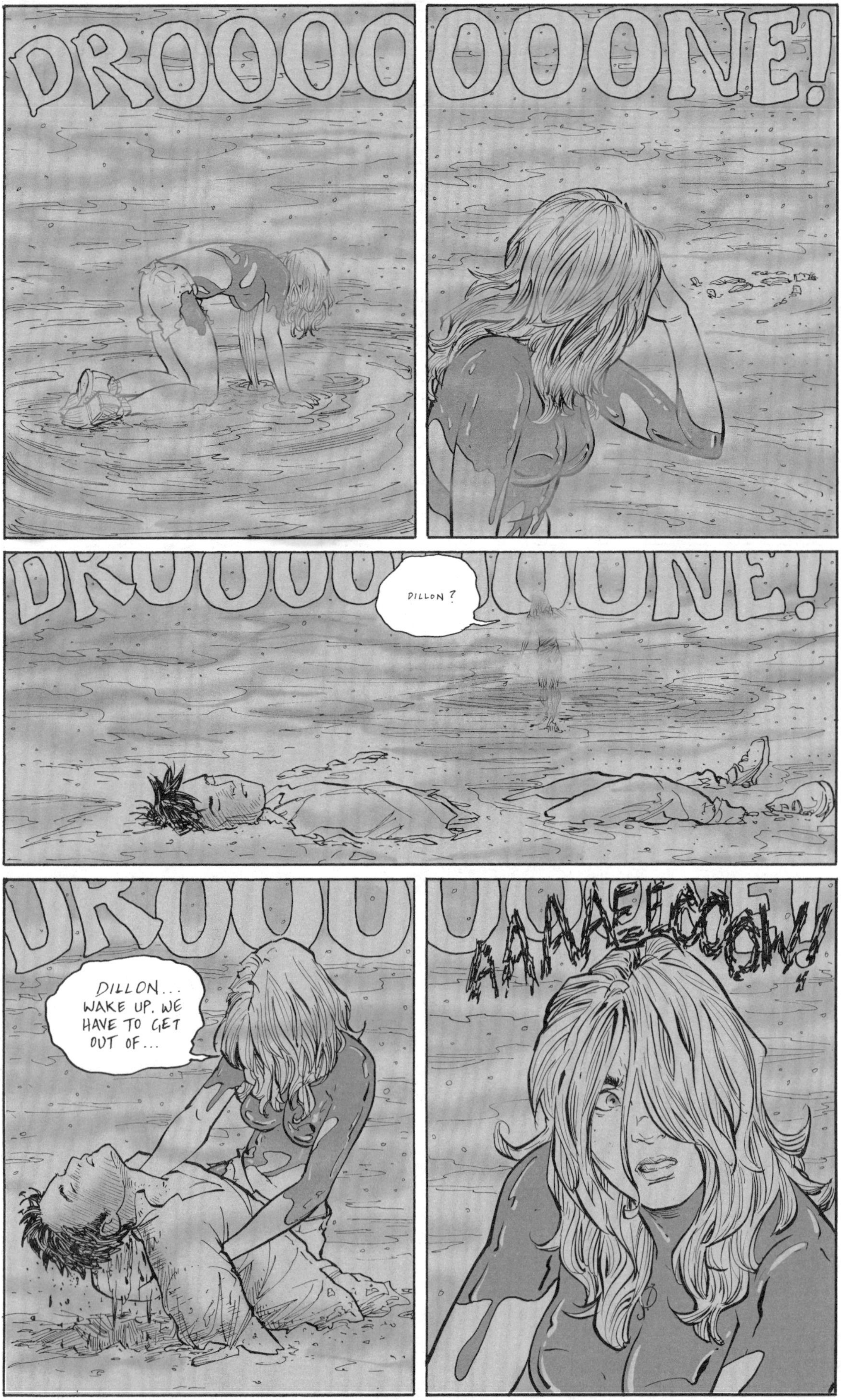
DROOOOOOOONE!
DROOOOOOOONE!
DILLON?
DILLON... WAKE UP. WE HAVE TO GET OUT OF...
AAAAEEOOOW!

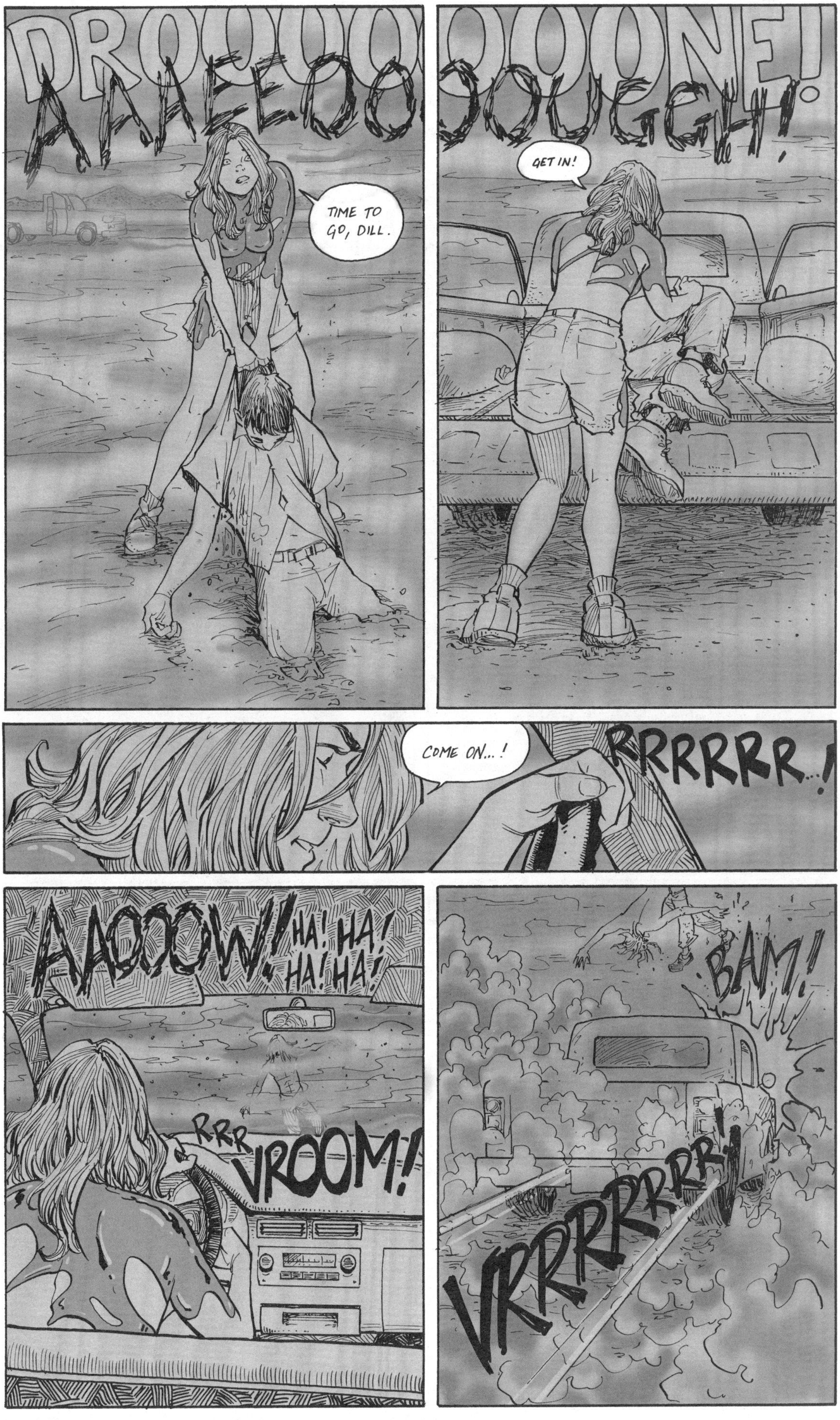
DROOOOOOOOONE!
AAAEEOOOOOUGGH!
TIME TO GO, DILL.
GET IN!
COME ON...!
RRRRRR...!
AAOOOW!
HA! HA! HA! HA!
RRR VROOM!
BAM!
VRRRRRRRR!

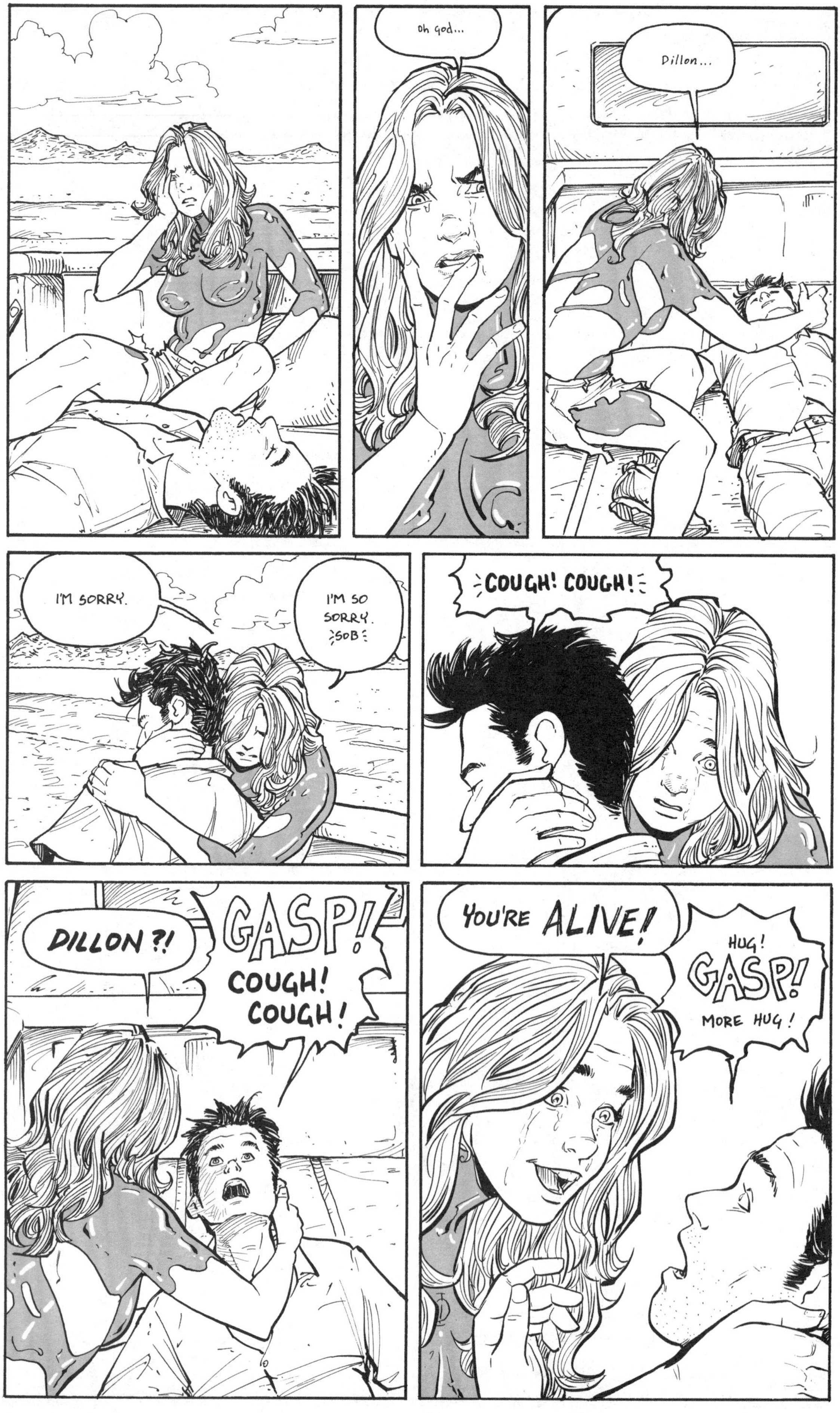

Oh god...
Dillon...
I'M SORRY.
I'M SO SORRY. SOB
COUGH! COUGH!
DILLON?!
GASP! COUGH! COUGH!
YOU'RE ALIVE!
HUG! GASP! MORE HUG!

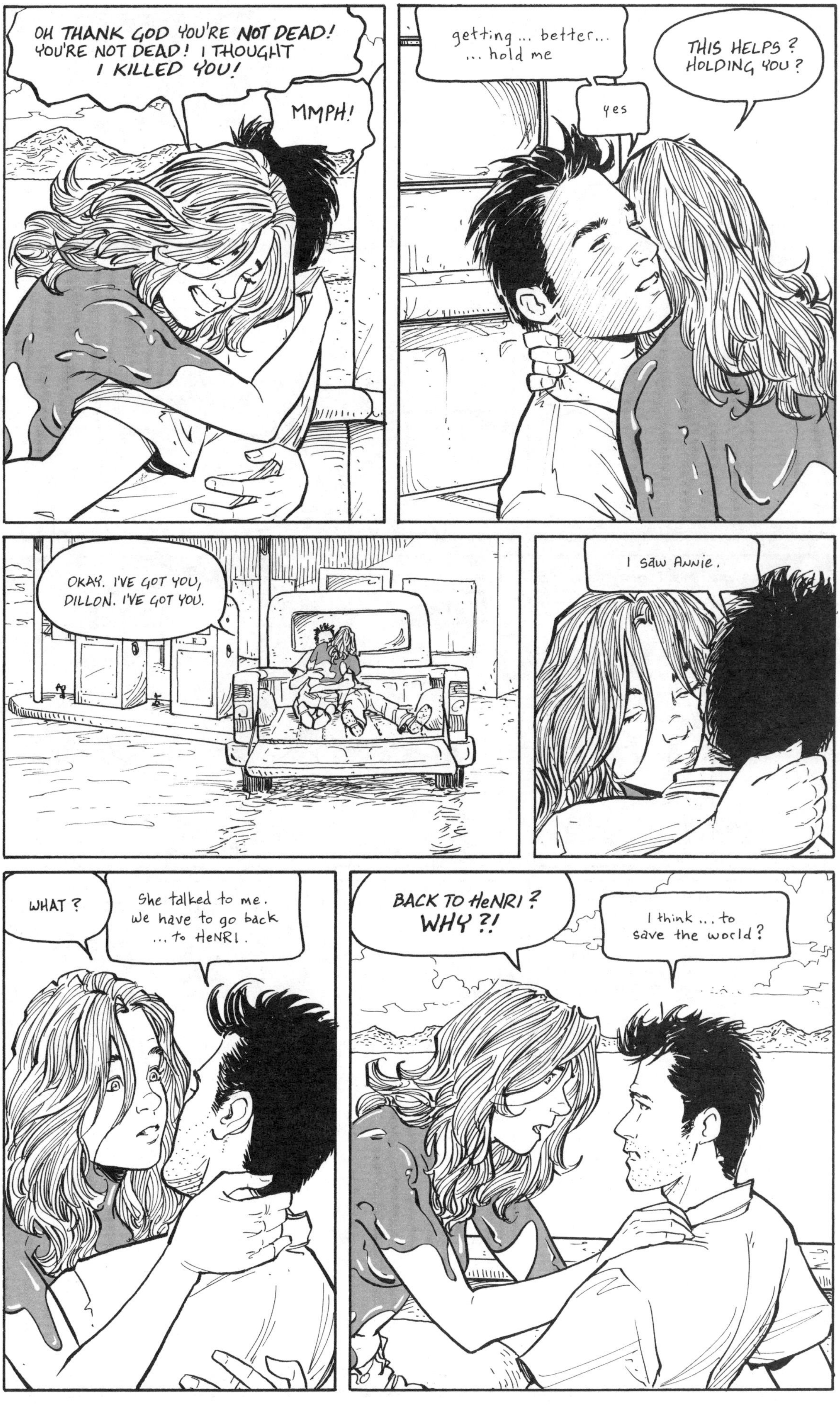
OH THANK GOD YOU'RE NOT DEAD! YOU'RE NOT DEAD! I THOUGHT I KILLED YOU!
MMPH!
getting ... better... ... hold me
yes
THIS HELPS? HOLDING YOU?
OKAY. I'VE GOT YOU, DILLON. I'VE GOT YOU.
I saw Annie.
WHAT?
She talked to me. We have to go back ... to HeNRI.
BACK TO HeNRI? WHY?!
I think ... to save the world?

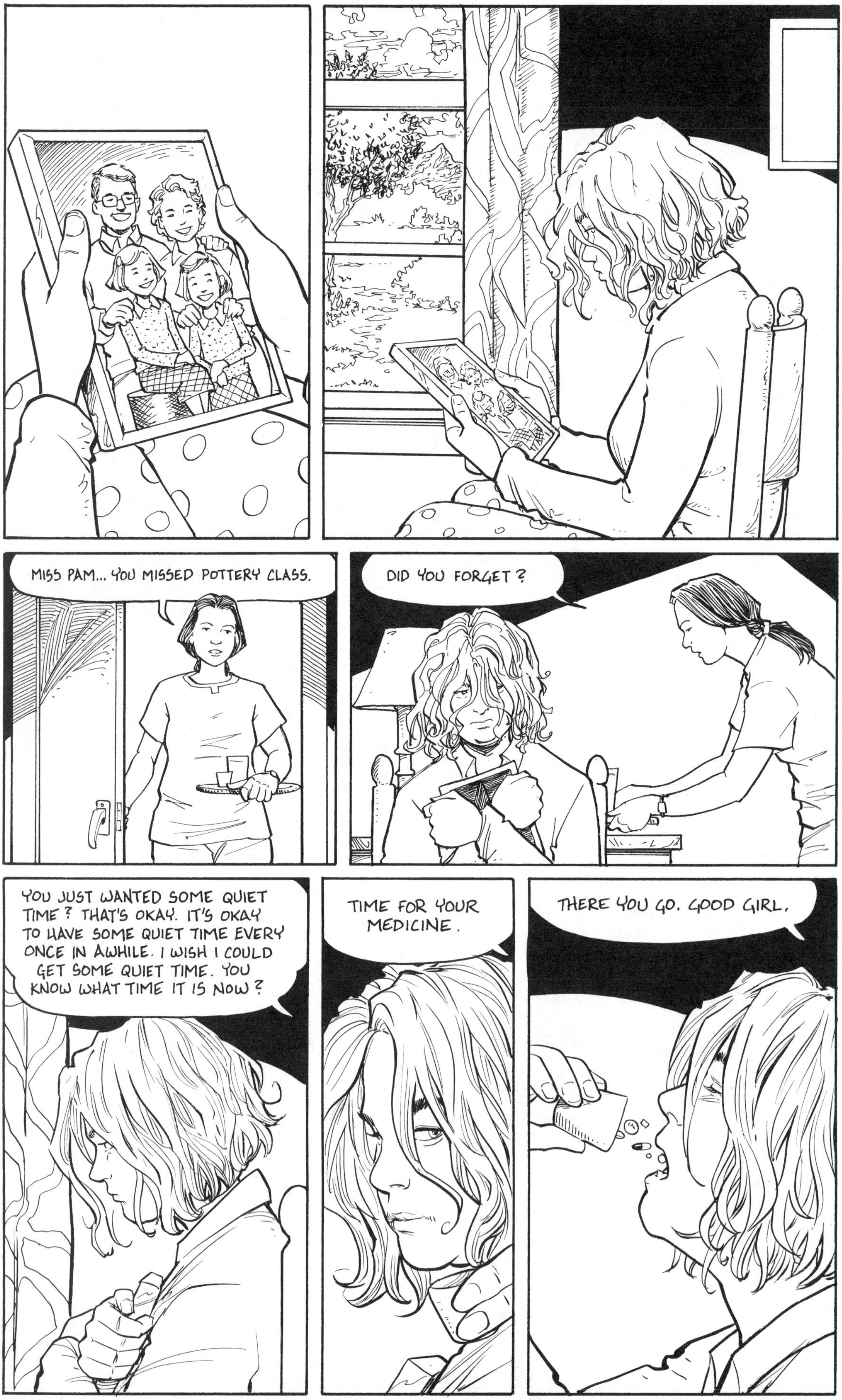
MISS PAM... YOU MISSED POTTERY CLASS.
DID YOU FORGET?
YOU JUST WANTED SOME QUIET TIME? THAT'S OKAY. IT'S OKAY TO HAVE SOME QUIET TIME EVERY ONCE IN AWHILE. I WISH I COULD GET SOME QUIET TIME. YOU KNOW WHAT TIME IT IS NOW?
TIME FOR YOUR MEDICINE.
THERE YOU GO. GOOD GIRL.

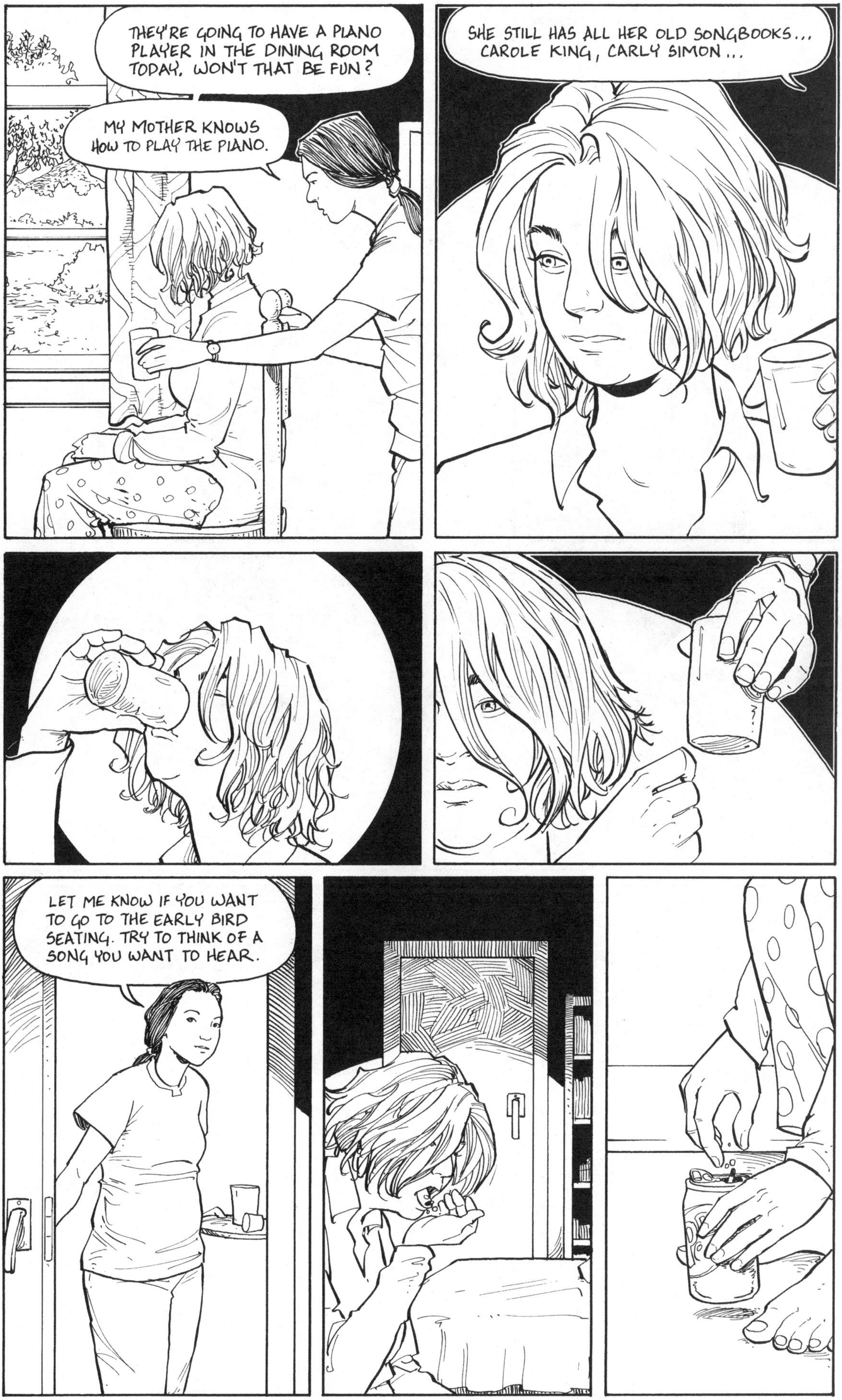
THEY'RE GOING TO HAVE A PIANO PLAYER IN THE DINING ROOM TODAY. WON'T THAT BE FUN?
MY MOTHER KNOWS HOW TO PLAY THE PIANO.
SHE STILL HAS ALL HER OLD SONGBOOKS... CAROLE KING, CARLY SIMON...
LET ME KNOW IF YOU WANT TO GO TO THE EARLY BIRD SEATING. TRY TO THINK OF A SONG YOU WANT TO HEAR.

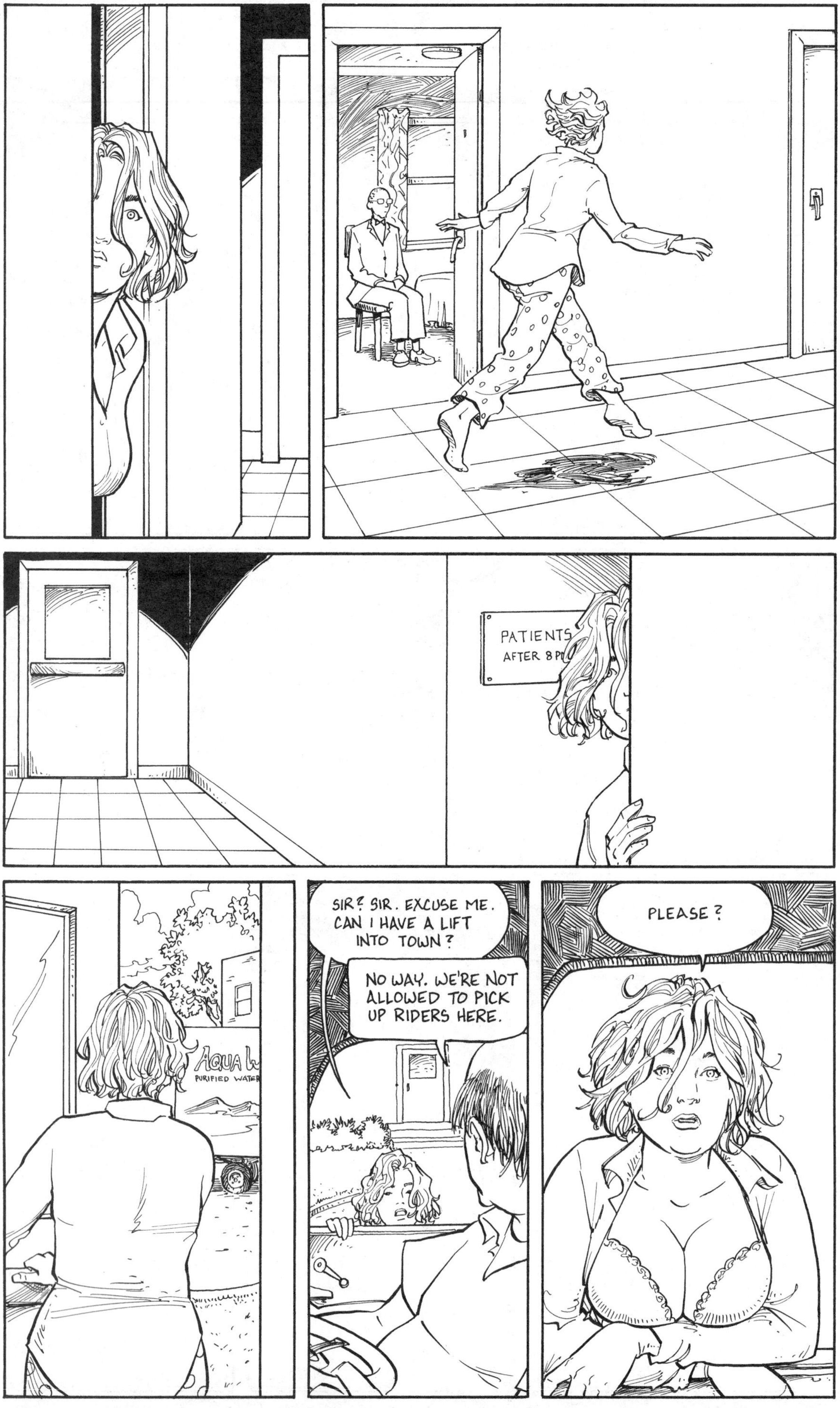
PATIENTS
AFTER 8 P
AQUA W
PURIFIED WATER
SIR? SIR. EXCUSE ME. CAN I HAVE A LIFT INTO TOWN?
NO WAY. WE'RE NOT ALLOWED TO PICK UP RIDERS HERE.
PLEASE?

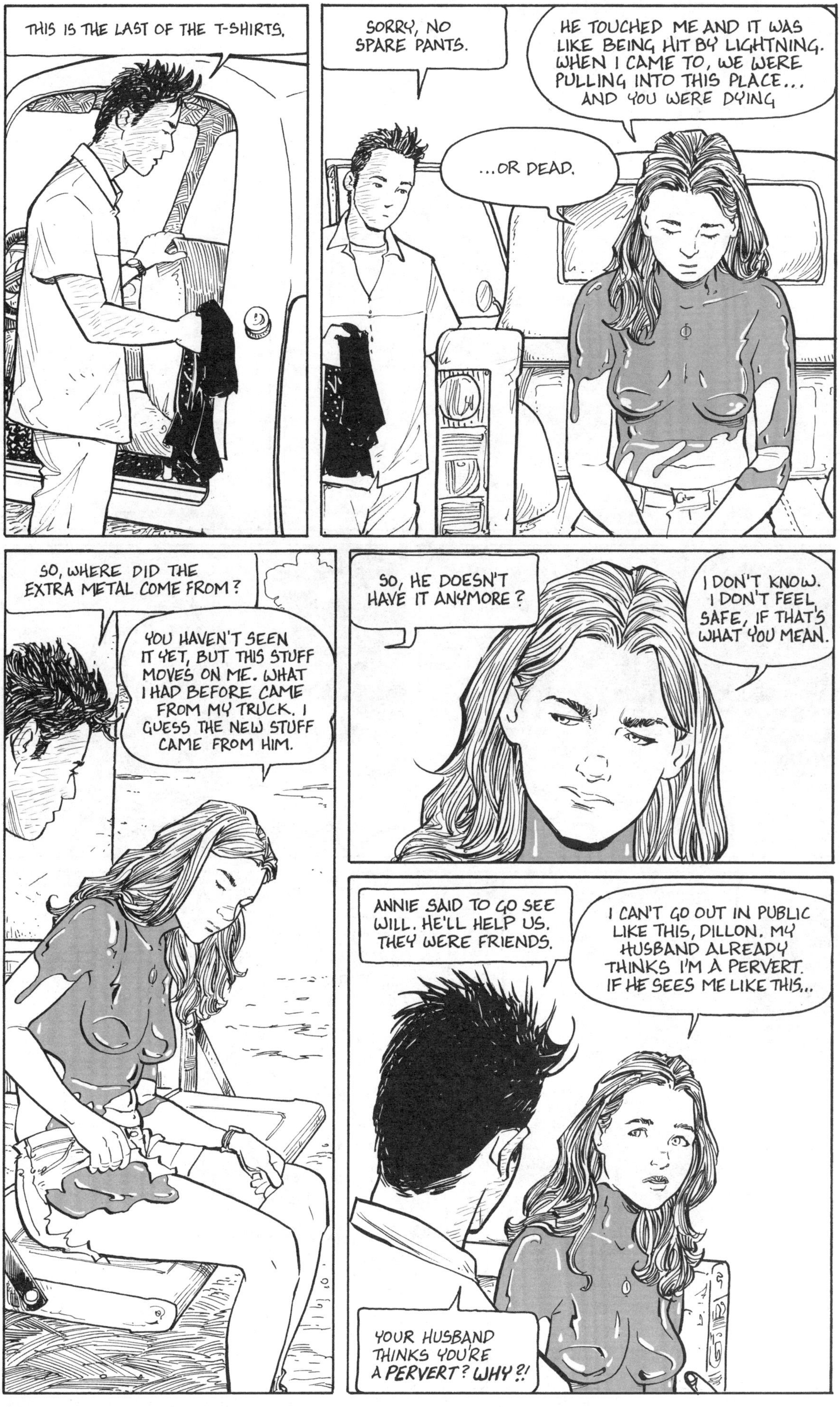
THIS IS THE LAST OF THE T-SHIRTS.
SORRY, NO SPARE PANTS.
HE TOUCHED ME AND IT WAS LIKE BEING HIT BY LIGHTNING. WHEN I CAME TO, WE WERE PULLING INTO THIS PLACE... AND YOU WERE DYING
...OR DEAD.
SO, WHERE DID THE EXTRA METAL COME FROM?
YOU HAVEN'T SEEN IT YET, BUT THIS STUFF MOVES ON ME. WHAT I HAD BEFORE CAME FROM MY TRUCK. I GUESS THE NEW STUFF CAME FROM HIM.
SO, HE DOESN'T HAVE IT ANYMORE?
I DON'T KNOW. I DON'T FEEL SAFE, IF THAT'S WHAT YOU MEAN.
ANNIE SAID TO GO SEE WILL. HE'LL HELP US. THEY WERE FRIENDS.
I CAN'T GO OUT IN PUBLIC LIKE THIS, DILLON. MY HUSBAND ALREADY THINKS I'M A PERVERT. IF HE SEES ME LIKE THIS...
YOUR HUSBAND THINKS YOU'RE A PERVERT? WHY?!

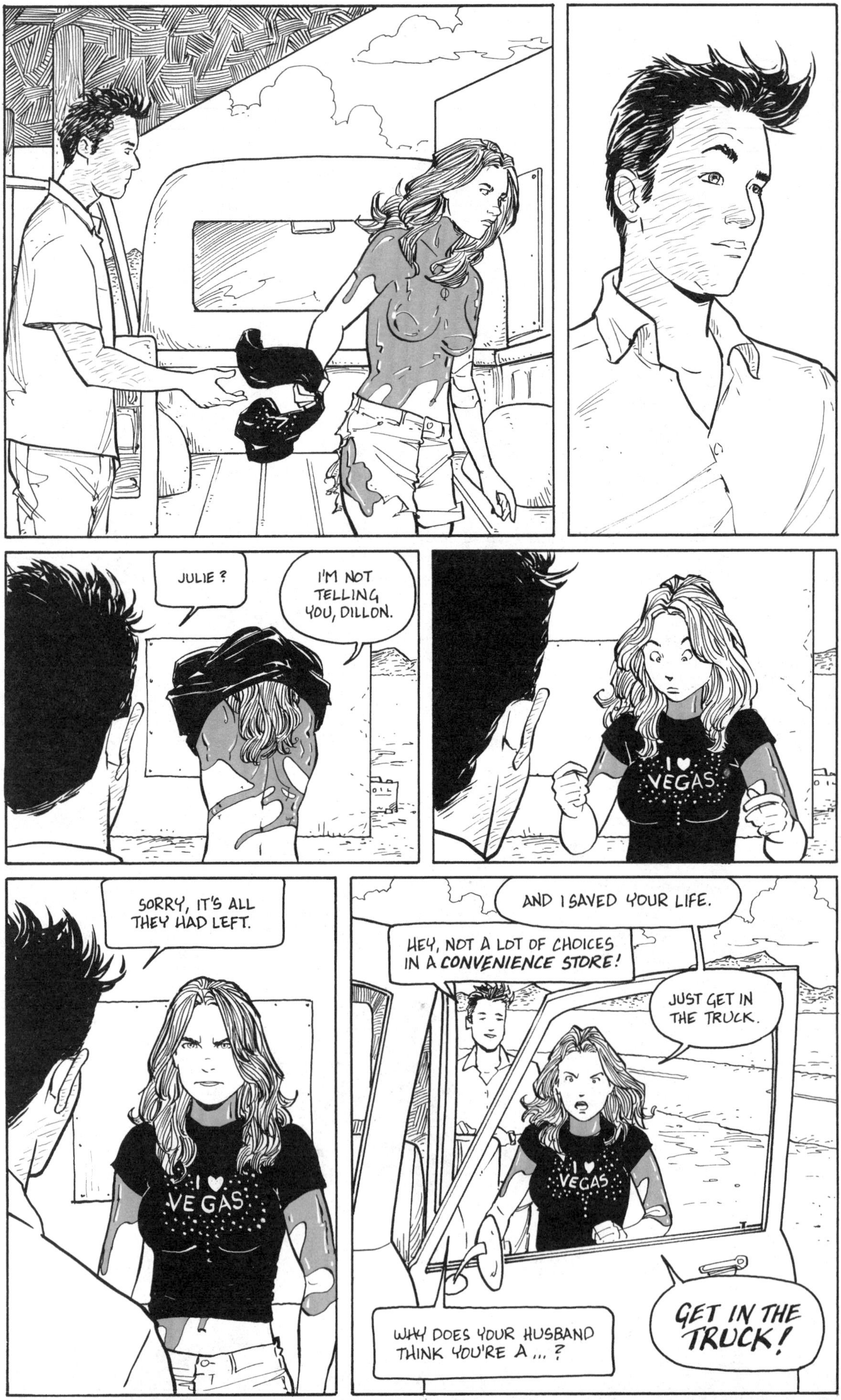
JULIE ?
I'M NOT TELLING YOU, DILLON.
SORRY, IT'S ALL THEY HAD LEFT.
AND I SAVED YOUR LIFE.
HEY, NOT A LOT OF CHOICES IN A CONVENIENCE STORE!
JUST GET IN THE TRUCK.
WHY DOES YOUR HUSBAND THINK YOU'RE A ... ?
GET IN THE TRUCK!
I ♥ VEGAS

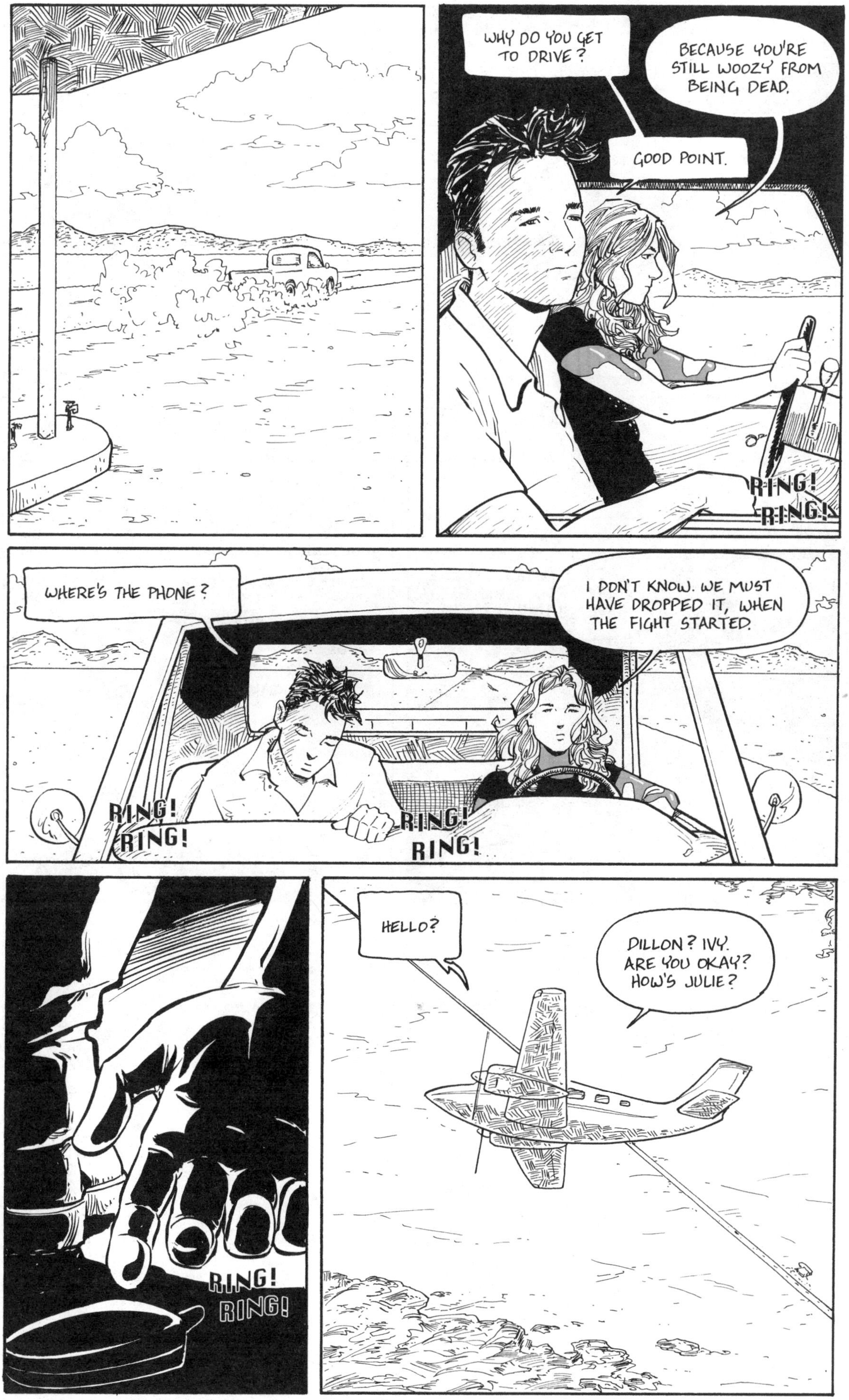
WHY DO YOU GET TO DRIVE?
BECAUSE YOU'RE STILL WOOZY FROM BEING DEAD.
GOOD POINT.
RING! RING!
WHERE'S THE PHONE?
I DON'T KNOW. WE MUST HAVE DROPPED IT, WHEN THE FIGHT STARTED.
RING! RING!
RING! RING!
RING! RING!
HELLO?
DILLON? IVY. ARE YOU OKAY? HOW'S JULIE?

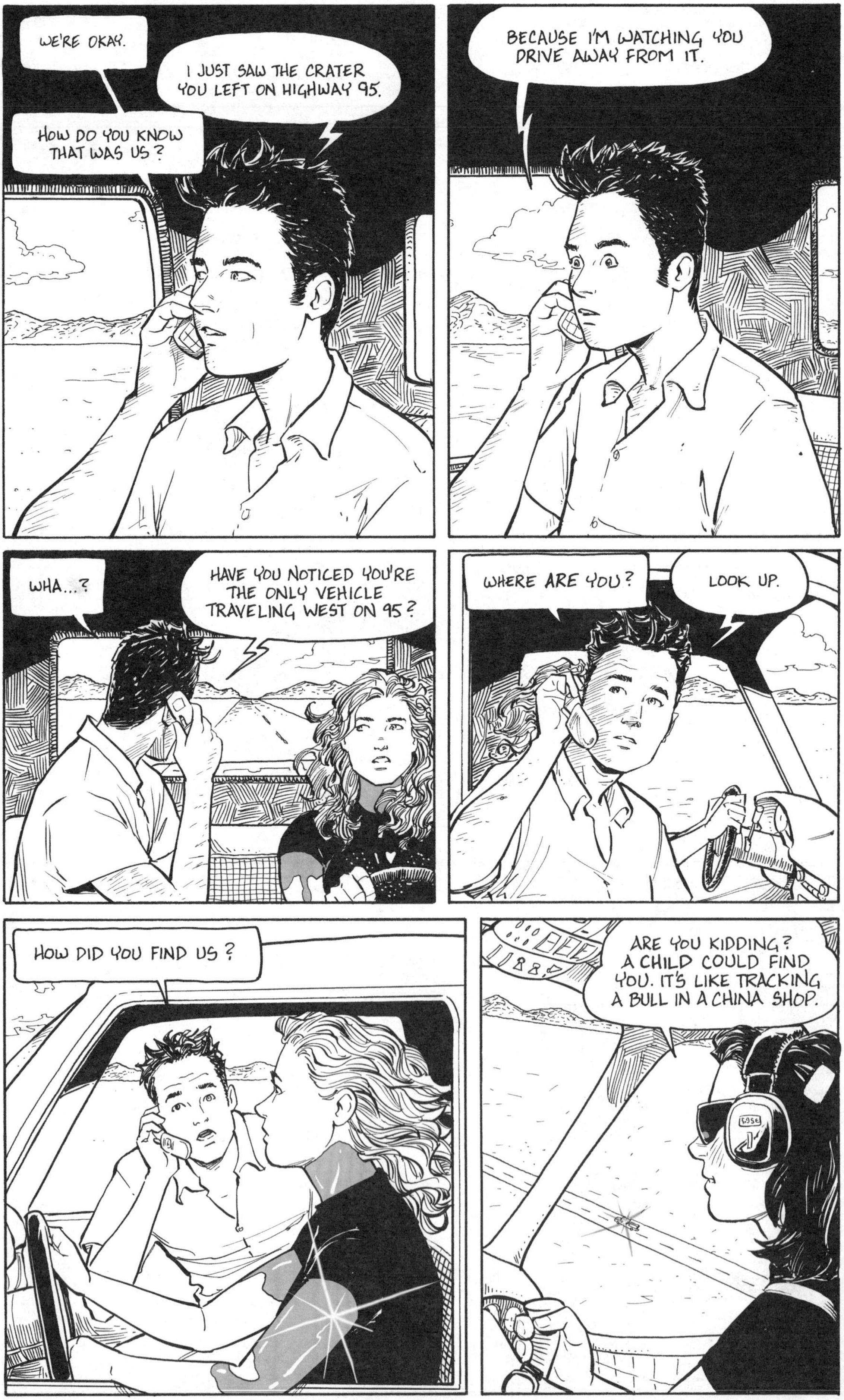
WE'RE OKAY.
I JUST SAW THE CRATER YOU LEFT ON HIGHWAY 95.
HOW DO YOU KNOW THAT WAS US?
BECAUSE I'M WATCHING YOU DRIVE AWAY FROM IT.
WHA...?
HAVE YOU NOTICED YOU'RE THE ONLY VEHICLE TRAVELING WEST ON 95?
WHERE ARE YOU?
LOOK UP.
HOW DID YOU FIND US?
ARE YOU KIDDING? A CHILD COULD FIND YOU. IT'S LIKE TRACKING A BULL IN A CHINA SHOP.

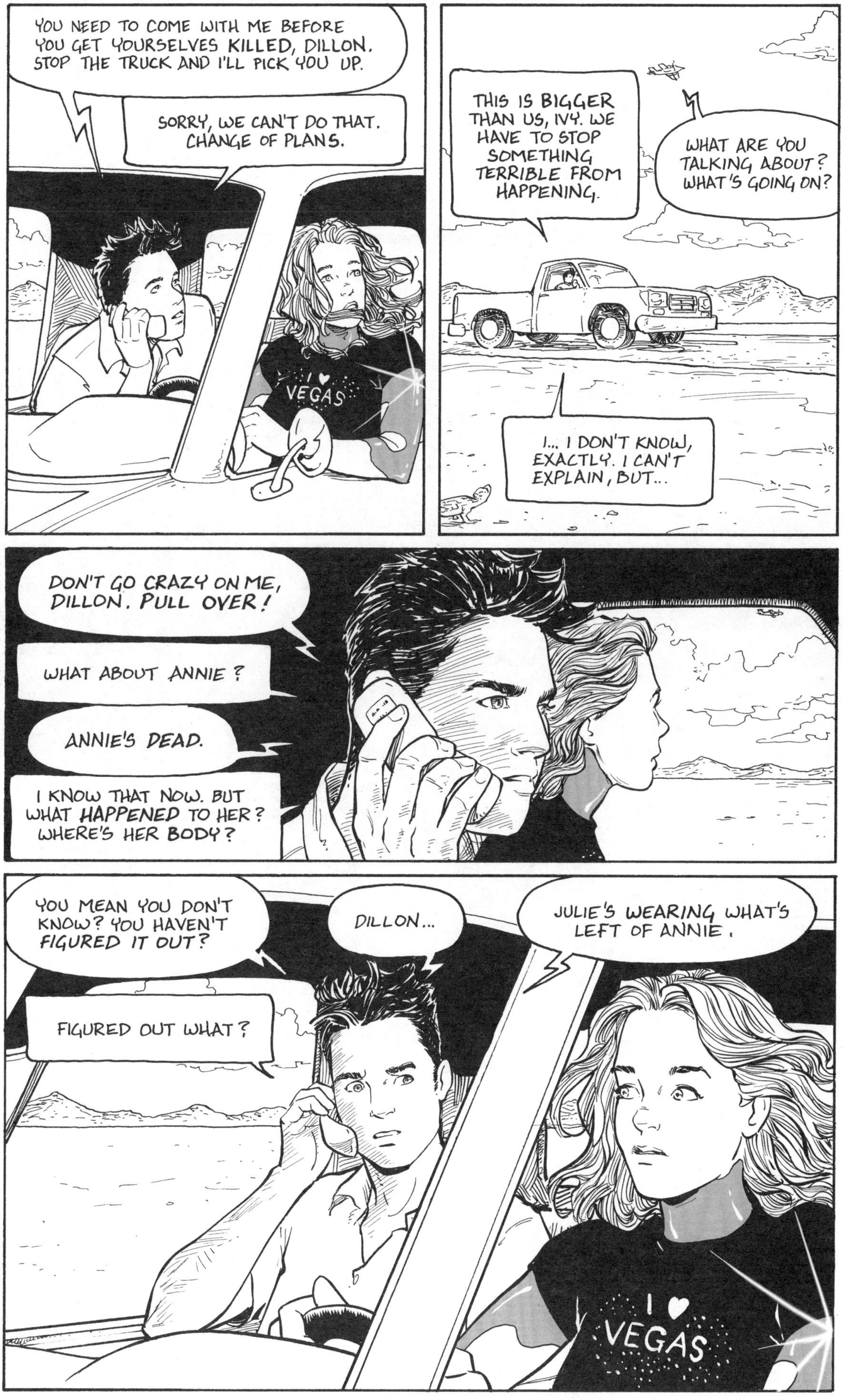
YOU NEED TO COME WITH ME BEFORE YOU GET YOURSELVES KILLED, DILLON. STOP THE TRUCK AND I'LL PICK YOU UP.
SORRY, WE CAN'T DO THAT. CHANGE OF PLANS.
THIS IS BIGGER THAN US, IVY. WE HAVE TO STOP SOMETHING TERRIBLE FROM HAPPENING.
WHAT ARE YOU TALKING ABOUT? WHAT'S GOING ON?
I... I DON'T KNOW, EXACTLY. I CAN'T EXPLAIN, BUT...
DON'T GO CRAZY ON ME, DILLON. PULL OVER!
WHAT ABOUT ANNIE?
ANNIE'S DEAD.
I KNOW THAT NOW. BUT WHAT HAPPENED TO HER? WHERE'S HER BODY?
YOU MEAN YOU DON'T KNOW? YOU HAVEN'T FIGURED IT OUT?
FIGURED OUT WHAT?
DILLON...
JULIE'S WEARING WHAT'S LEFT OF ANNIE.
I ♥ VEGAS

War would end if the dead could return.
—Stanley Baldwin

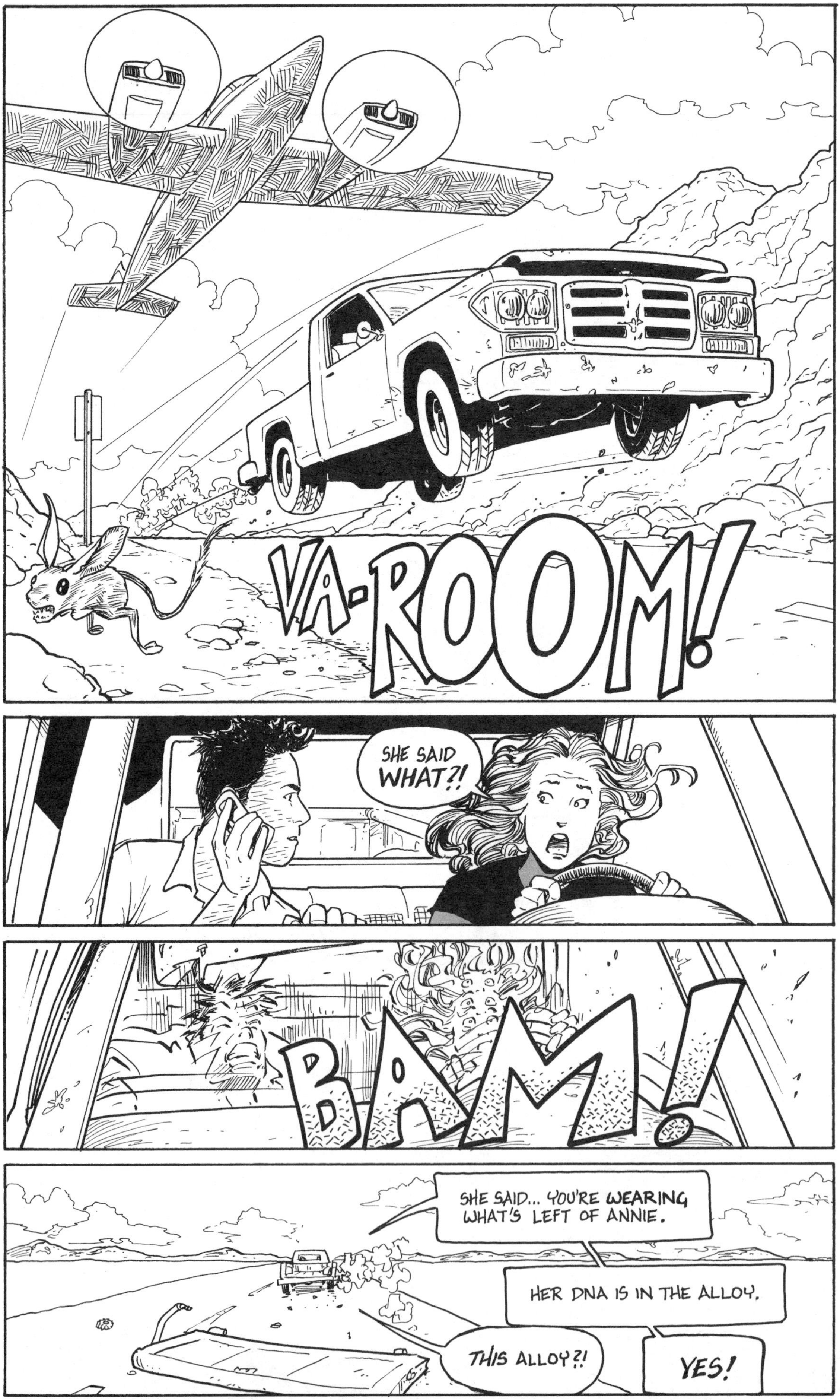
VA-ROOM!
SHE SAID WHAT?!
BAM!
SHE SAID... YOU'RE WEARING WHAT'S LEFT OF ANNIE.
HER DNA IS IN THE ALLOY.
THIS ALLOY?!
YES!

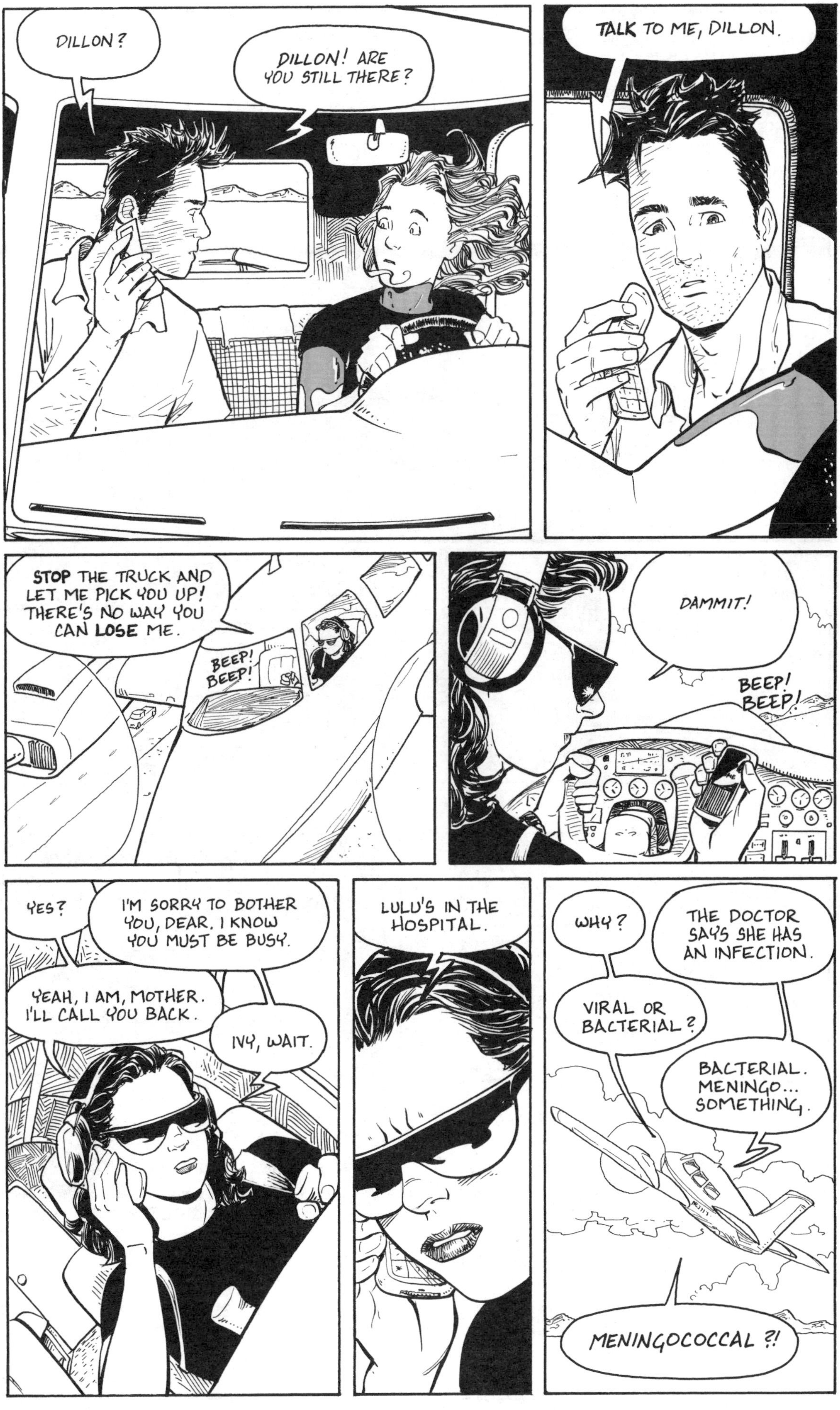
DILLON?
DILLON! ARE YOU STILL THERE?
TALK TO ME, DILLON.
STOP THE TRUCK AND LET ME PICK YOU UP! THERE'S NO WAY YOU CAN LOSE ME.
BEEP! BEEP!
DAMMIT!
BEEP! BEEP!
YES?
I'M SORRY TO BOTHER YOU, DEAR. I KNOW YOU MUST BE BUSY.
YEAH, I AM, MOTHER. I'LL CALL YOU BACK.
IVY, WAIT.
LULU'S IN THE HOSPITAL.
WHY?
THE DOCTOR SAYS SHE HAS AN INFECTION.
VIRAL OR BACTERIAL?
BACTERIAL. MENINGO... SOMETHING.
MENINGOCOCCAL?!

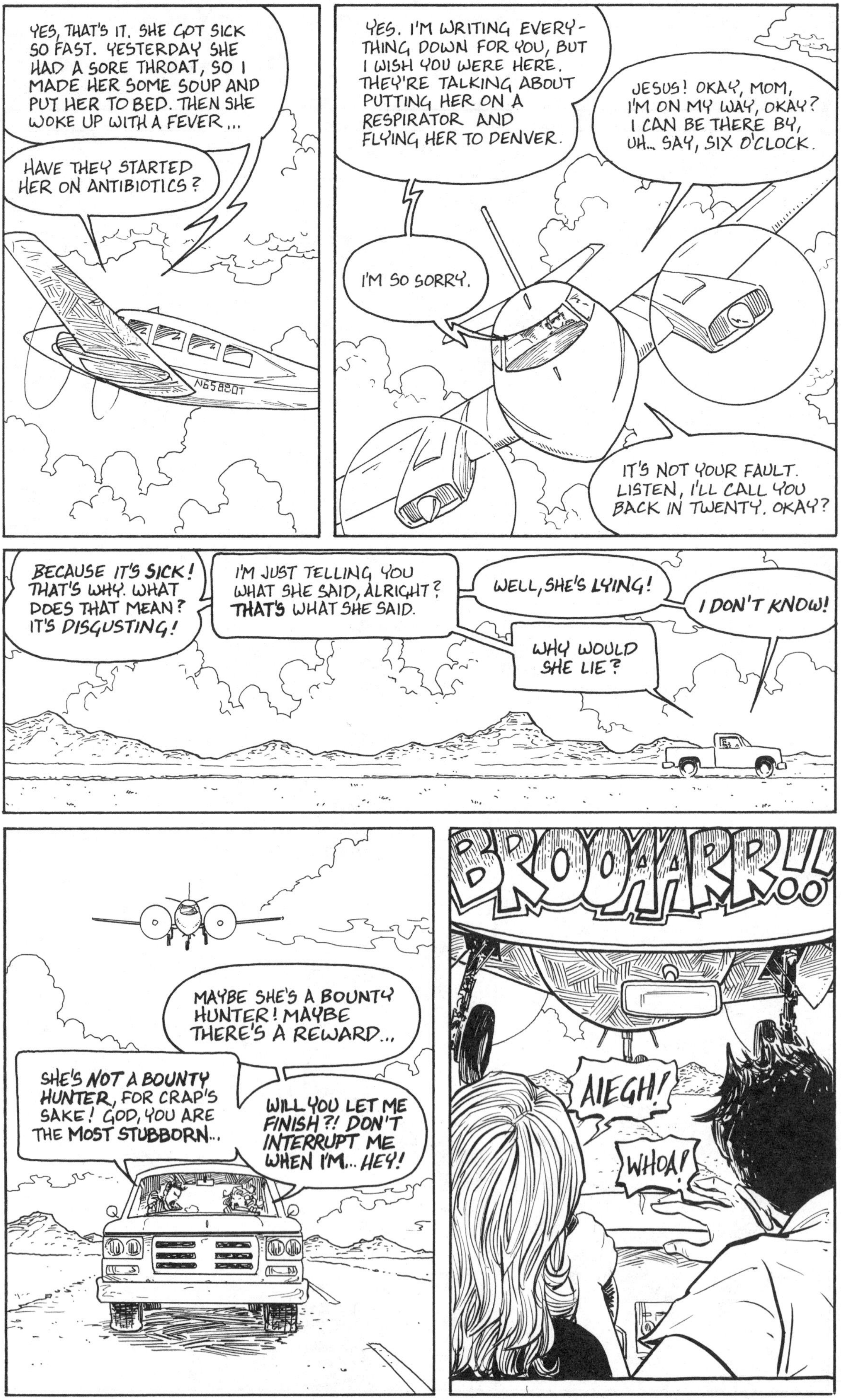

YES, THAT'S IT. SHE GOT SICK SO FAST. YESTERDAY SHE HAD A SORE THROAT, SO I MADE HER SOME SOUP AND PUT HER TO BED. THEN SHE WOKE UP WITH A FEVER...
HAVE THEY STARTED HER ON ANTIBIOTICS?
YES. I'M WRITING EVERY-THING DOWN FOR YOU, BUT I WISH YOU WERE HERE. THEY'RE TALKING ABOUT PUTTING HER ON A RESPIRATOR AND FLYING HER TO DENVER.
JESUS! OKAY, MOM, I'M ON MY WAY, OKAY? I CAN BE THERE BY, UH... SAY, SIX O'CLOCK.
I'M SO SORRY.
IT'S NOT YOUR FAULT. LISTEN, I'LL CALL YOU BACK IN TWENTY. OKAY?
BECAUSE IT'S SICK! THAT'S WHY. WHAT DOES THAT MEAN? IT'S DISGUSTING!
I'M JUST TELLING YOU WHAT SHE SAID, ALRIGHT? THAT'S WHAT SHE SAID.
WELL, SHE'S LYING!
WHY WOULD SHE LIE?
I DON'T KNOW!
MAYBE SHE'S A BOUNTY HUNTER! MAYBE THERE'S A REWARD...
SHE'S NOT A BOUNTY HUNTER, FOR CRAP'S SAKE! GOD, YOU ARE THE MOST STUBBORN...
WILL YOU LET ME FINISH?! DON'T INTERRUPT ME WHEN I'M... HEY!
BROOAARR!!
AIEGH!
WHOA!

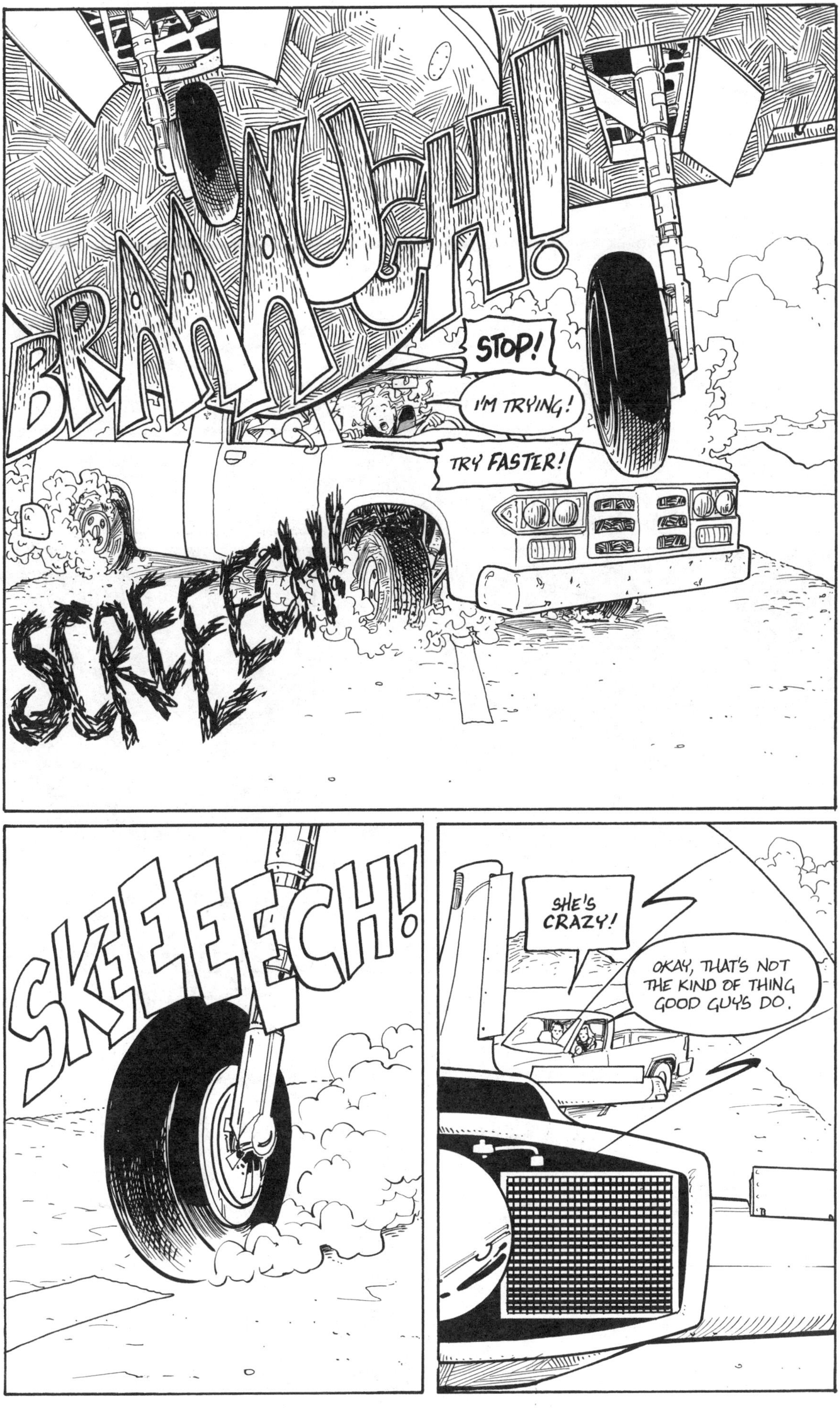
BRAAAUGH!
STOP!
I'M TRYING!
TRY FASTER!
SCREEECH!
SKEEEECH!
SHE'S CRAZY!
OKAY, THAT'S NOT THE KIND OF THING GOOD GUYS DO.

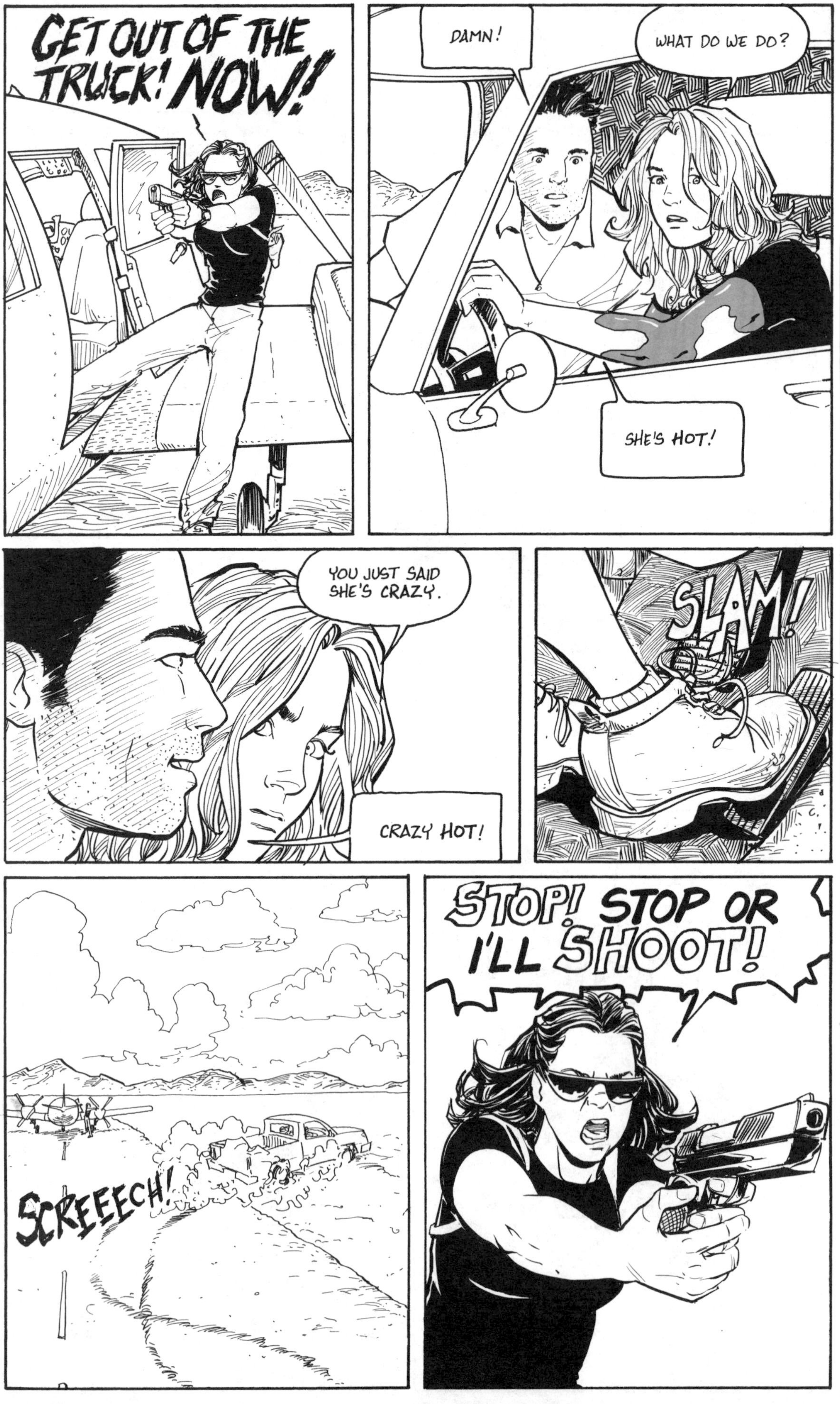
GET OUT OF THE TRUCK! NOW!!
DAMN!
WHAT DO WE DO?
SHE'S HOT!
YOU JUST SAID SHE'S CRAZY.
CRAZY HOT!
SLAM!
SCREEECH!
STOP! STOP OR I'LL SHOOT!

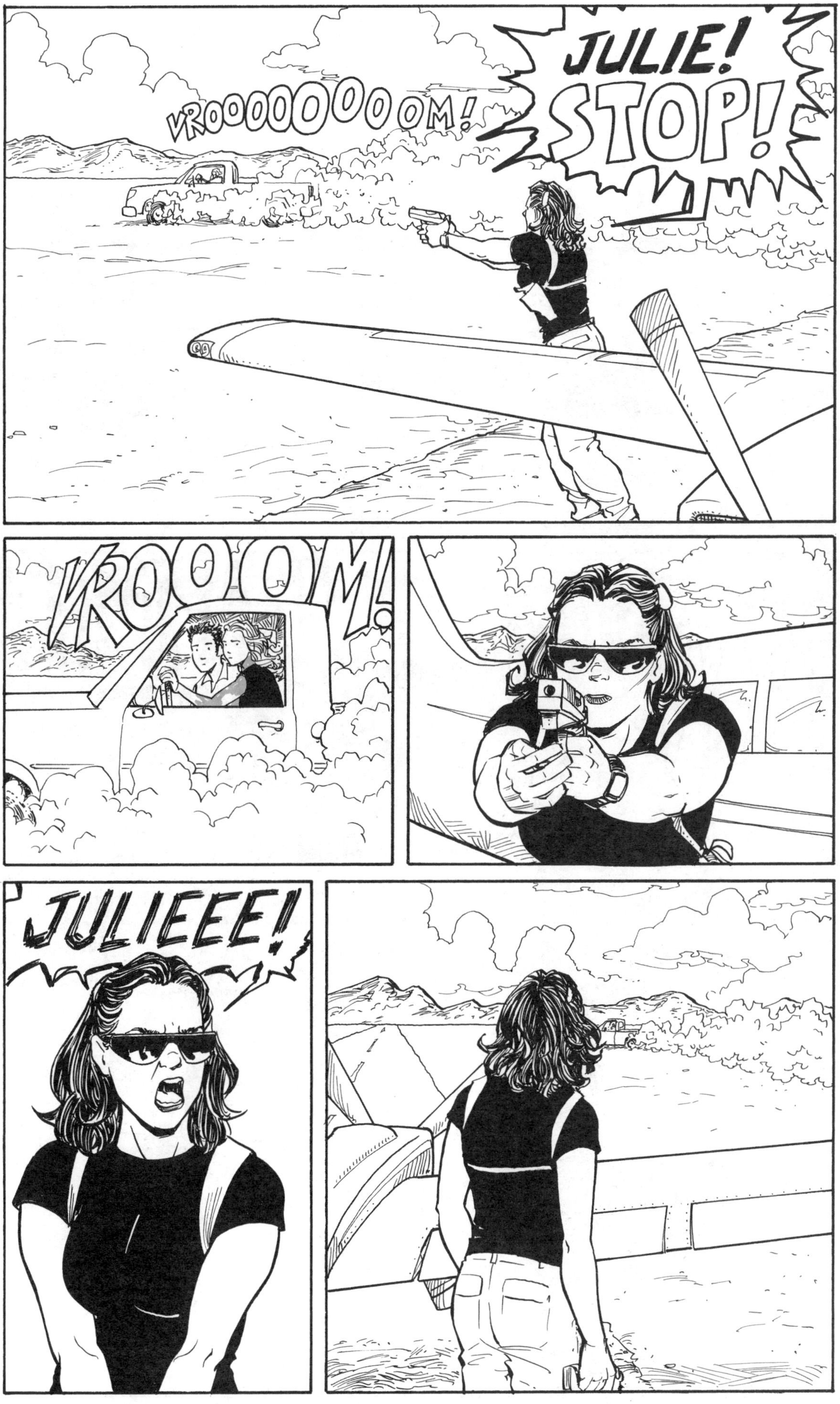
VROOOOOOOOOM!
JULIE! STOP!
VROOOOM!
JULIEEE!

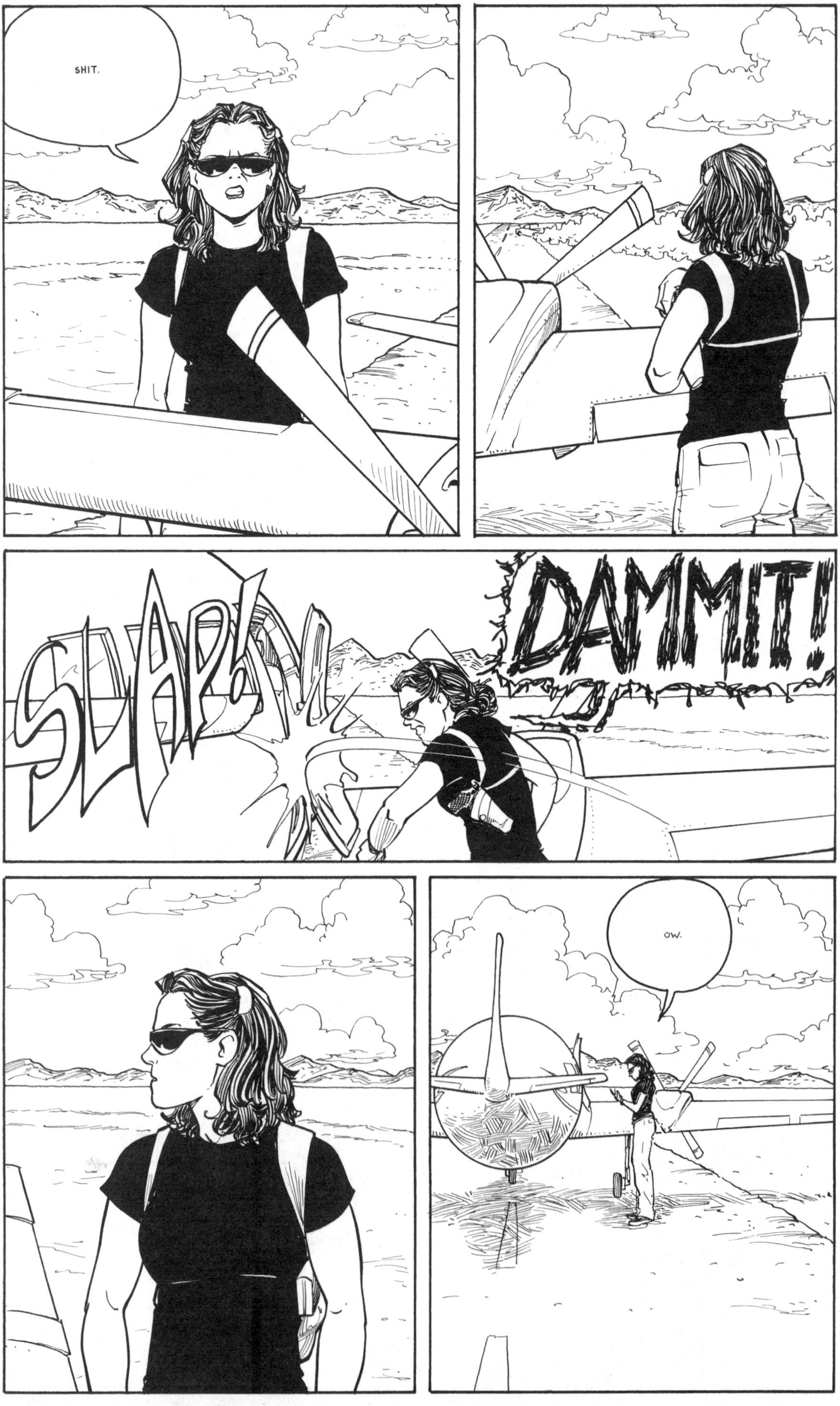
SHIT.
SLAP!
DAMMIT!
OW.

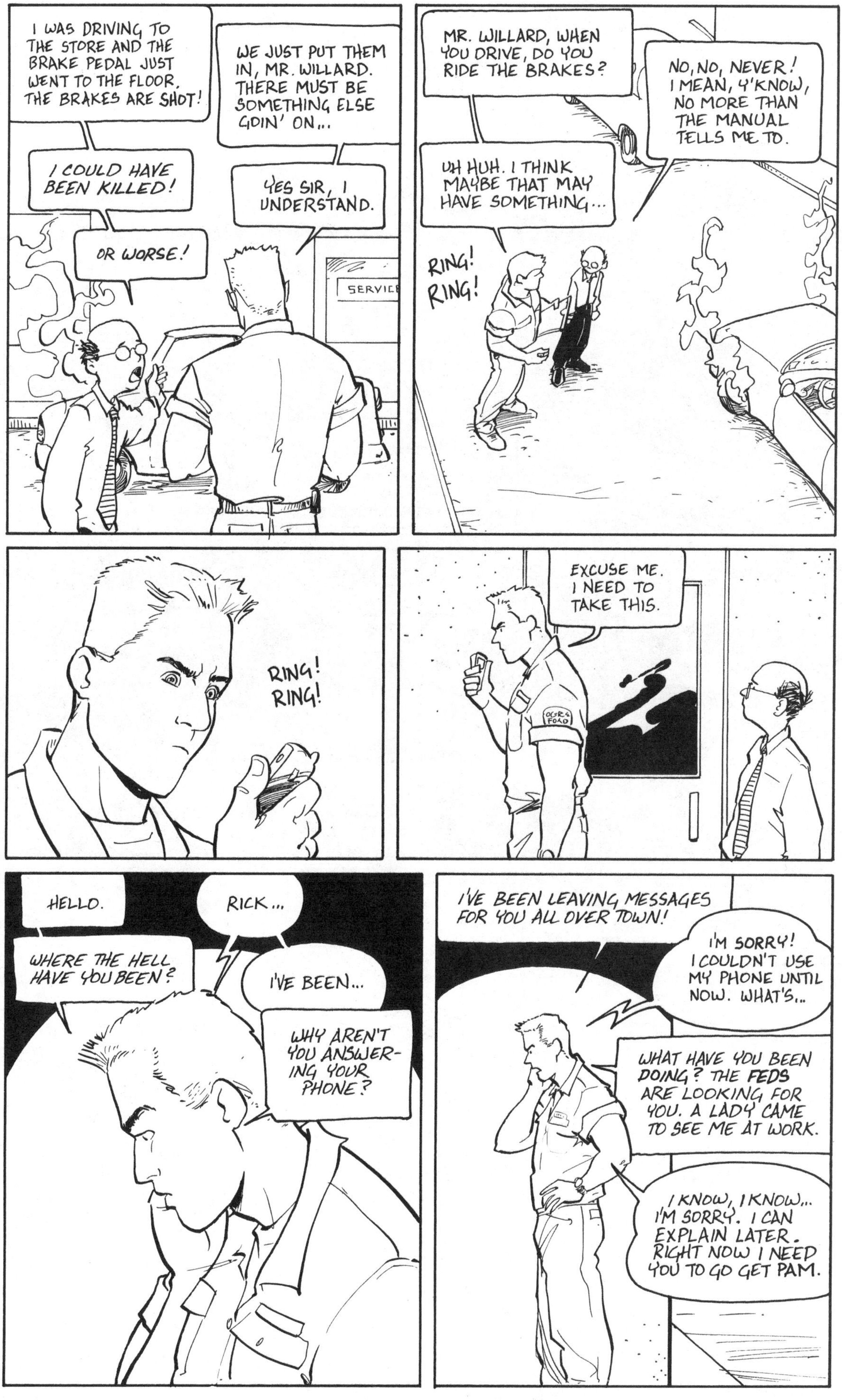
I WAS DRIVING TO THE STORE AND THE BRAKE PEDAL JUST WENT TO THE FLOOR. THE BRAKES ARE SHOT!
WE JUST PUT THEM IN, MR. WILLARD. THERE MUST BE SOMETHING ELSE GOIN' ON...
I COULD HAVE BEEN KILLED!
YES SIR, I UNDERSTAND.
OR WORSE!
MR. WILLARD, WHEN YOU DRIVE, DO YOU RIDE THE BRAKES?
NO, NO, NEVER! I MEAN, Y'KNOW, NO MORE THAN THE MANUAL TELLS ME TO.
UH HUH. I THINK MAYBE THAT MAY HAVE SOMETHING...
RING! RING!
RING! RING!
EXCUSE ME. I NEED TO TAKE THIS.
HELLO.
RICK...
WHERE THE HELL HAVE YOU BEEN?
I'VE BEEN...
WHY AREN'T YOU ANSWERING YOUR PHONE?
I'VE BEEN LEAVING MESSAGES FOR YOU ALL OVER TOWN!
I'M SORRY! I COULDN'T USE MY PHONE UNTIL NOW. WHAT'S...
WHAT HAVE YOU BEEN DOING? THE FEDS ARE LOOKING FOR YOU. A LADY CAME TO SEE ME AT WORK.
I KNOW, I KNOW... I'M SORRY. I CAN EXPLAIN LATER. RIGHT NOW I NEED YOU TO GO GET PAM.

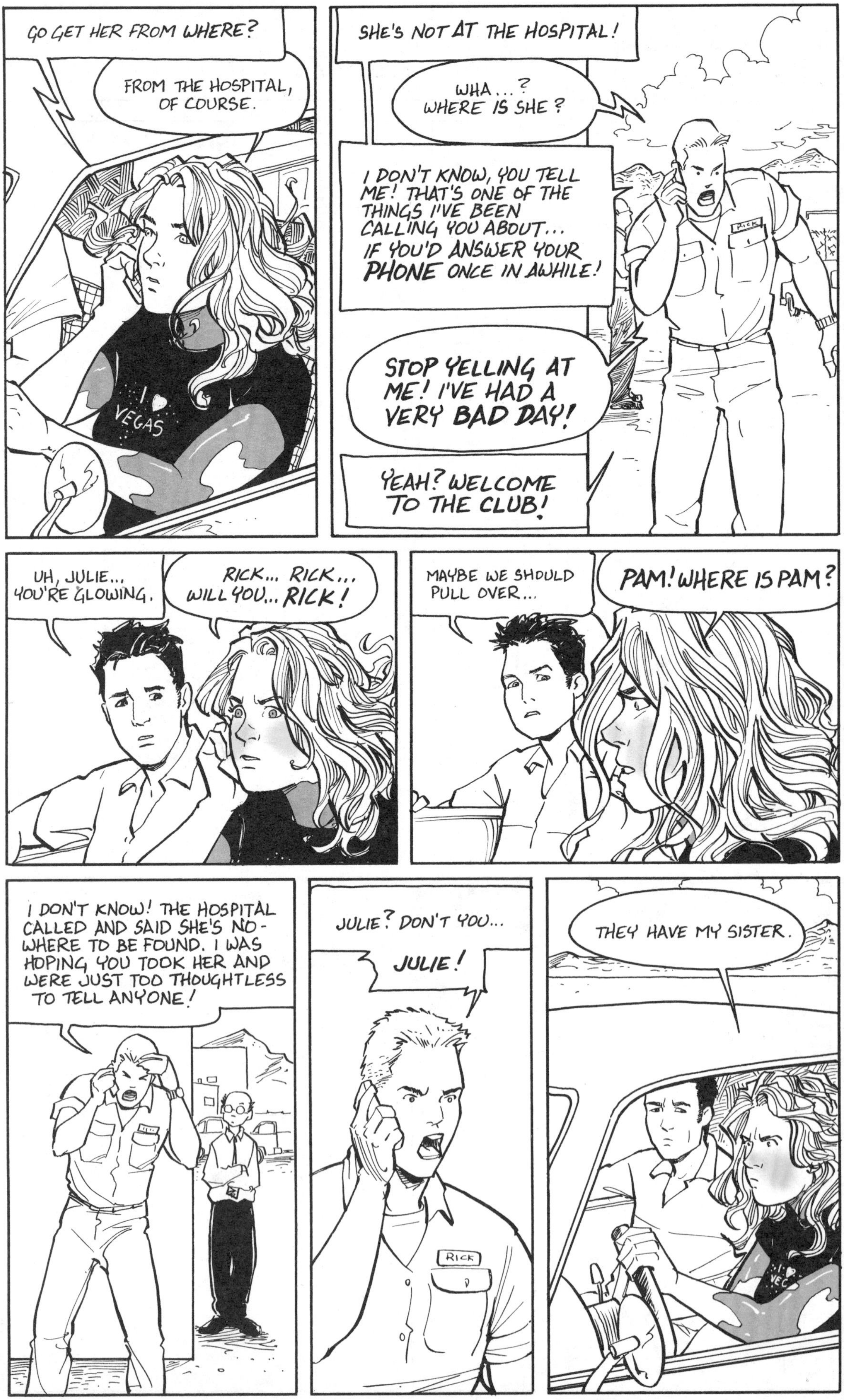
GO GET HER FROM WHERE?
FROM THE HOSPITAL, OF COURSE.
SHE'S NOT AT THE HOSPITAL!
WHA...? WHERE IS SHE?
I DON'T KNOW, YOU TELL ME! THAT'S ONE OF THE THINGS I'VE BEEN CALLING YOU ABOUT... IF YOU'D ANSWER YOUR PHONE ONCE IN AWHILE!
STOP YELLING AT ME! I'VE HAD A VERY BAD DAY!
YEAH? WELCOME TO THE CLUB!
UH, JULIE... YOU'RE GLOWING.
RICK... RICK... WILL YOU... RICK!
MAYBE WE SHOULD PULL OVER...
PAM! WHERE IS PAM?
I DON'T KNOW! THE HOSPITAL CALLED AND SAID SHE'S NO-WHERE TO BE FOUND. I WAS HOPING YOU TOOK HER AND WERE JUST TOO THOUGHTLESS TO TELL ANYONE!
JULIE? DON'T YOU...
JULIE!
THEY HAVE MY SISTER.

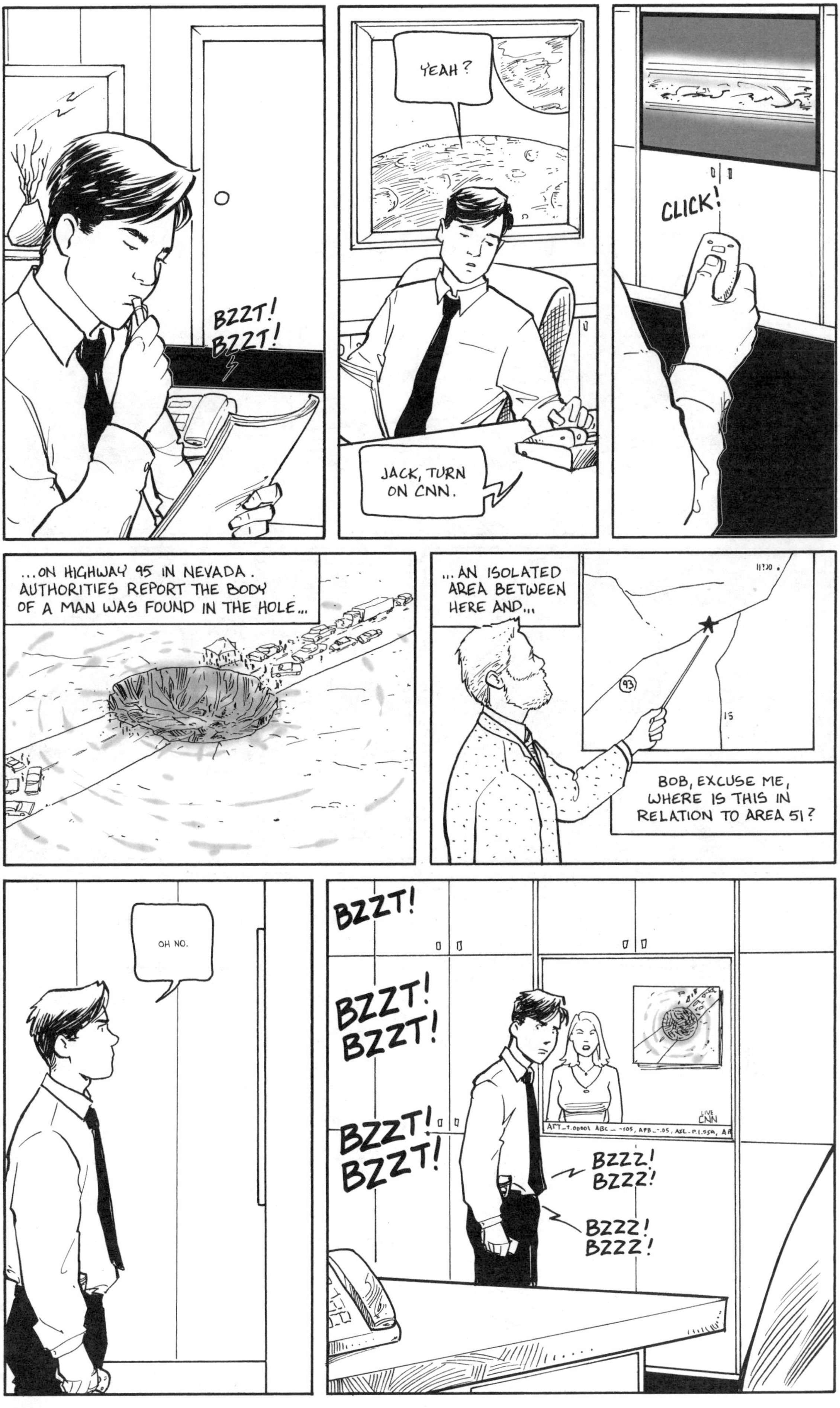
BZZT!
BZZT!
YEAH?
JACK, TURN ON CNN.
CLICK!
...ON HIGHWAY 95 IN NEVADA. AUTHORITIES REPORT THE BODY OF A MAN WAS FOUND IN THE HOLE...
...AN ISOLATED AREA BETWEEN HERE AND...
93
15
BOB, EXCUSE ME, WHERE IS THIS IN RELATION TO AREA 51?
OH NO.
BZZT!
BZZT!
BZZT!
BZZT!
BZZT!
BZZZ!
BZZZ!
BZZZ!
BZZZ!

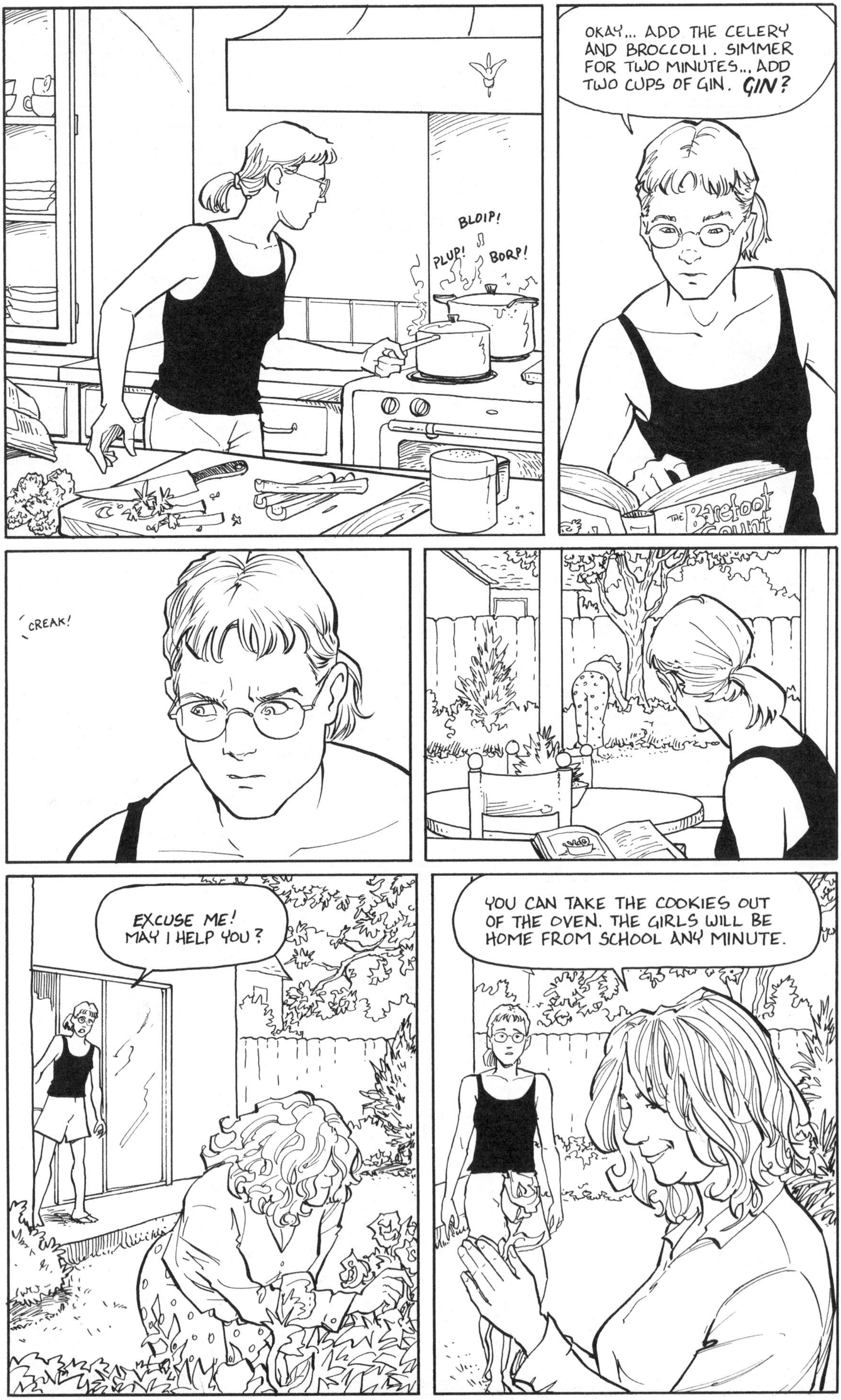
BLOIP!
PLUP!
BORP!
OKAY... ADD THE CELERY AND BROCCOLI. SIMMER FOR TWO MINUTES... ADD TWO CUPS OF GIN. GIN?
THE Barefoot Count
CREAK!
EXCUSE ME! MAY I HELP YOU?
YOU CAN TAKE THE COOKIES OUT OF THE OVEN. THE GIRLS WILL BE HOME FROM SCHOOL ANY MINUTE.

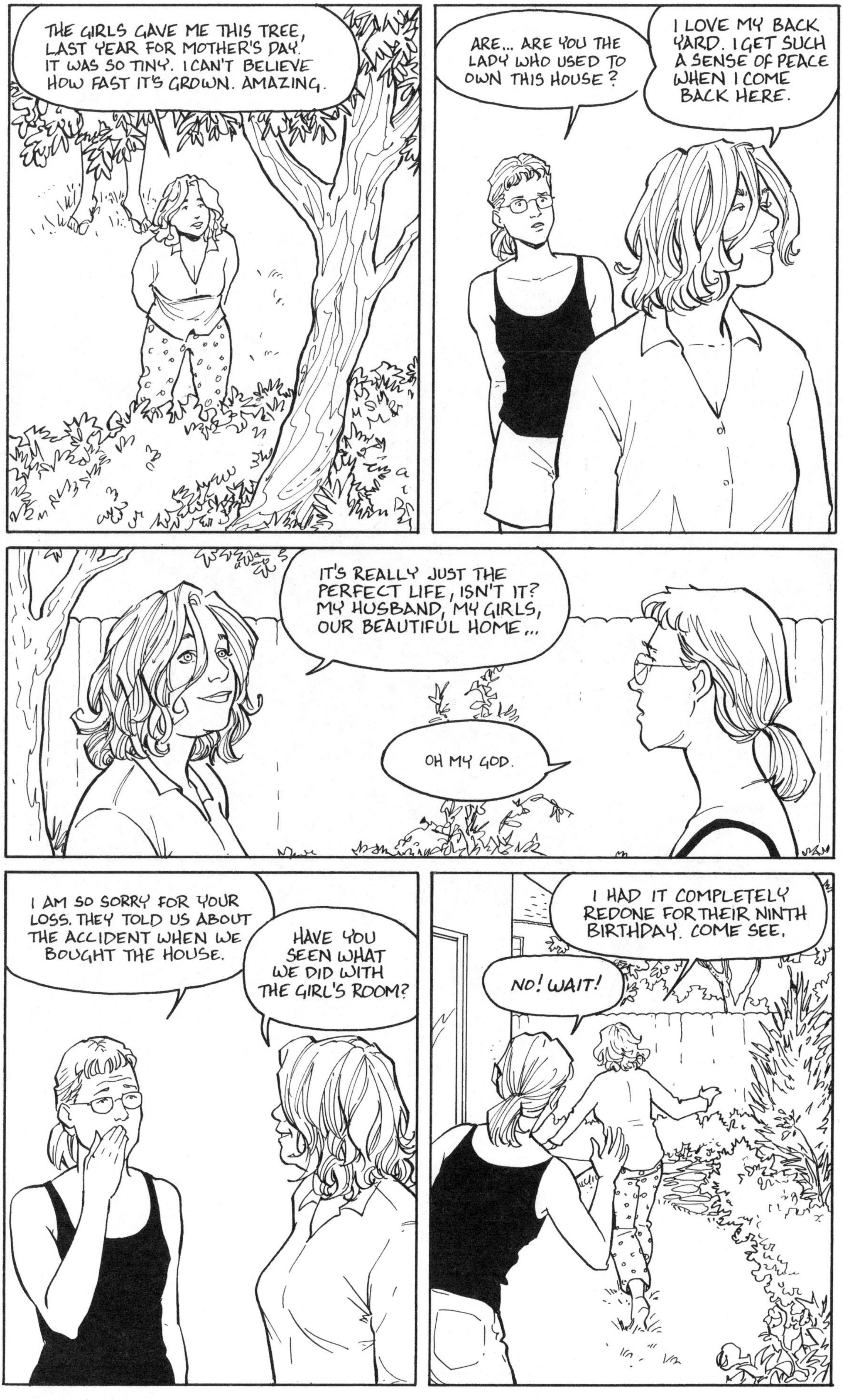
THE GIRLS GAVE ME THIS TREE, LAST YEAR FOR MOTHER'S DAY. IT WAS SO TINY. I CAN'T BELIEVE HOW FAST IT'S GROWN. AMAZING.
ARE... ARE YOU THE LADY WHO USED TO OWN THIS HOUSE?
I LOVE MY BACK YARD. I GET SUCH A SENSE OF PEACE WHEN I COME BACK HERE.
IT'S REALLY JUST THE PERFECT LIFE, ISN'T IT? MY HUSBAND, MY GIRLS, OUR BEAUTIFUL HOME...
OH MY GOD.
I AM SO SORRY FOR YOUR LOSS. THEY TOLD US ABOUT THE ACCIDENT WHEN WE BOUGHT THE HOUSE.
HAVE YOU SEEN WHAT WE DID WITH THE GIRL'S ROOM?
I HAD IT COMPLETELY REDONE FOR THEIR NINTH BIRTHDAY. COME SEE.
NO! WAIT!

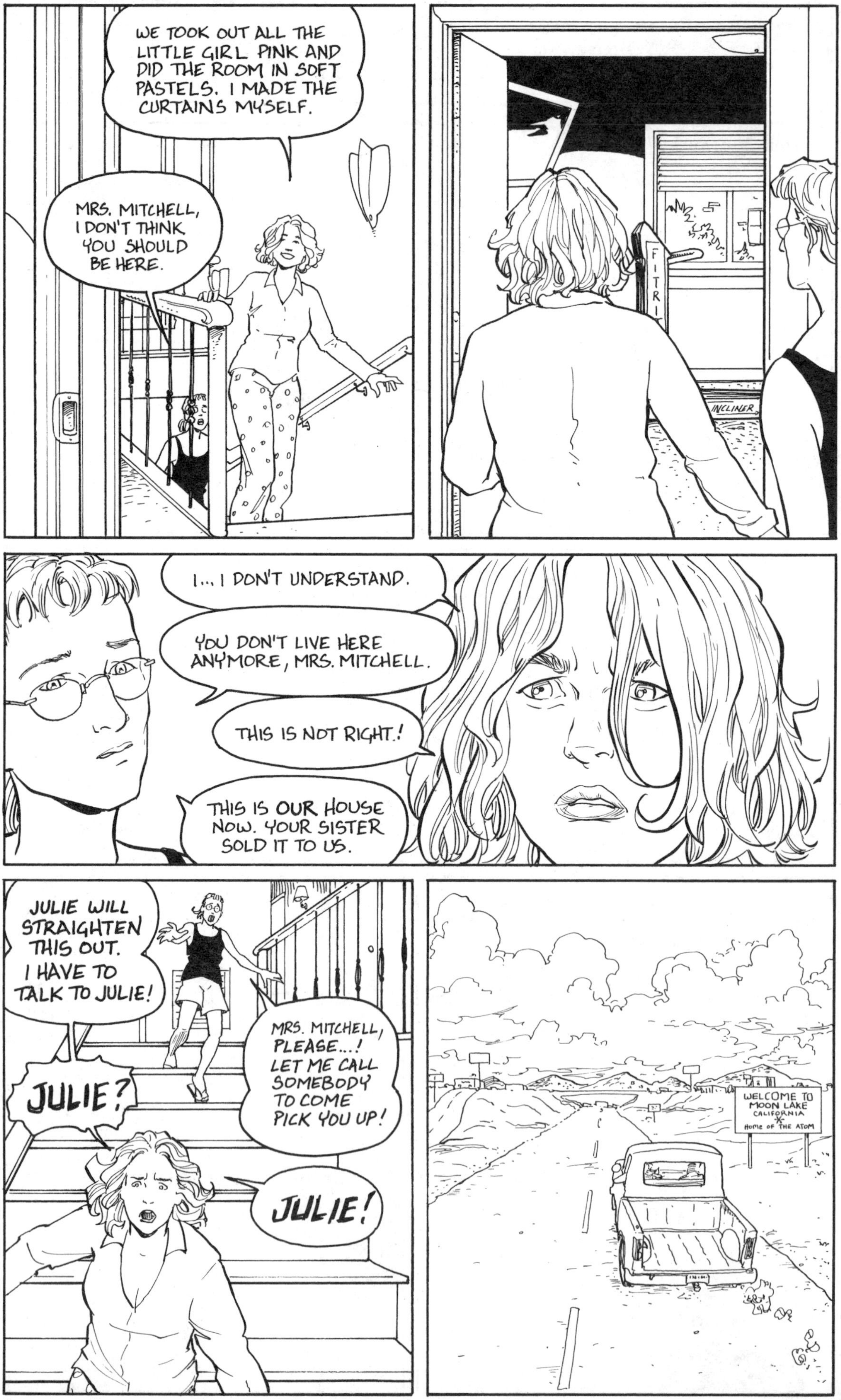
WE TOOK OUT ALL THE LITTLE GIRL PINK AND DID THE ROOM IN SOFT PASTELS. I MADE THE CURTAINS MYSELF.
MRS. MITCHELL, I DON'T THINK YOU SHOULD BE HERE.
INCLINER
I... I DON'T UNDERSTAND.
YOU DON'T LIVE HERE ANYMORE, MRS. MITCHELL.
THIS IS NOT RIGHT.!
THIS IS OUR HOUSE NOW. YOUR SISTER SOLD IT TO US.
JULIE WILL STRAIGHTEN THIS OUT. I HAVE TO TALK TO JULIE!
JULIE?
MRS. MITCHELL, PLEASE...! LET ME CALL SOMEBODY TO COME PICK YOU UP!
JULIE!
WELCOME TO MOON LAKE CALIFORNIA HOME OF THE ATOM

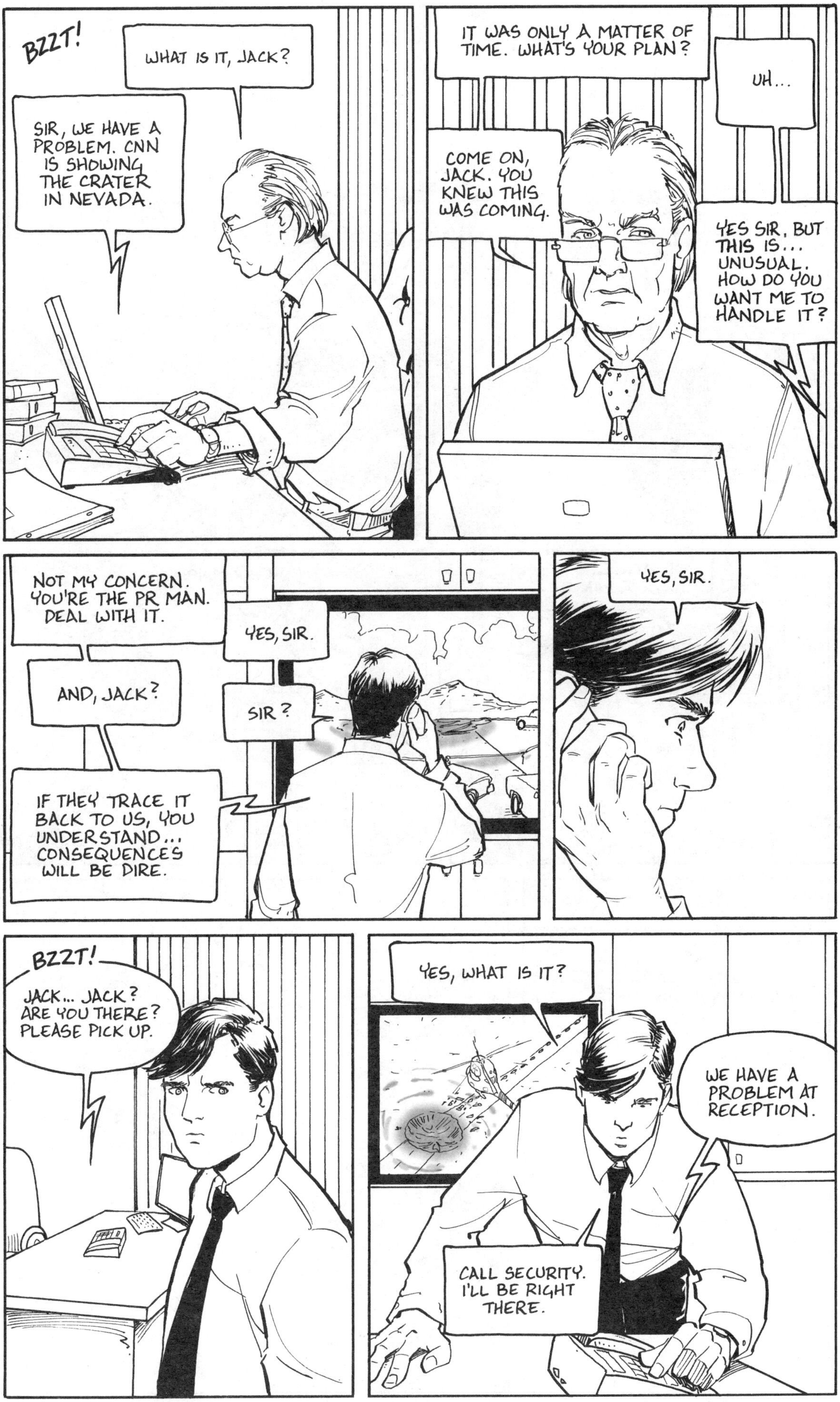
BZZT!
WHAT IS IT, JACK?
SIR, WE HAVE A PROBLEM. CNN IS SHOWING THE CRATER IN NEVADA.
IT WAS ONLY A MATTER OF TIME. WHAT'S YOUR PLAN?
UH...
COME ON, JACK. YOU KNEW THIS WAS COMING.
YES SIR, BUT THIS IS... UNUSUAL. HOW DO YOU WANT ME TO HANDLE IT?
NOT MY CONCERN. YOU'RE THE PR MAN. DEAL WITH IT.
YES, SIR.
AND, JACK?
SIR?
IF THEY TRACE IT BACK TO US, YOU UNDERSTAND... CONSEQUENCES WILL BE DIRE.
YES, SIR.
BZZT!
JACK... JACK? ARE YOU THERE? PLEASE PICK UP.
YES, WHAT IS IT?
WE HAVE A PROBLEM AT RECEPTION.
CALL SECURITY. I'LL BE RIGHT THERE.

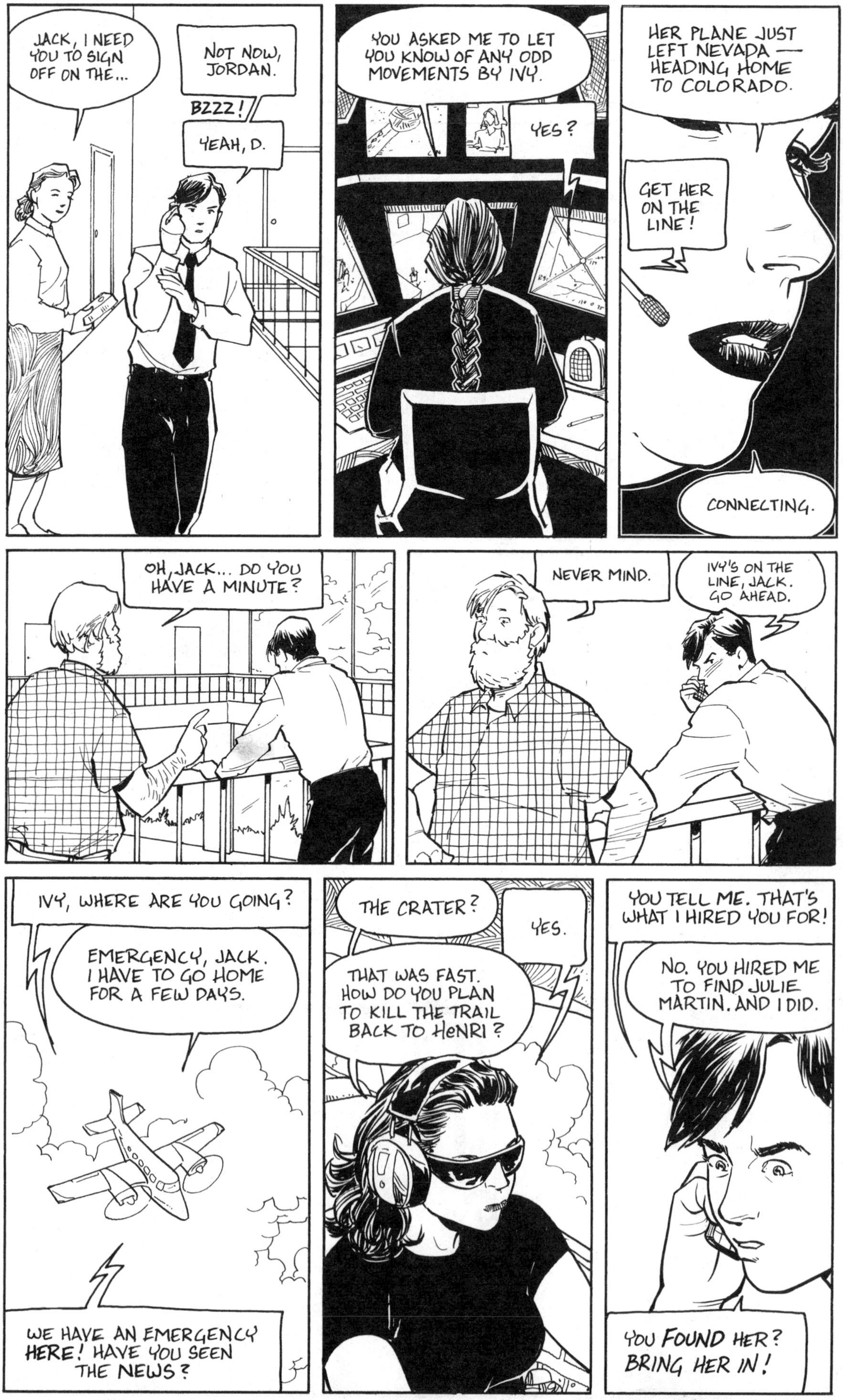
JACK, I NEED YOU TO SIGN OFF ON THE...
NOT NOW, JORDAN.
BZZZ!
YEAH, D.
YOU ASKED ME TO LET YOU KNOW OF ANY ODD MOVEMENTS BY IVY.
YES?
HER PLANE JUST LEFT NEVADA — HEADING HOME TO COLORADO.
GET HER ON THE LINE!
CONNECTING.
OH, JACK... DO YOU HAVE A MINUTE?
NEVER MIND.
IVY'S ON THE LINE, JACK. GO AHEAD.
IVY, WHERE ARE YOU GOING?
EMERGENCY, JACK. I HAVE TO GO HOME FOR A FEW DAYS.
WE HAVE AN EMERGENCY HERE! HAVE YOU SEEN THE NEWS?
THE CRATER?
YES.
THAT WAS FAST. HOW DO YOU PLAN TO KILL THE TRAIL BACK TO HENRI?
YOU TELL ME. THAT'S WHAT I HIRED YOU FOR!
NO. YOU HIRED ME TO FIND JULIE MARTIN. AND I DID.
YOU FOUND HER? BRING HER IN!

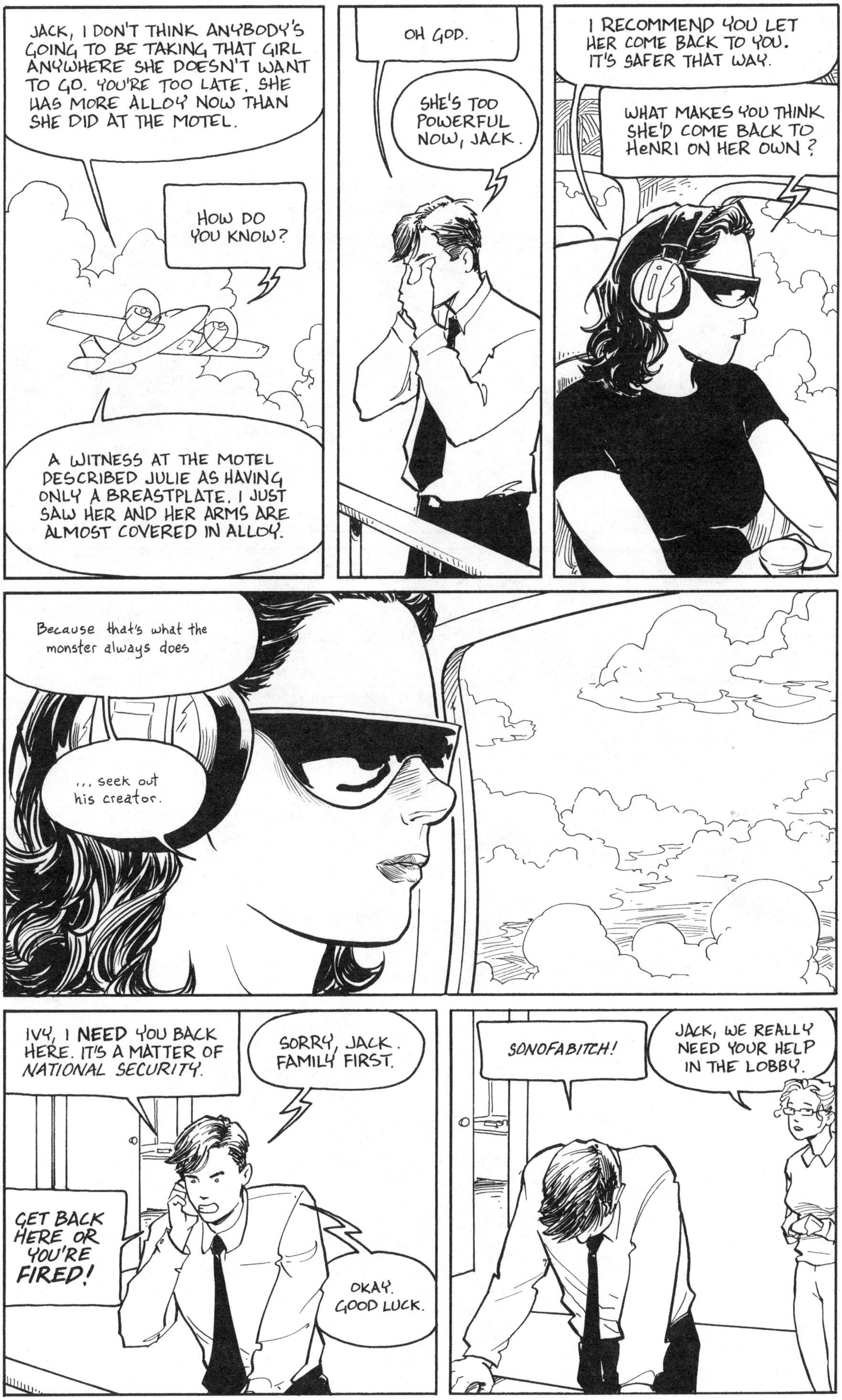
JACK, I DON'T THINK ANYBODY'S GOING TO BE TAKING THAT GIRL ANYWHERE SHE DOESN'T WANT TO GO. YOU'RE TOO LATE. SHE HAS MORE ALLOY NOW THAN SHE DID AT THE MOTEL.
HOW DO YOU KNOW?
A WITNESS AT THE MOTEL DESCRIBED JULIE AS HAVING ONLY A BREASTPLATE. I JUST SAW HER AND HER ARMS ARE ALMOST COVERED IN ALLOY.
OH GOD.
SHE'S TOO POWERFUL NOW, JACK.
I RECOMMEND YOU LET HER COME BACK TO YOU. IT'S SAFER THAT WAY.
WHAT MAKES YOU THINK SHE'D COME BACK TO HENRI ON HER OWN?
Because that's what the monster always does
... seek out his creator.
IVY, I NEED YOU BACK HERE. IT'S A MATTER OF NATIONAL SECURITY.
SORRY, JACK. FAMILY FIRST.
GET BACK HERE OR YOU'RE FIRED!
OKAY. GOOD LUCK.
SONOFABITCH!
JACK, WE REALLY NEED YOUR HELP IN THE LOBBY.

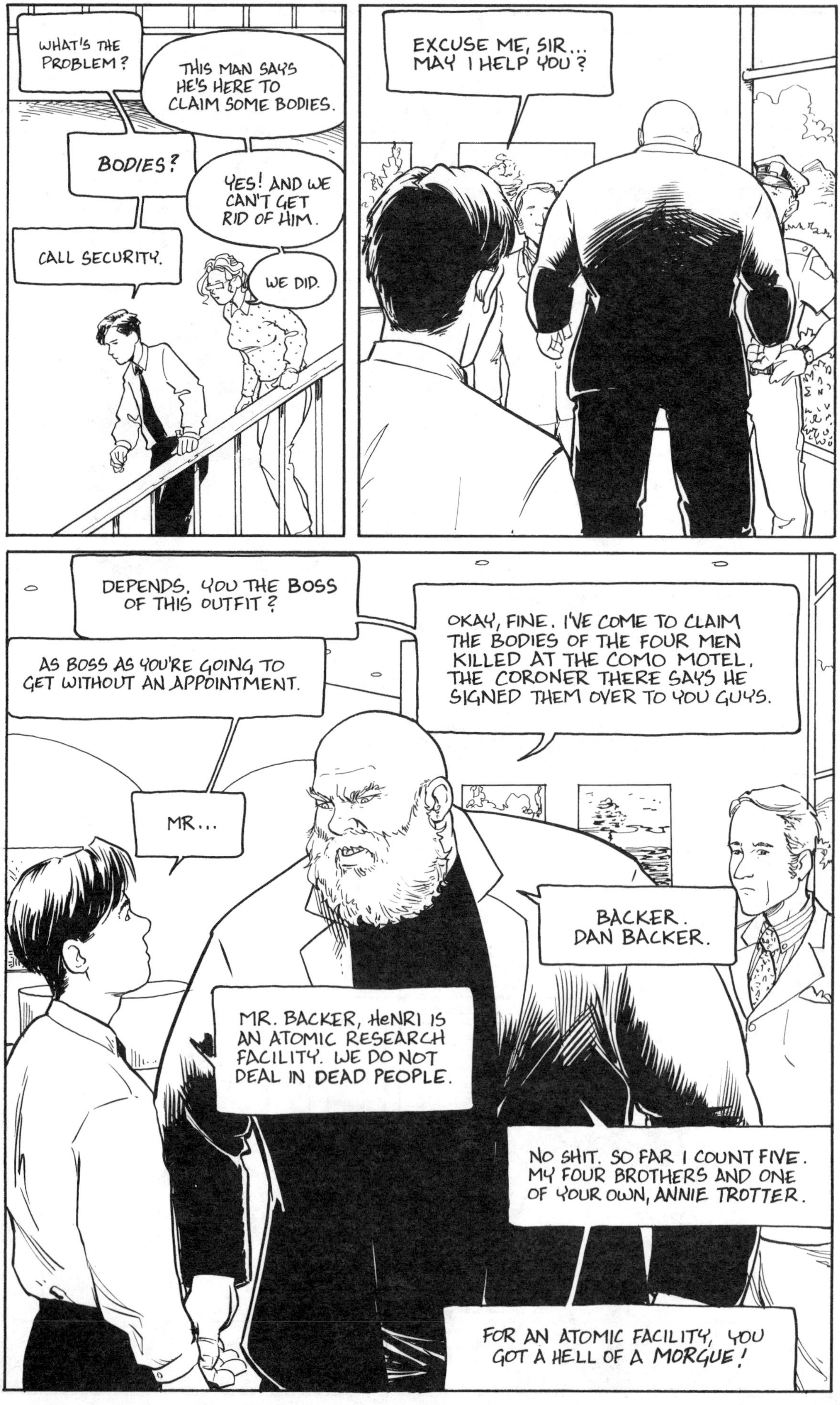
WHAT'S THE PROBLEM?
THIS MAN SAYS HE'S HERE TO CLAIM SOME BODIES.
BODIES?
YES! AND WE CAN'T GET RID OF HIM.
CALL SECURITY.
WE DID.
EXCUSE ME, SIR... MAY I HELP YOU?
DEPENDS. YOU THE BOSS OF THIS OUTFIT?
AS BOSS AS YOU'RE GOING TO GET WITHOUT AN APPOINTMENT.
OKAY, FINE. I'VE COME TO CLAIM THE BODIES OF THE FOUR MEN KILLED AT THE COMO MOTEL. THE CORONER THERE SAYS HE SIGNED THEM OVER TO YOU GUYS.
MR...
BACKER. DAN BACKER.
MR. BACKER, HeNRI IS AN ATOMIC RESEARCH FACILITY. WE DO NOT DEAL IN DEAD PEOPLE.
NO SHIT. SO FAR I COUNT FIVE. MY FOUR BROTHERS AND ONE OF YOUR OWN, ANNIE TROTTER.
FOR AN ATOMIC FACILITY, YOU GOT A HELL OF A MORGUE!

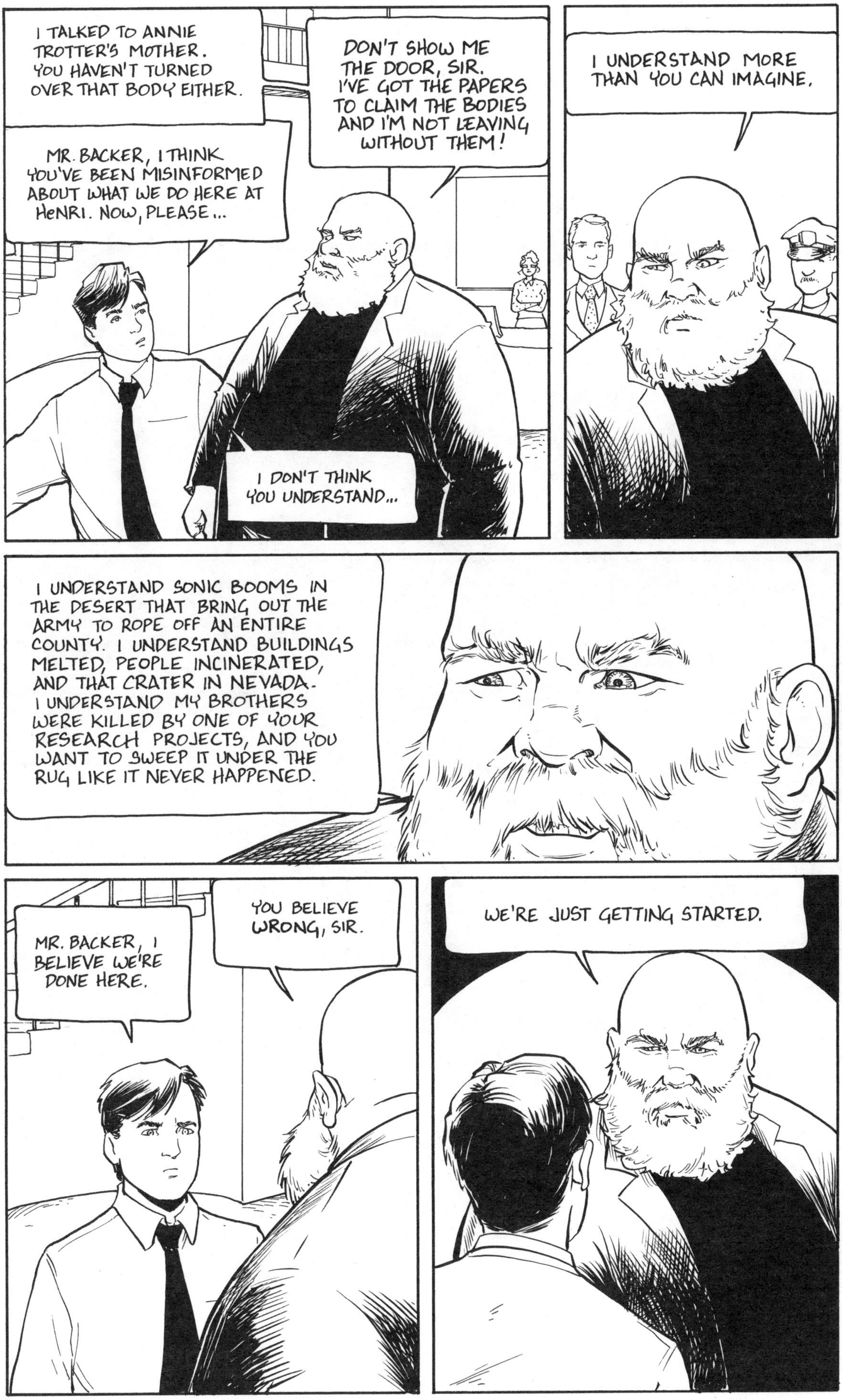
I TALKED TO ANNIE TROTTER'S MOTHER. YOU HAVEN'T TURNED OVER THAT BODY EITHER.
MR. BACKER, I THINK YOU'VE BEEN MISINFORMED ABOUT WHAT WE DO HERE AT HeNRI. NOW, PLEASE...
DON'T SHOW ME THE DOOR, SIR. I'VE GOT THE PAPERS TO CLAIM THE BODIES AND I'M NOT LEAVING WITHOUT THEM!
I DON'T THINK YOU UNDERSTAND...
I UNDERSTAND MORE THAN YOU CAN IMAGINE.
I UNDERSTAND SONIC BOOMS IN THE DESERT THAT BRING OUT THE ARMY TO ROPE OFF AN ENTIRE COUNTY. I UNDERSTAND BUILDINGS MELTED, PEOPLE INCINERATED, AND THAT CRATER IN NEVADA. I UNDERSTAND MY BROTHERS WERE KILLED BY ONE OF YOUR RESEARCH PROJECTS, AND YOU WANT TO SWEEP IT UNDER THE RUG LIKE IT NEVER HAPPENED.
MR. BACKER, I BELIEVE WE'RE DONE HERE.
YOU BELIEVE WRONG, SIR.
WE'RE JUST GETTING STARTED.

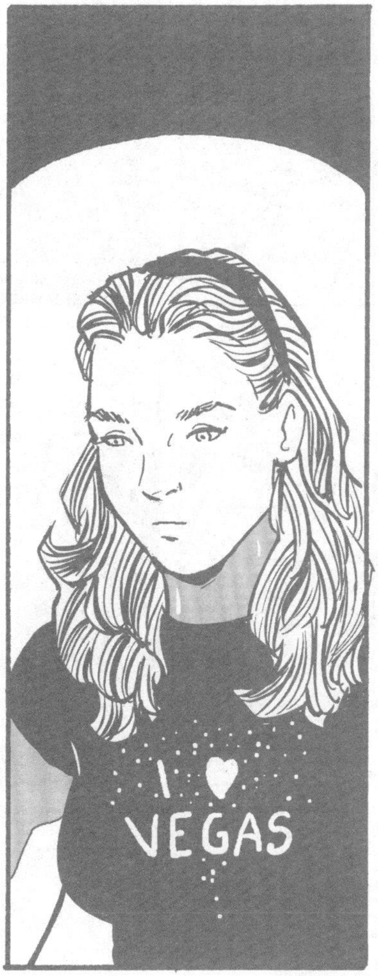
I ♥
VEGAS

You cannot simultaneously prevent and prepare for war.
—Albert Einstein

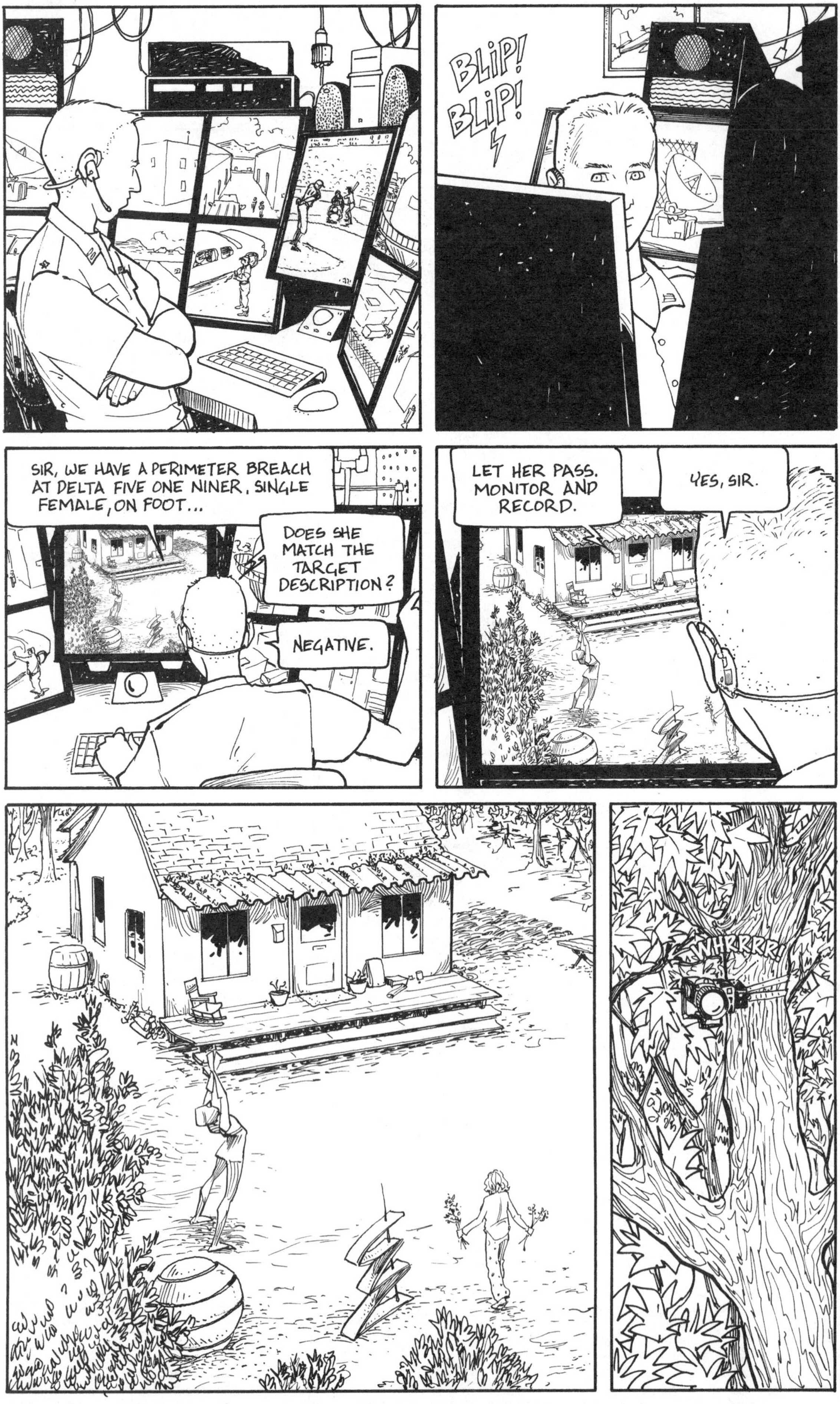
BLIP! BLIP!
SIR, WE HAVE A PERIMETER BREACH AT DELTA FIVE ONE NINER, SINGLE FEMALE, ON FOOT...
DOES SHE MATCH THE TARGET DESCRIPTION?
NEGATIVE.
LET HER PASS. MONITOR AND RECORD.
YES, SIR.
WHRRRR

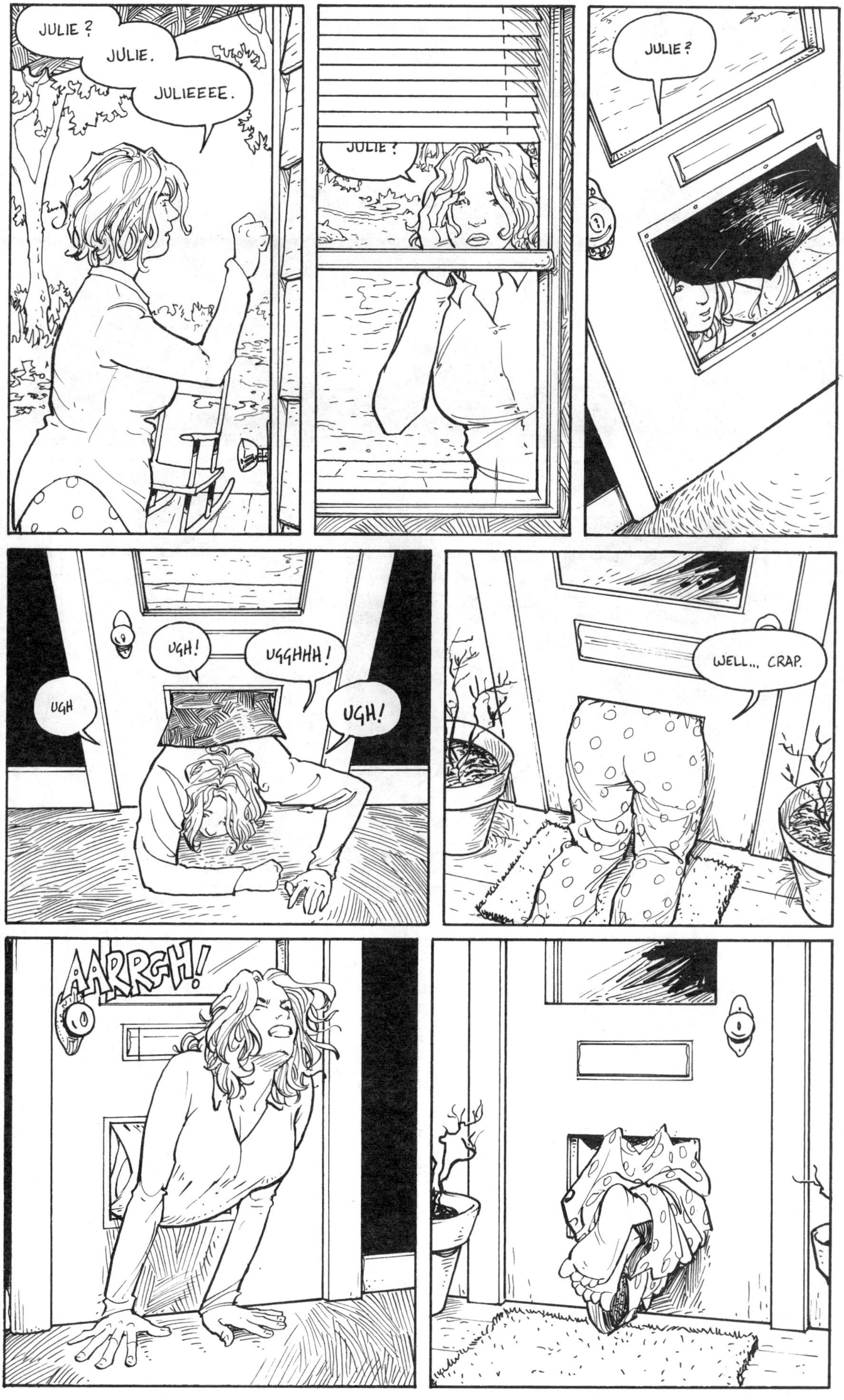
JULIE?
JULIE.
JULIEEEE.
JULIE?
JULIE?
UGH
UGH!
UGGHHH!
UGH!
WELL... CRAP.
AARRGH!

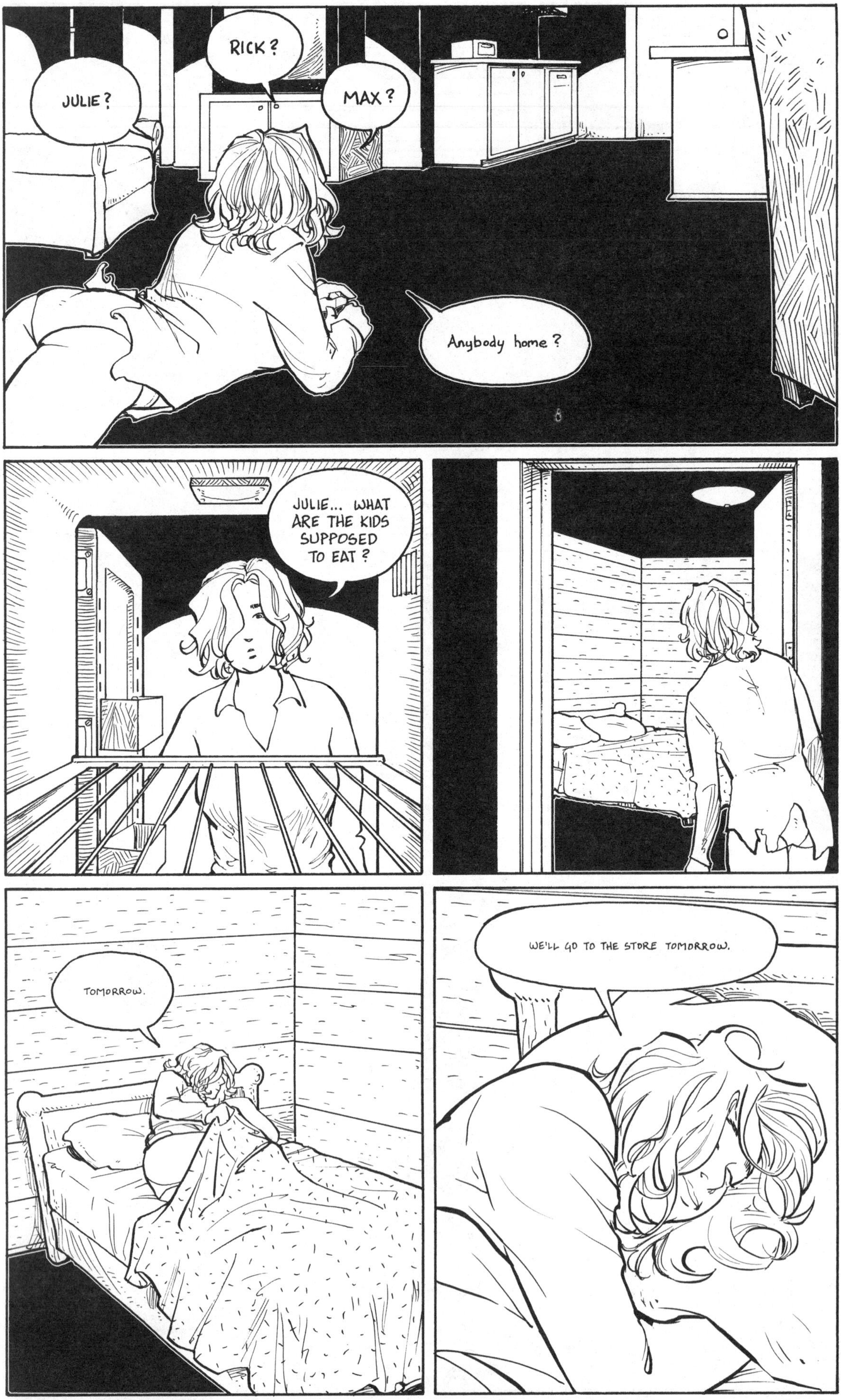
JULIE?
RICK?
MAX?
Anybody home?
JULIE... WHAT ARE THE KIDS SUPPOSED TO EAT?
TOMORROW.
WE'LL GO TO THE STORE TOMORROW.

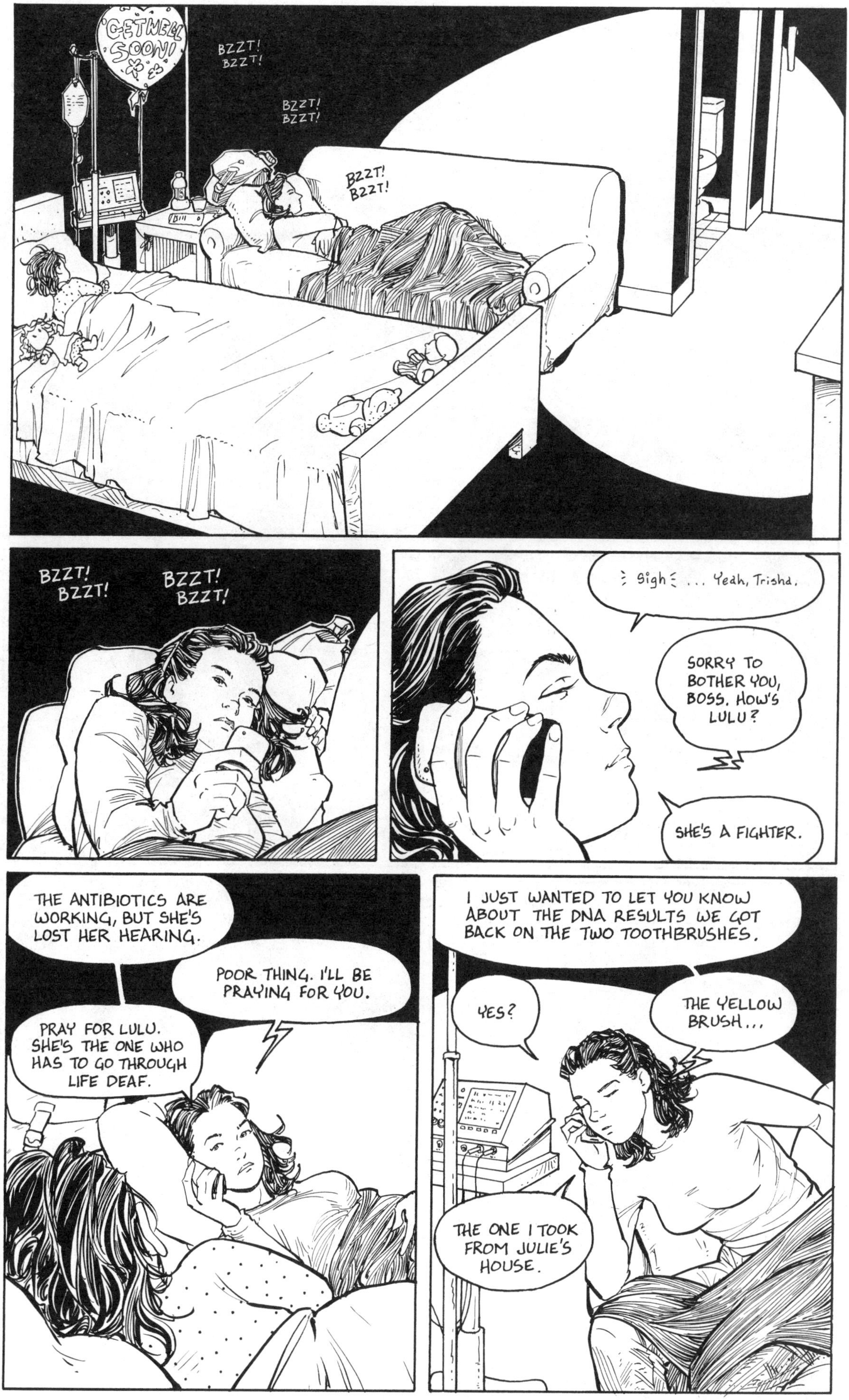
GET WELL SOON!
BZZT! BZZT!
BZZT! BZZT!
BZZT! BZZT!
BZZT! BZZT!
BZZT! BZZT!
Sigh ... Yeah, Trisha.
SORRY TO BOTHER YOU, BOSS. HOW'S LULU?
SHE'S A FIGHTER.
THE ANTIBIOTICS ARE WORKING, BUT SHE'S LOST HER HEARING.
POOR THING. I'LL BE PRAYING FOR YOU.
PRAY FOR LULU. SHE'S THE ONE WHO HAS TO GO THROUGH LIFE DEAF.
I JUST WANTED TO LET YOU KNOW ABOUT THE DNA RESULTS WE GOT BACK ON THE TWO TOOTHBRUSHES.
YES?
THE YELLOW BRUSH...
THE ONE I TOOK FROM JULIE'S HOUSE.

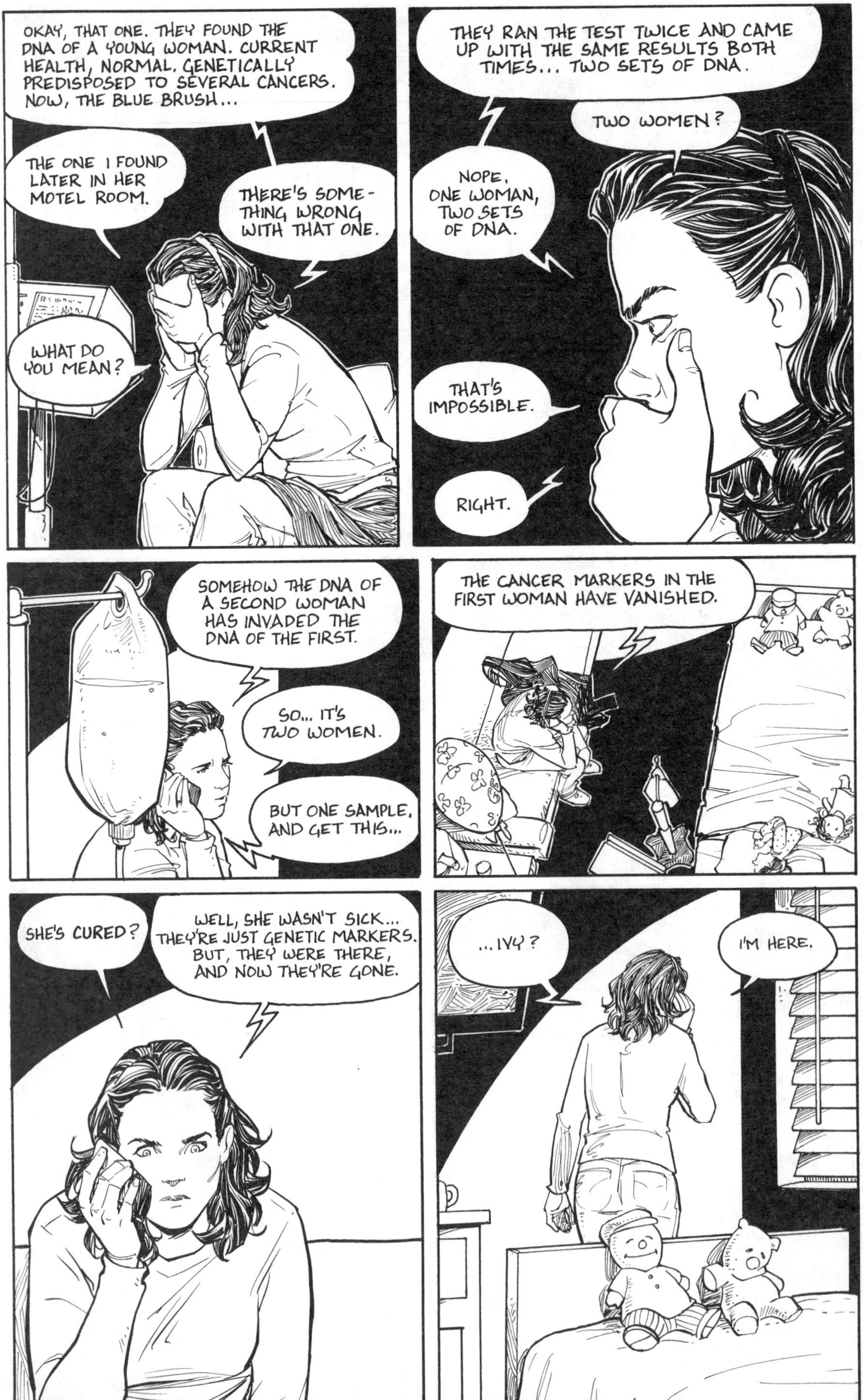

OKAY, THAT ONE. THEY FOUND THE DNA OF A YOUNG WOMAN. CURRENT HEALTH, NORMAL. GENETICALLY PREDISPOSED TO SEVERAL CANCERS. NOW, THE BLUE BRUSH...
THE ONE I FOUND LATER IN HER MOTEL ROOM.
THERE'S SOMETHING WRONG WITH THAT ONE.
WHAT DO YOU MEAN?
THEY RAN THE TEST TWICE AND CAME UP WITH THE SAME RESULTS BOTH TIMES... TWO SETS OF DNA.
TWO WOMEN?
NOPE. ONE WOMAN, TWO SETS OF DNA.
THAT'S IMPOSSIBLE.
RIGHT.
SOMEHOW THE DNA OF A SECOND WOMAN HAS INVADED THE DNA OF THE FIRST.
SO... IT'S TWO WOMEN.
BUT ONE SAMPLE, AND GET THIS...
THE CANCER MARKERS IN THE FIRST WOMAN HAVE VANISHED.
SHE'S CURED?
WELL, SHE WASN'T SICK... THEY'RE JUST GENETIC MARKERS. BUT, THEY WERE THERE, AND NOW THEY'RE GONE.
...IVY?
I'M HERE.

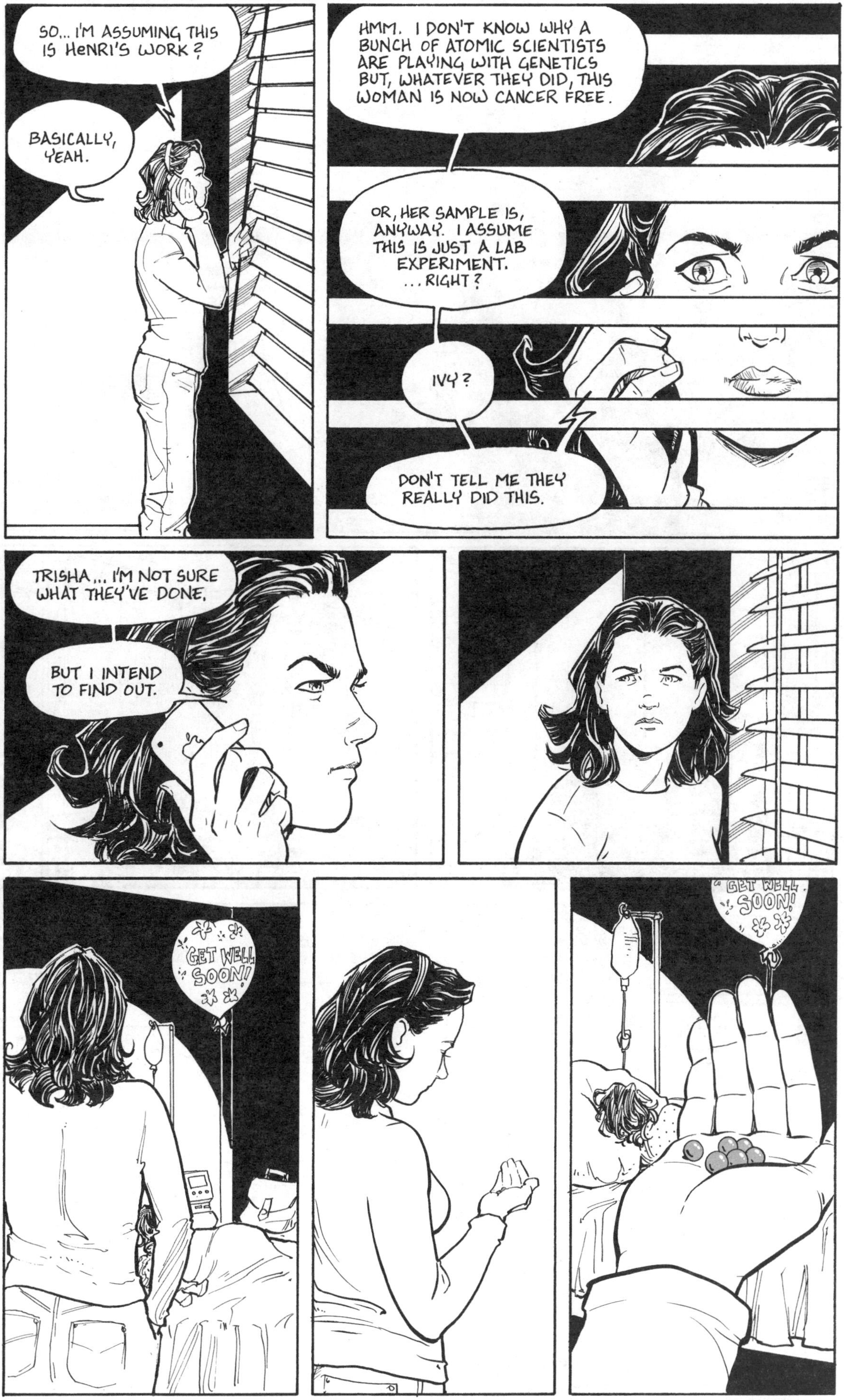
SO... I'M ASSUMING THIS IS HENRI'S WORK?
BASICALLY, YEAH.
HMM. I DON'T KNOW WHY A BUNCH OF ATOMIC SCIENTISTS ARE PLAYING WITH GENETICS BUT, WHATEVER THEY DID, THIS WOMAN IS NOW CANCER FREE.
OR, HER SAMPLE IS, ANYWAY. I ASSUME THIS IS JUST A LAB EXPERIMENT. ...RIGHT?
IVY?
DON'T TELL ME THEY REALLY DID THIS.
TRISHA... I'M NOT SURE WHAT THEY'VE DONE.
BUT I INTEND TO FIND OUT.
GET WELL SOON!
GET WELL SOON!

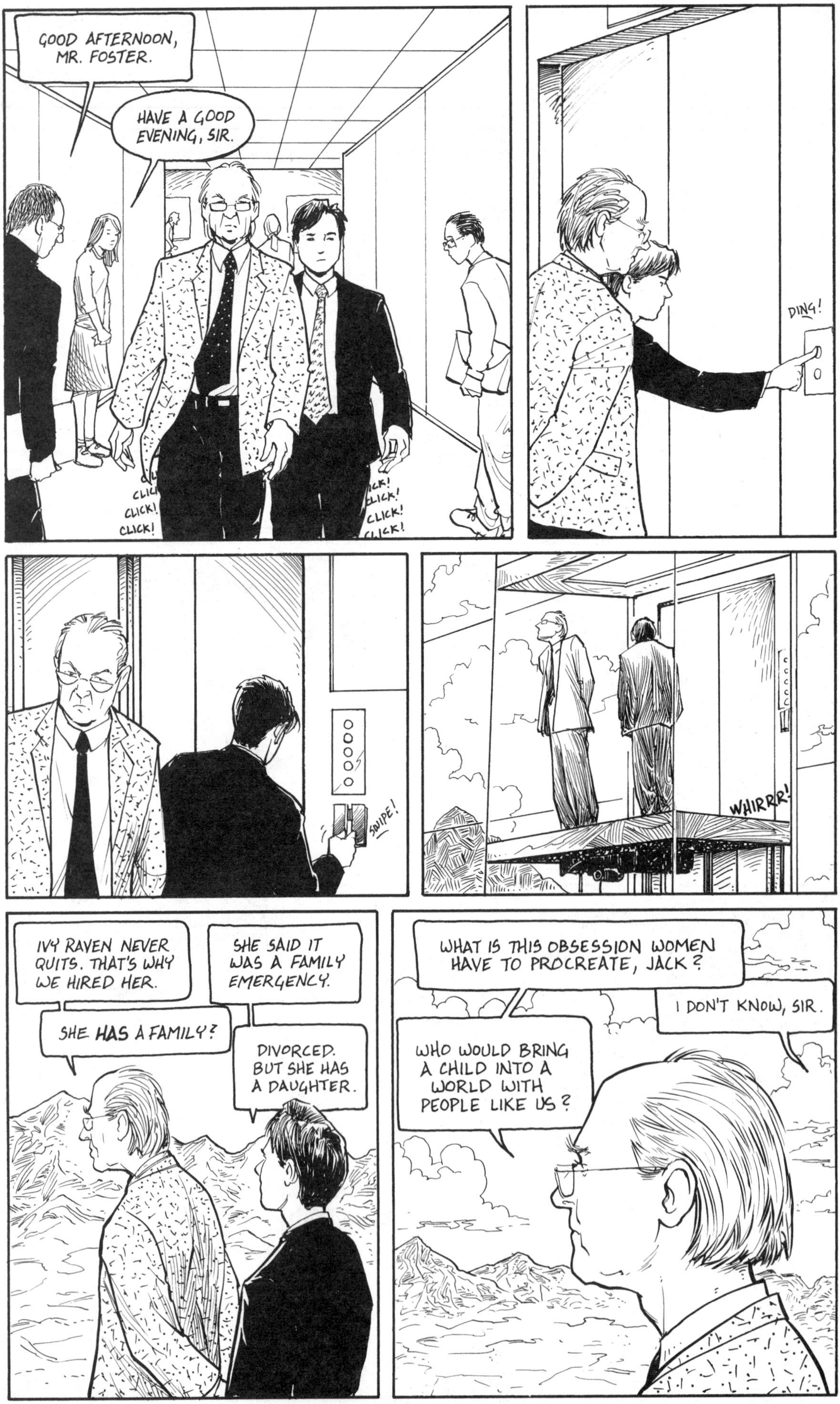
GOOD AFTERNOON, MR. FOSTER.
HAVE A GOOD EVENING, SIR.
CLICK! CLICK! CLICK!
CLICK! CLICK! CLICK!
DING!
SWIPE!
WHIRRR!
IVY RAVEN NEVER QUITS. THAT'S WHY WE HIRED HER.
SHE HAS A FAMILY?
SHE SAID IT WAS A FAMILY EMERGENCY.
DIVORCED. BUT SHE HAS A DAUGHTER.
WHAT IS THIS OBSESSION WOMEN HAVE TO PROCREATE, JACK?
WHO WOULD BRING A CHILD INTO A WORLD WITH PEOPLE LIKE US?
I DON'T KNOW, SIR.

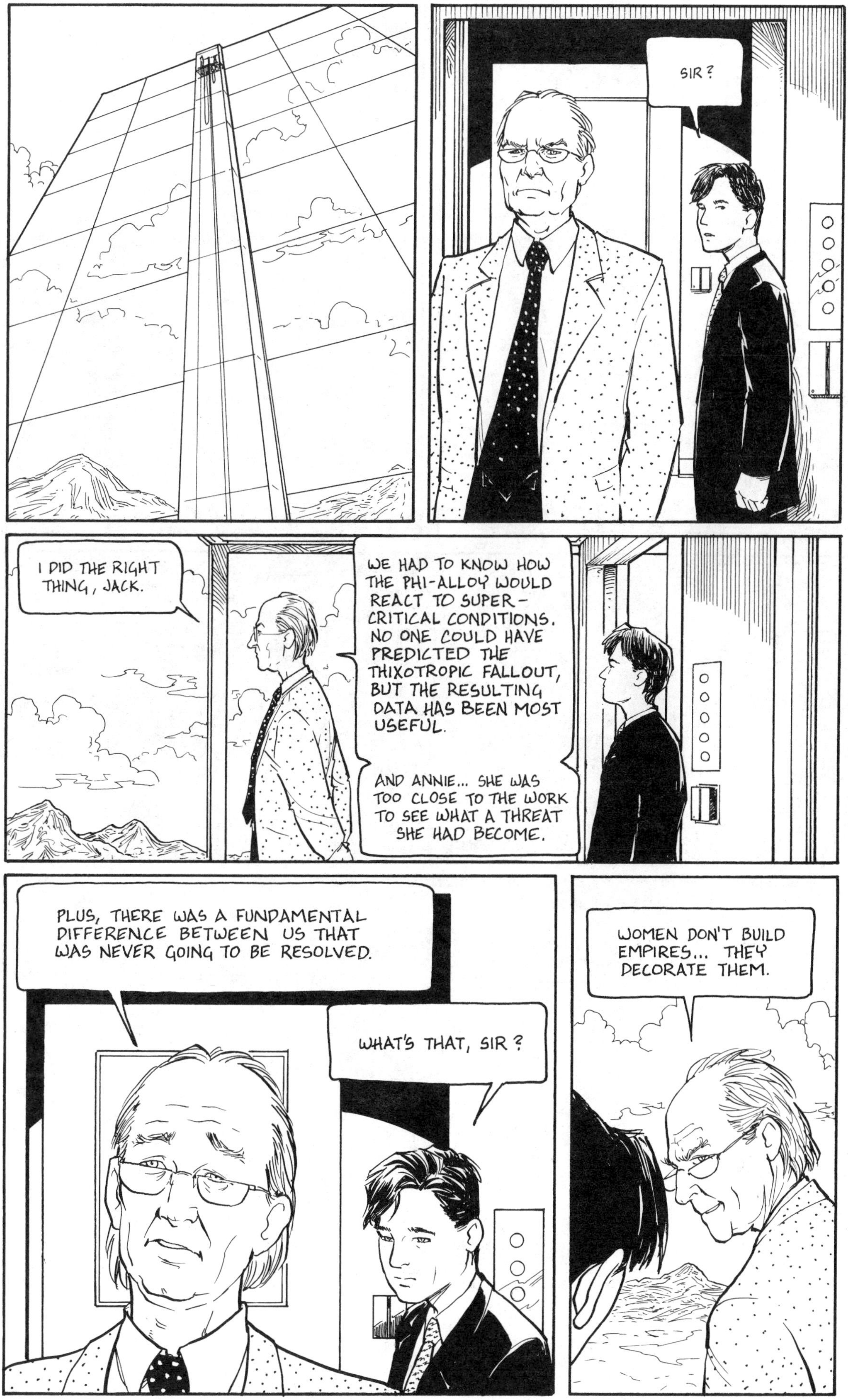
SIR?
I DID THE RIGHT THING, JACK.
WE HAD TO KNOW HOW THE PHI-ALLOY WOULD REACT TO SUPER-CRITICAL CONDITIONS. NO ONE COULD HAVE PREDICTED THE THIXOTROPIC FALLOUT, BUT THE RESULTING DATA HAS BEEN MOST USEFUL.
AND ANNIE... SHE WAS TOO CLOSE TO THE WORK TO SEE WHAT A THREAT SHE HAD BECOME.
PLUS, THERE WAS A FUNDAMENTAL DIFFERENCE BETWEEN US THAT WAS NEVER GOING TO BE RESOLVED.
WHAT'S THAT, SIR?
WOMEN DON'T BUILD EMPIRES... THEY DECORATE THEM.

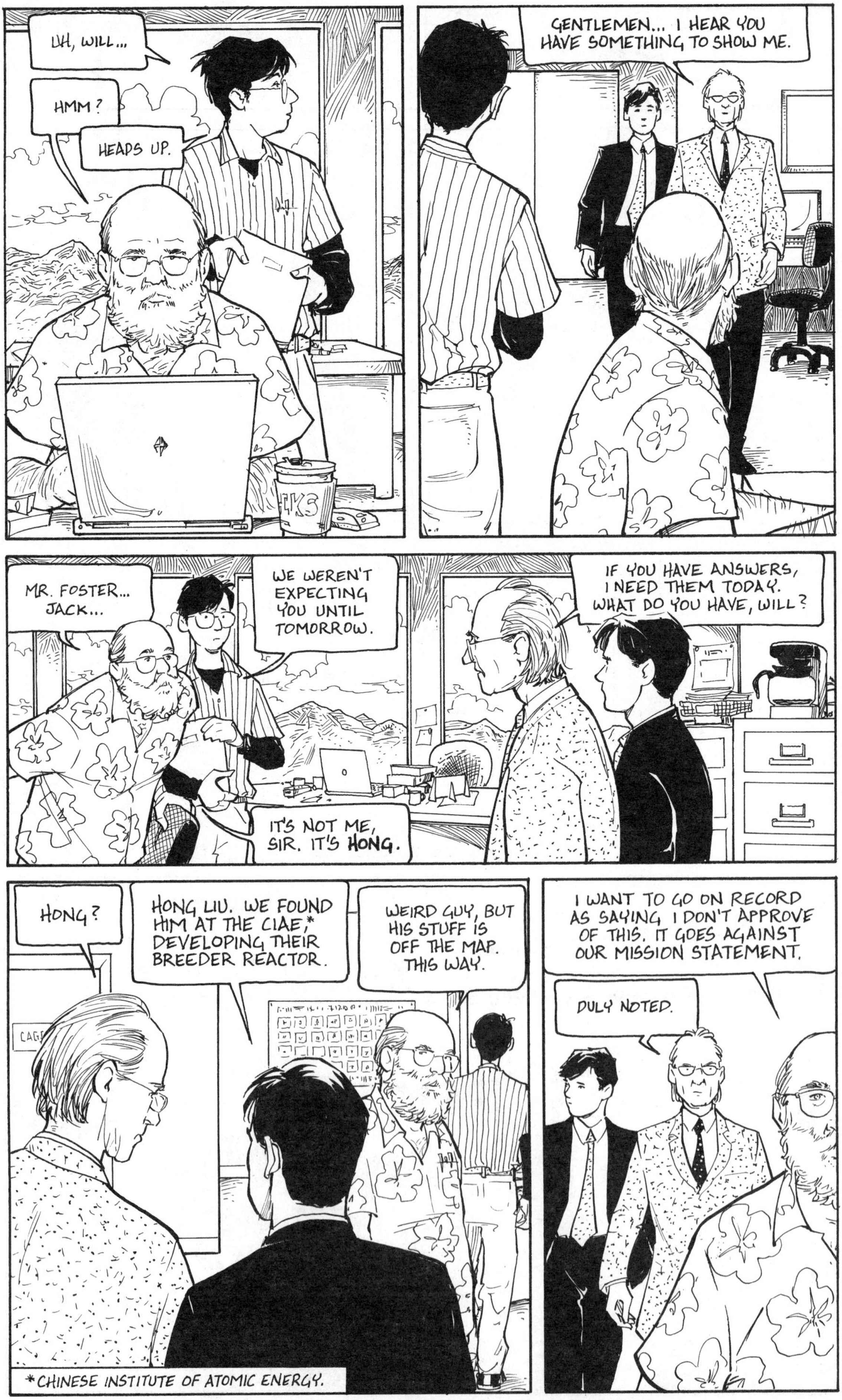

UH, WILL...
HMM?
HEADS UP.
GENTLEMEN... I HEAR YOU HAVE SOMETHING TO SHOW ME.
MR. FOSTER... JACK...
WE WEREN'T EXPECTING YOU UNTIL TOMORROW.
IF YOU HAVE ANSWERS, I NEED THEM TODAY. WHAT DO YOU HAVE, WILL?
IT'S NOT ME, SIR. IT'S **HONG**.
HONG?
HONG LIU. WE FOUND HIM AT THE CIAE,* DEVELOPING THEIR BREEDER REACTOR.
WEIRD GUY, BUT HIS STUFF IS OFF THE MAP. THIS WAY.
*CHINESE INSTITUTE OF ATOMIC ENERGY.
I WANT TO GO ON RECORD AS SAYING I DON'T APPROVE OF THIS. IT GOES AGAINST OUR MISSION STATEMENT.
DULY NOTED.

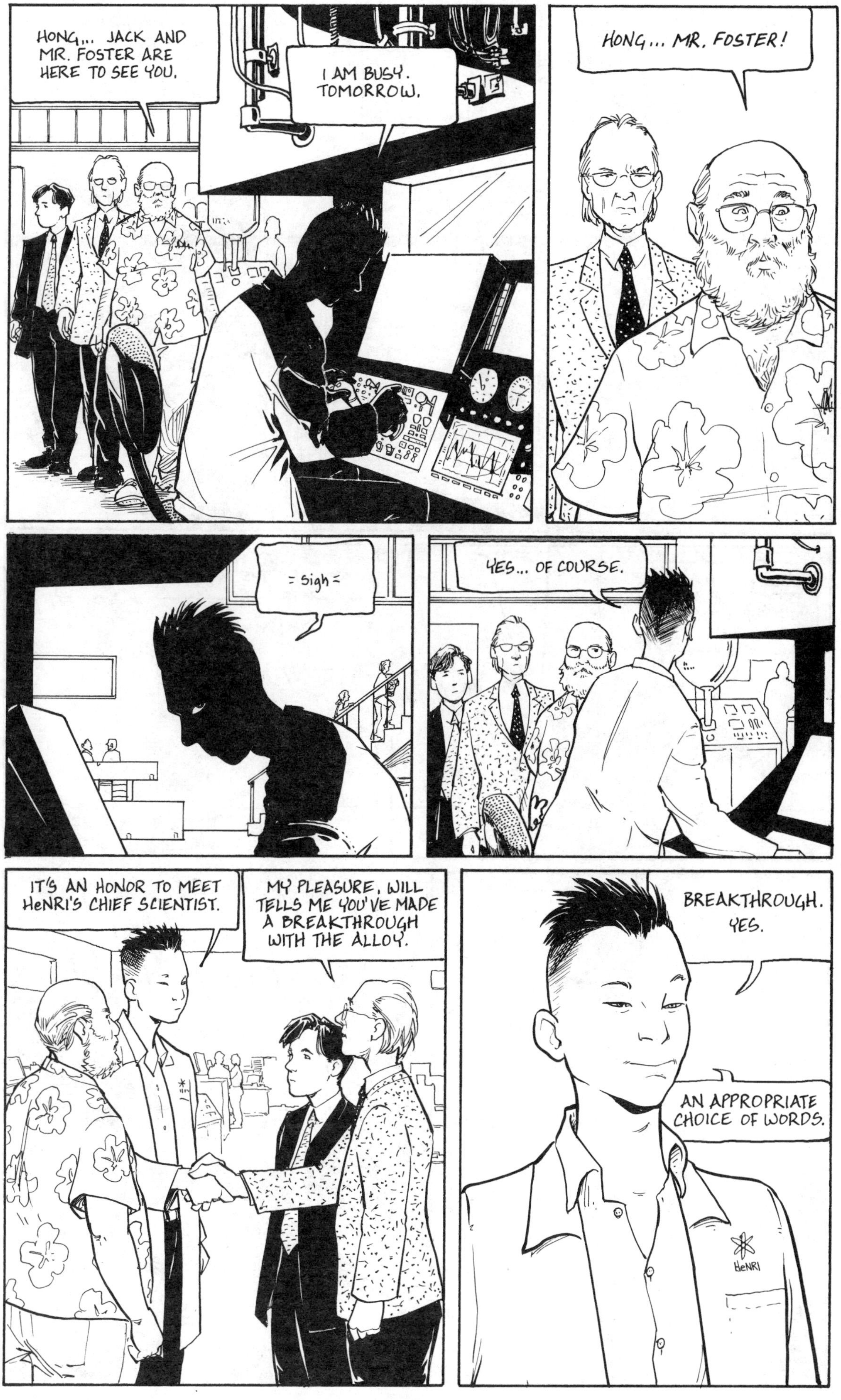
HONG... JACK AND MR. FOSTER ARE HERE TO SEE YOU.
I AM BUSY. TOMORROW.
HONG... MR. FOSTER!
= sigh =
YES... OF COURSE.
IT'S AN HONOR TO MEET HeNRI'S CHIEF SCIENTIST.
MY PLEASURE. WILL TELLS ME YOU'VE MADE A BREAKTHROUGH WITH THE ALLOY.
BREAKTHROUGH. YES.
AN APPROPRIATE CHOICE OF WORDS.

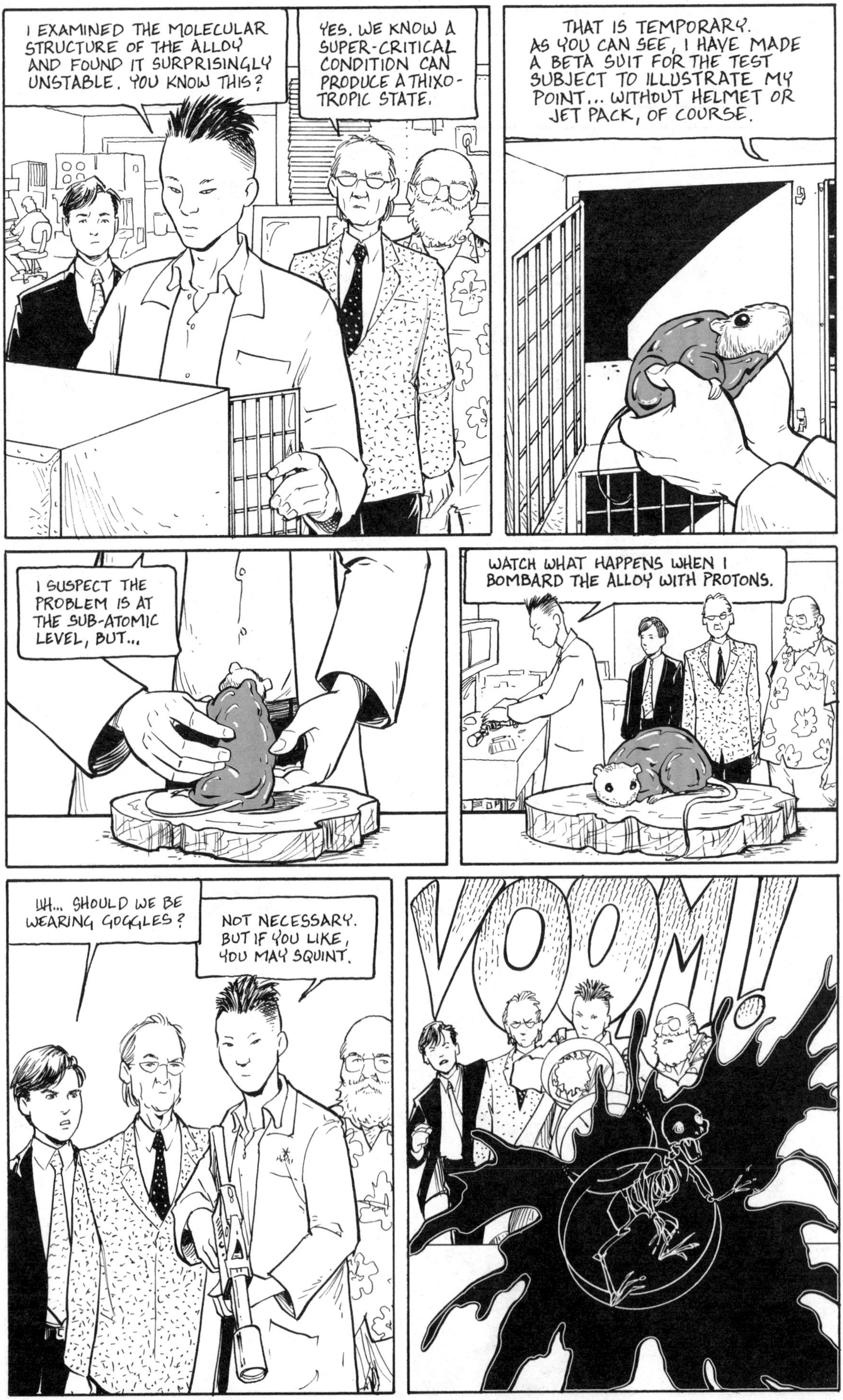
I EXAMINED THE MOLECULAR STRUCTURE OF THE ALLOY AND FOUND IT SURPRISINGLY UNSTABLE. YOU KNOW THIS?
YES. WE KNOW A SUPER-CRITICAL CONDITION CAN PRODUCE A THIXO-TROPIC STATE.
THAT IS TEMPORARY. AS YOU CAN SEE, I HAVE MADE A BETA SUIT FOR THE TEST SUBJECT TO ILLUSTRATE MY POINT... WITHOUT HELMET OR JET PACK, OF COURSE.
I SUSPECT THE PROBLEM IS AT THE SUB-ATOMIC LEVEL, BUT...
WATCH WHAT HAPPENS WHEN I BOMBARD THE ALLOY WITH PROTONS.
UH... SHOULD WE BE WEARING GOGGLES?
NOT NECESSARY. BUT IF YOU LIKE, YOU MAY SQUINT.
VOOM!

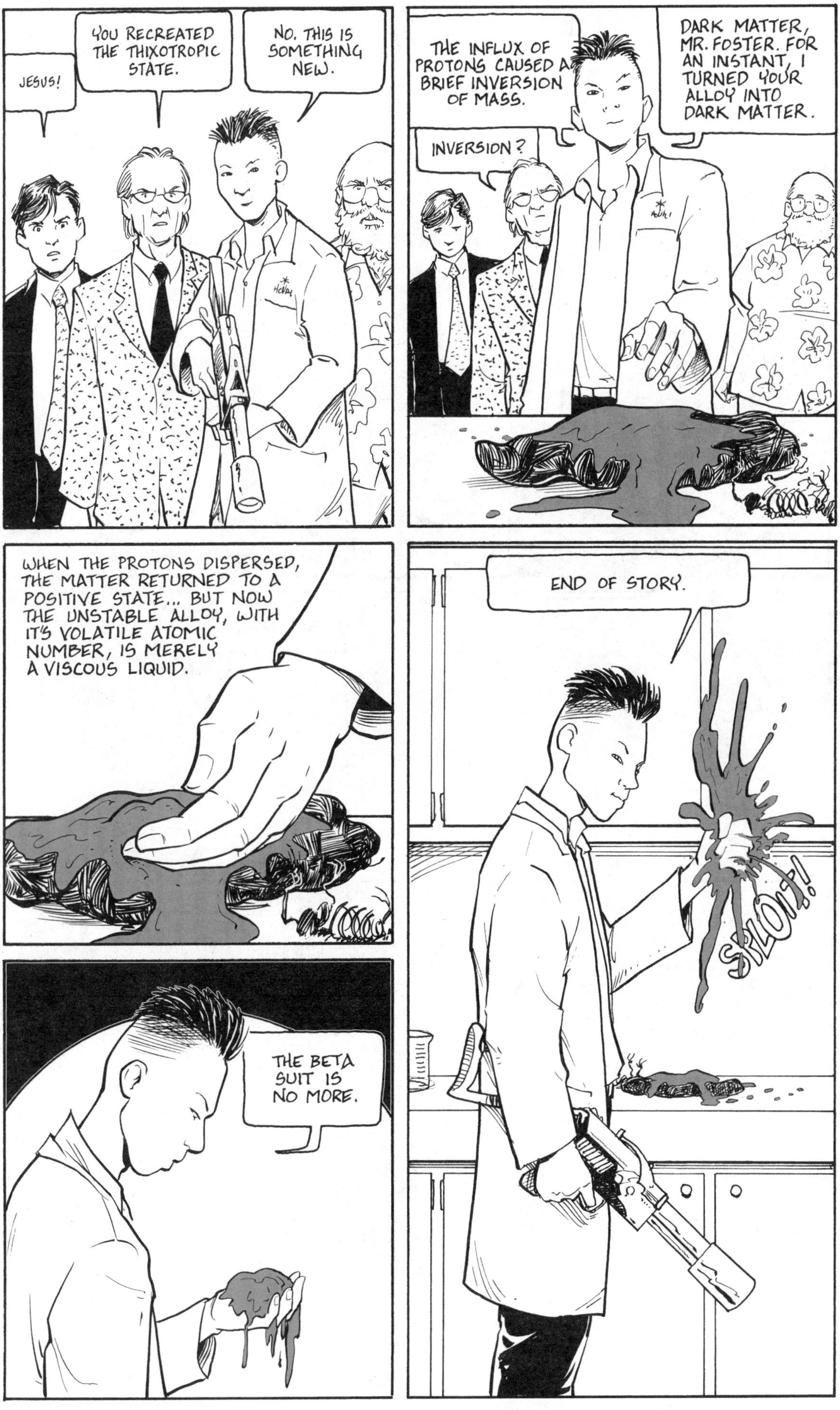
JESUS!
YOU RECREATED THE THIXOTROPIC STATE.
NO. THIS IS SOMETHING NEW.
THE INFLUX OF PROTONS CAUSED A BRIEF INVERSION OF MASS.
DARK MATTER, MR. FOSTER. FOR AN INSTANT, I TURNED YOUR ALLOY INTO DARK MATTER.
INVERSION?
WHEN THE PROTONS DISPERSED, THE MATTER RETURNED TO A POSITIVE STATE... BUT NOW THE UNSTABLE ALLOY, WITH IT'S VOLATILE ATOMIC NUMBER, IS MERELY A VISCOUS LIQUID.
THE BETA SUIT IS NO MORE.
END OF STORY.
SPLOITZ!

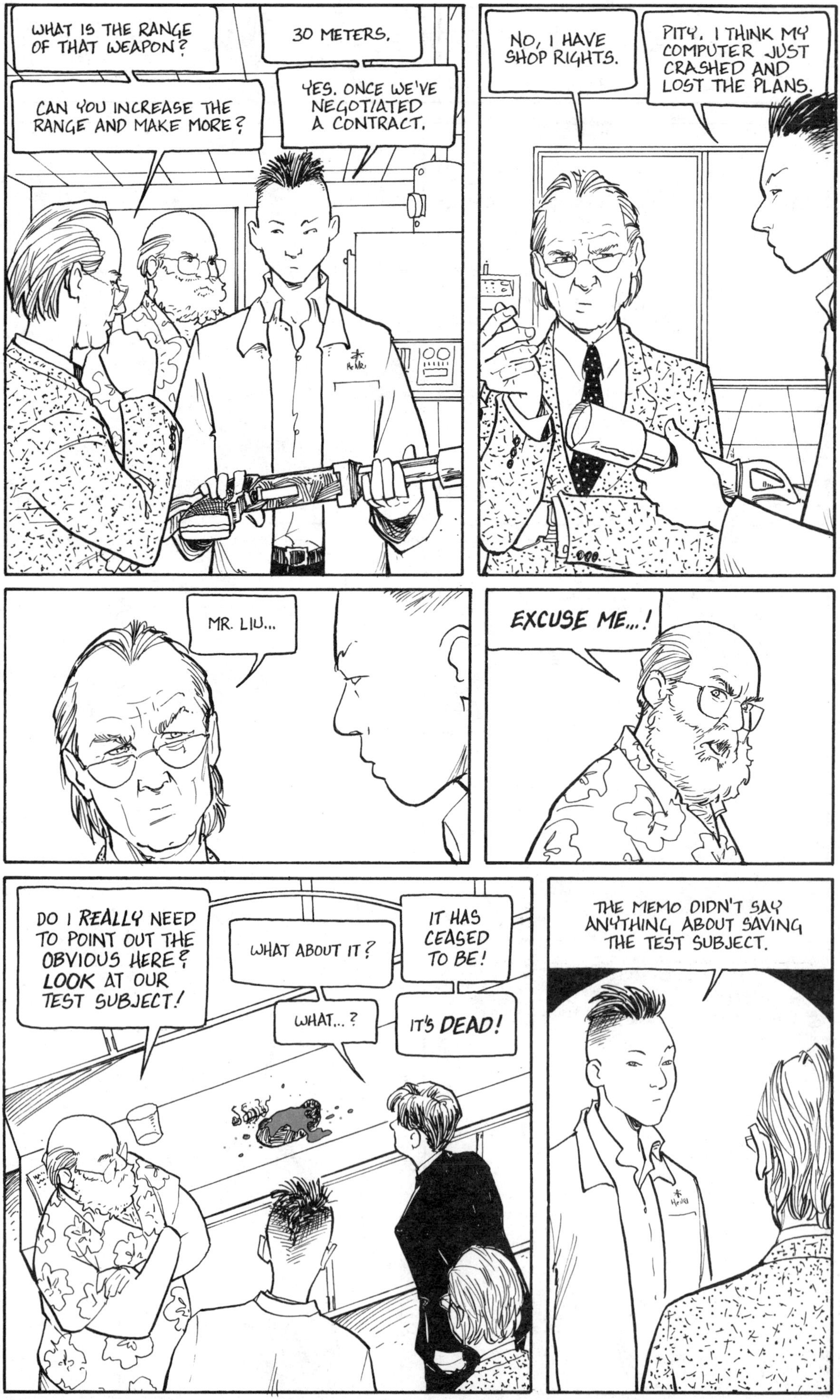
WHAT IS THE RANGE OF THAT WEAPON?
30 METERS.
CAN YOU INCREASE THE RANGE AND MAKE MORE?
YES. ONCE WE'VE NEGOTIATED A CONTRACT.
NO, I HAVE SHOP RIGHTS.
PITY. I THINK MY COMPUTER JUST CRASHED AND LOST THE PLANS.
MR. LIU...
EXCUSE ME...!
DO I REALLY NEED TO POINT OUT THE OBVIOUS HERE? LOOK AT OUR TEST SUBJECT!
WHAT ABOUT IT?
IT HAS CEASED TO BE!
WHAT...?
IT'S DEAD!
THE MEMO DIDN'T SAY ANYTHING ABOUT SAVING THE TEST SUBJECT.

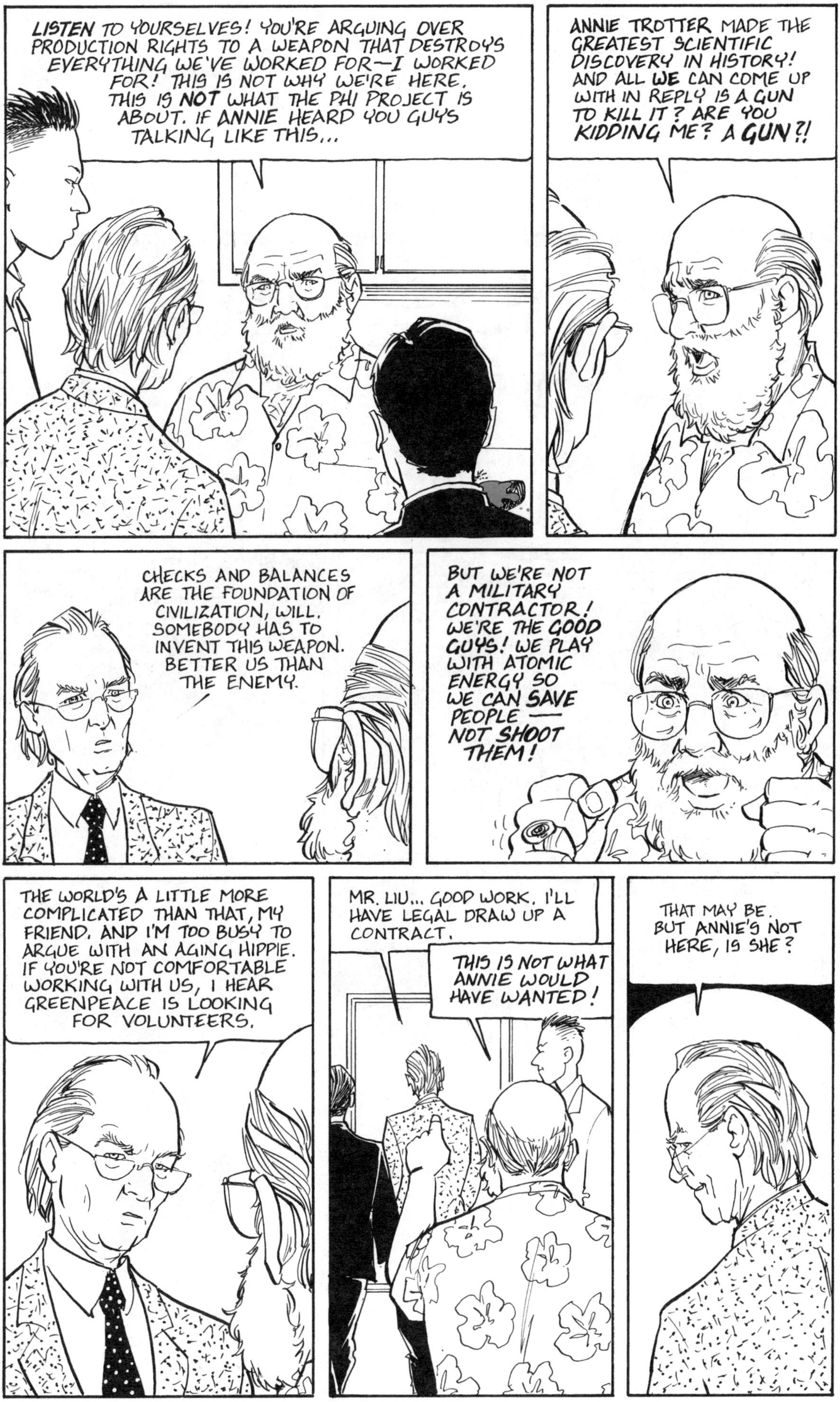
LISTEN TO YOURSELVES! YOU'RE ARGUING OVER PRODUCTION RIGHTS TO A WEAPON THAT DESTROYS EVERYTHING WE'VE WORKED FOR—I WORKED FOR! THIS IS NOT WHY WE'RE HERE. THIS IS NOT WHAT THE PHI PROJECT IS ABOUT. IF ANNIE HEARD YOU GUYS TALKING LIKE THIS...
ANNIE TROTTER MADE THE GREATEST SCIENTIFIC DISCOVERY IN HISTORY! AND ALL WE CAN COME UP WITH IN REPLY IS A GUN TO KILL IT? ARE YOU KIDDING ME? A GUN?!
CHECKS AND BALANCES ARE THE FOUNDATION OF CIVILIZATION, WILL. SOMEBODY HAS TO INVENT THIS WEAPON. BETTER US THAN THE ENEMY.
BUT WE'RE NOT A MILITARY CONTRACTOR! WE'RE THE GOOD GUYS! WE PLAY WITH ATOMIC ENERGY SO WE CAN SAVE PEOPLE — NOT SHOOT THEM!
THE WORLD'S A LITTLE MORE COMPLICATED THAN THAT, MY FRIEND. AND I'M TOO BUSY TO ARGUE WITH AN AGING HIPPIE. IF YOU'RE NOT COMFORTABLE WORKING WITH US, I HEAR GREENPEACE IS LOOKING FOR VOLUNTEERS.
MR. LIU... GOOD WORK. I'LL HAVE LEGAL DRAW UP A CONTRACT.
THIS IS NOT WHAT ANNIE WOULD HAVE WANTED!
THAT MAY BE. BUT ANNIE'S NOT HERE, IS SHE?

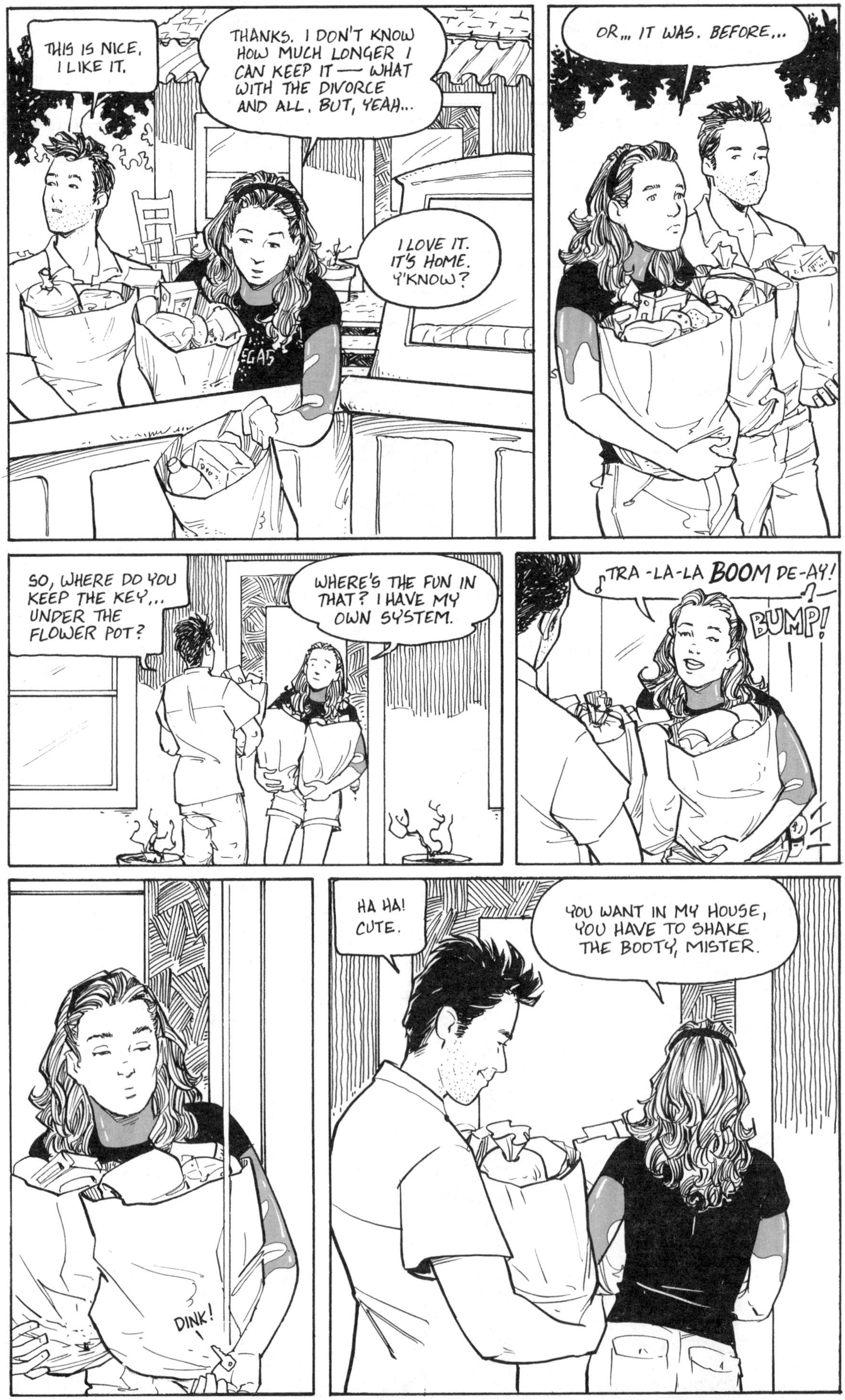
THIS IS NICE, I LIKE IT.
THANKS. I DON'T KNOW HOW MUCH LONGER I CAN KEEP IT — WHAT WITH THE DIVORCE AND ALL. BUT, YEAH...
I LOVE IT. IT'S HOME. Y'KNOW?
VEGAS
OR... IT WAS. BEFORE...
SO, WHERE DO YOU KEEP THE KEY... UNDER THE FLOWER POT?
WHERE'S THE FUN IN THAT? I HAVE MY OWN SYSTEM.
TRA-LA-LA BOOM DE-AY!
BUMP!
DINK!
HA HA! CUTE.
YOU WANT IN MY HOUSE, YOU HAVE TO SHAKE THE BOOTY, MISTER.

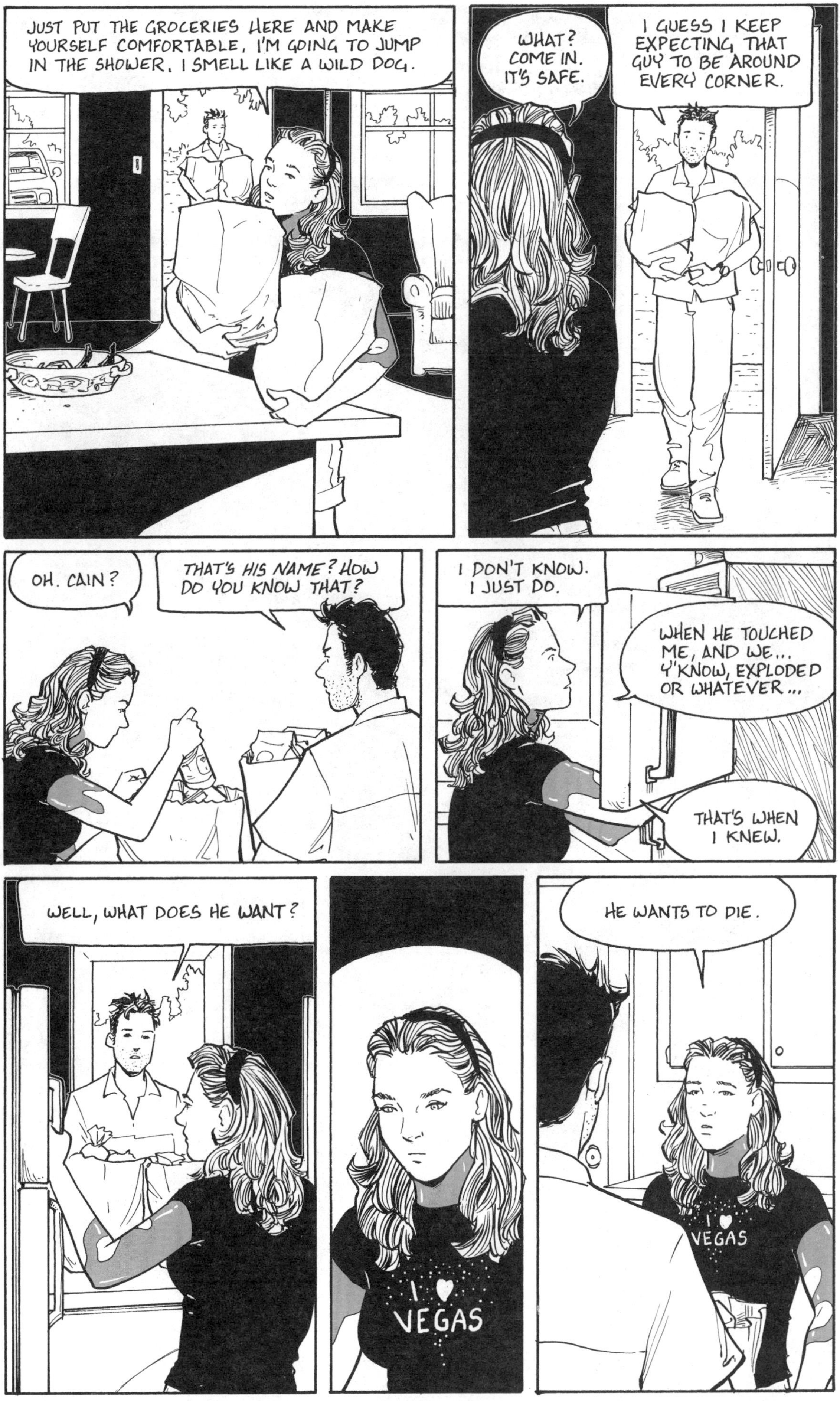
JUST PUT THE GROCERIES HERE AND MAKE YOURSELF COMFORTABLE, I'M GOING TO JUMP IN THE SHOWER. I SMELL LIKE A WILD DOG.
WHAT? COME IN. IT'S SAFE.
I GUESS I KEEP EXPECTING THAT GUY TO BE AROUND EVERY CORNER.
OH. CAIN?
THAT'S HIS NAME? HOW DO YOU KNOW THAT?
I DON'T KNOW. I JUST DO.
WHEN HE TOUCHED ME, AND WE... Y'KNOW, EXPLODED OR WHATEVER...
THAT'S WHEN I KNEW.
WELL, WHAT DOES HE WANT?
I ♥ VEGAS
HE WANTS TO DIE.
I ♥ VEGAS

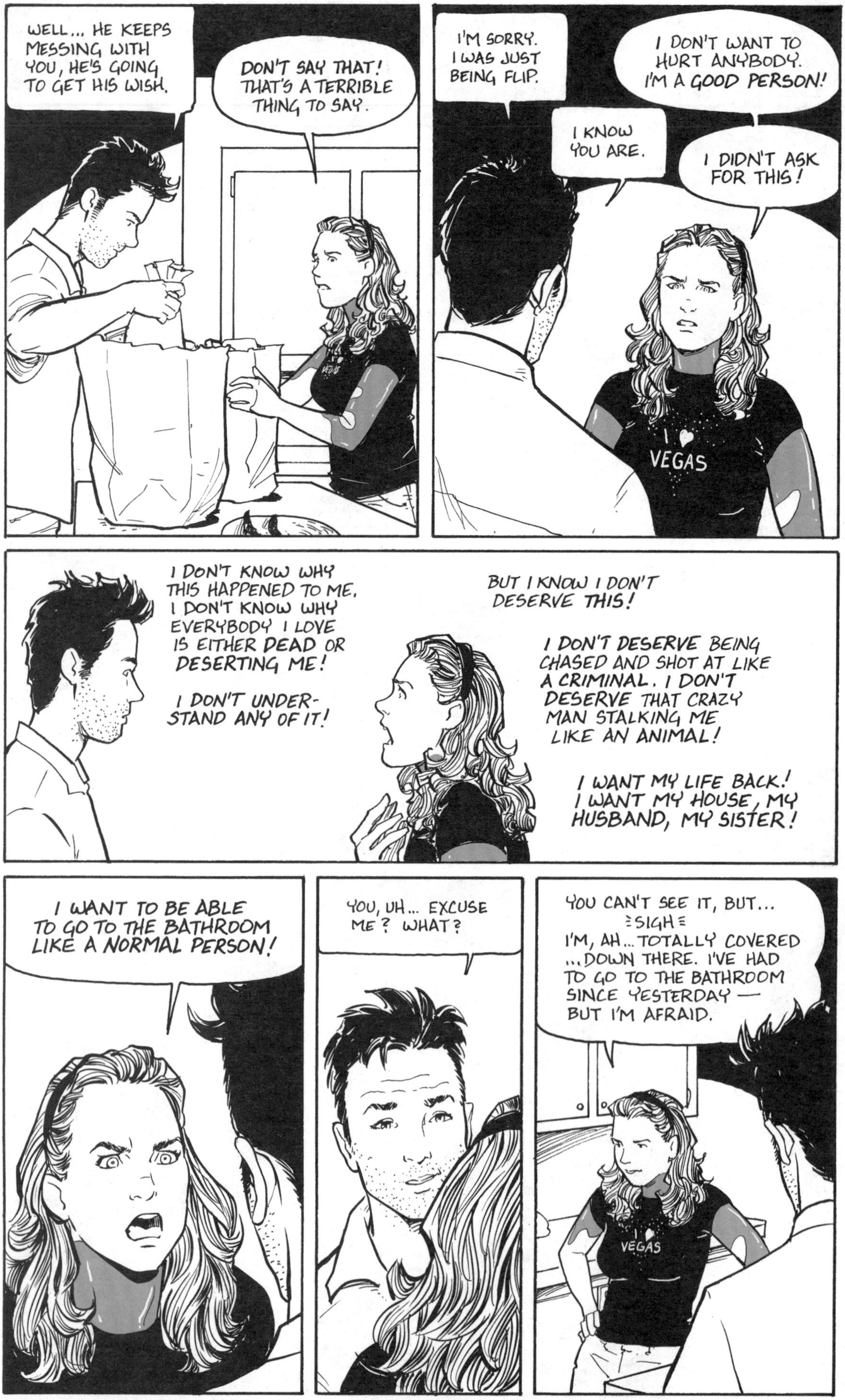
WELL... HE KEEPS MESSING WITH YOU, HE'S GOING TO GET HIS WISH.
DON'T SAY THAT! THAT'S A TERRIBLE THING TO SAY.
I'M SORRY. I WAS JUST BEING FLIP.
I DON'T WANT TO HURT ANYBODY. I'M A GOOD PERSON!
I KNOW YOU ARE.
I DIDN'T ASK FOR THIS!
I DON'T KNOW WHY THIS HAPPENED TO ME. I DON'T KNOW WHY EVERYBODY I LOVE IS EITHER DEAD OR DESERTING ME!
I DON'T UNDER-STAND ANY OF IT!
BUT I KNOW I DON'T DESERVE THIS!
I DON'T DESERVE BEING CHASED AND SHOT AT LIKE A CRIMINAL. I DON'T DESERVE THAT CRAZY MAN STALKING ME LIKE AN ANIMAL!
I WANT MY LIFE BACK! I WANT MY HOUSE, MY HUSBAND, MY SISTER!
I WANT TO BE ABLE TO GO TO THE BATHROOM LIKE A NORMAL PERSON!
YOU, UH... EXCUSE ME? WHAT?
YOU CAN'T SEE IT, BUT... SIGH I'M, AH... TOTALLY COVERED ...DOWN THERE. I'VE HAD TO GO TO THE BATHROOM SINCE YESTERDAY — BUT I'M AFRAID.

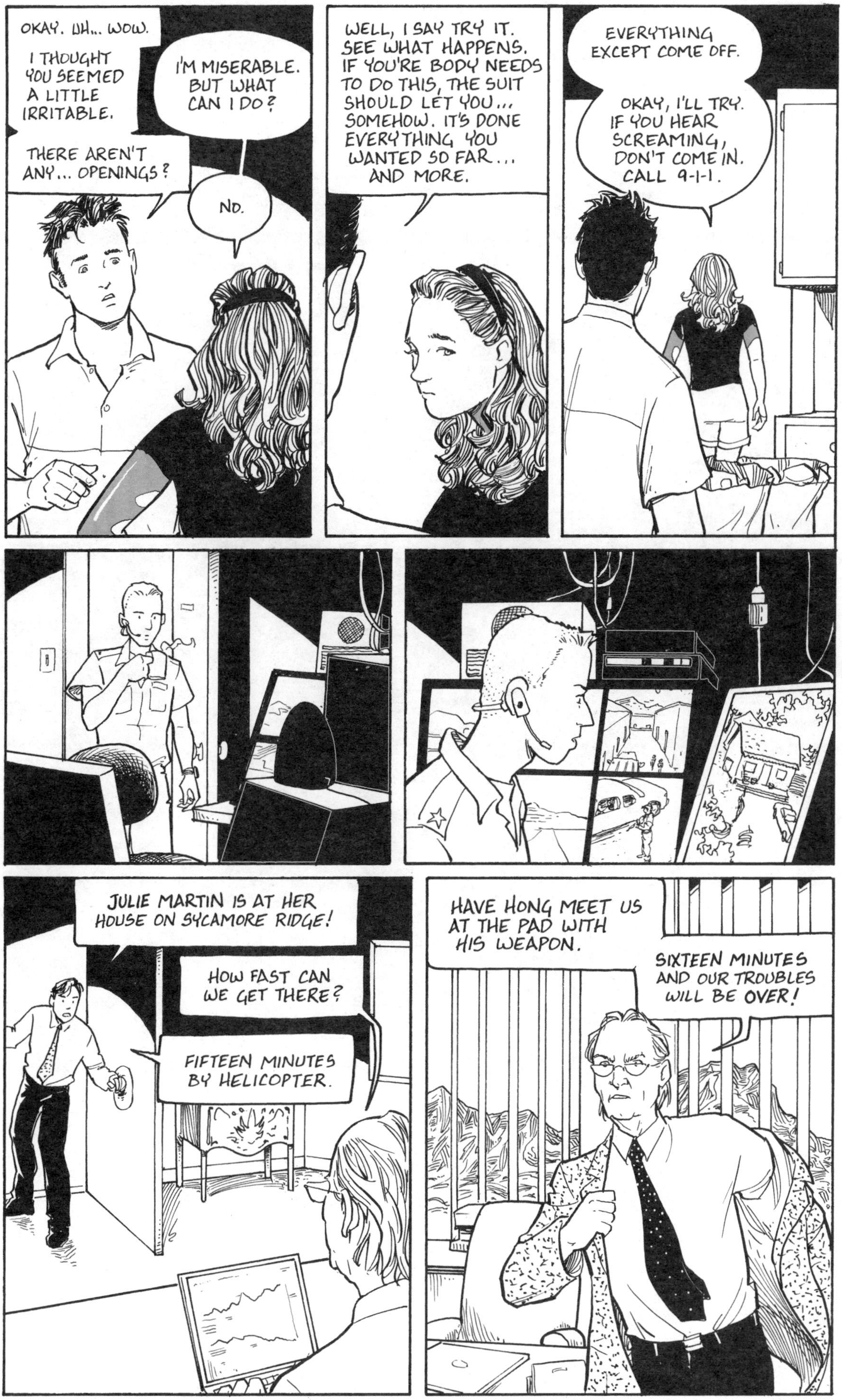
OKAY. UH... WOW.
I THOUGHT YOU SEEMED A LITTLE IRRITABLE.
I'M MISERABLE. BUT WHAT CAN I DO?
THERE AREN'T ANY... OPENINGS?
NO.
WELL, I SAY TRY IT. SEE WHAT HAPPENS. IF YOU'RE BODY NEEDS TO DO THIS, THE SUIT SHOULD LET YOU... SOMEHOW. IT'S DONE EVERYTHING YOU WANTED SO FAR... AND MORE.
EVERYTHING EXCEPT COME OFF.
OKAY, I'LL TRY. IF YOU HEAR SCREAMING, DON'T COME IN. CALL 9-1-1.
JULIE MARTIN IS AT HER HOUSE ON SYCAMORE RIDGE!
HOW FAST CAN WE GET THERE?
FIFTEEN MINUTES BY HELICOPTER.
HAVE HONG MEET US AT THE PAD WITH HIS WEAPON.
SIXTEEN MINUTES AND OUR TROUBLES WILL BE OVER!

In nuclear war all men are cremated equal.
—Dexter Gordon

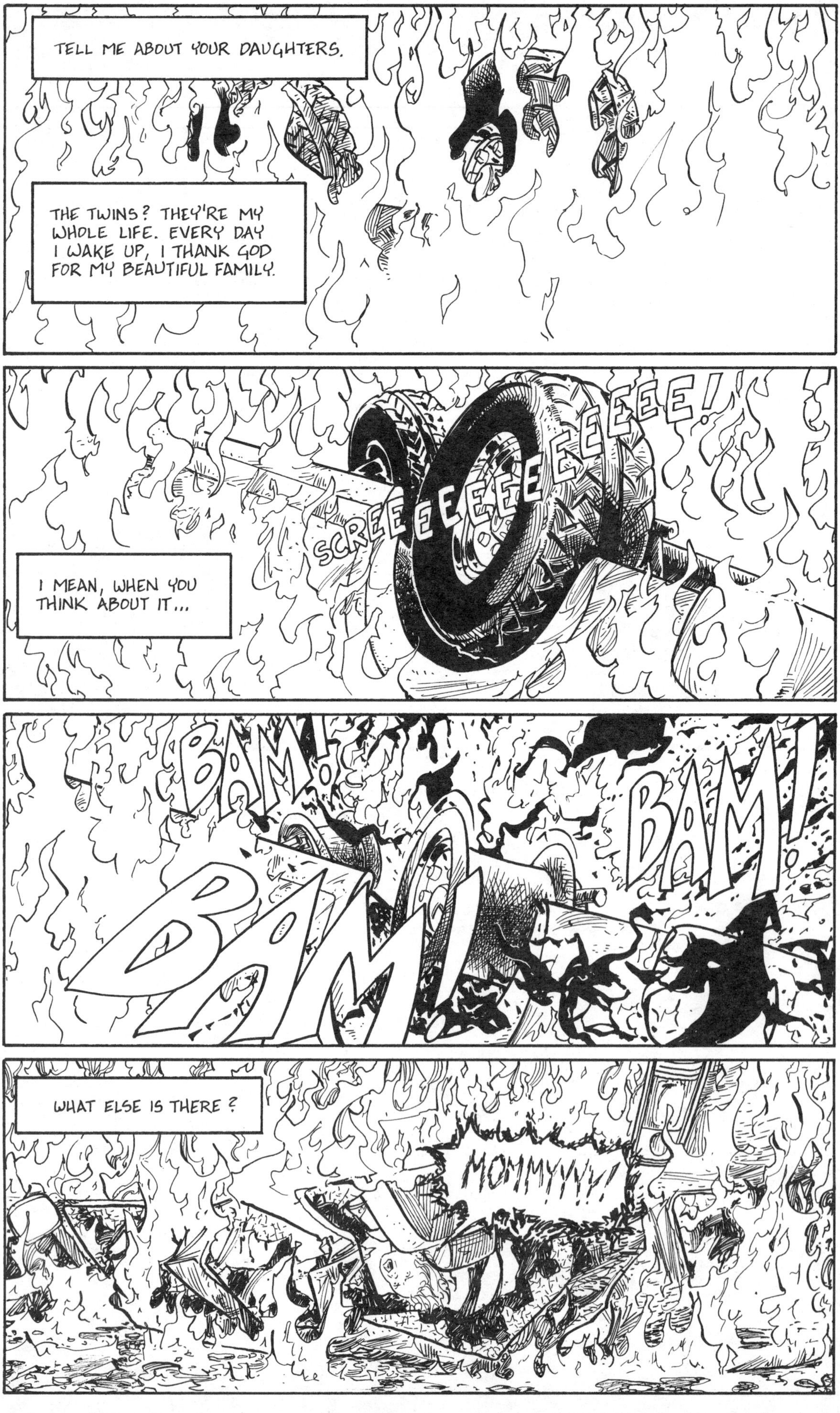
TELL ME ABOUT YOUR DAUGHTERS.
THE TWINS? THEY'RE MY WHOLE LIFE. EVERY DAY I WAKE UP, I THANK GOD FOR MY BEAUTIFUL FAMILY.
SCREEEEEEEEEEEEE!
I MEAN, WHEN YOU THINK ABOUT IT...
BAM!
BAM!
BAM!
WHAT ELSE IS THERE?
MOMMYYY!

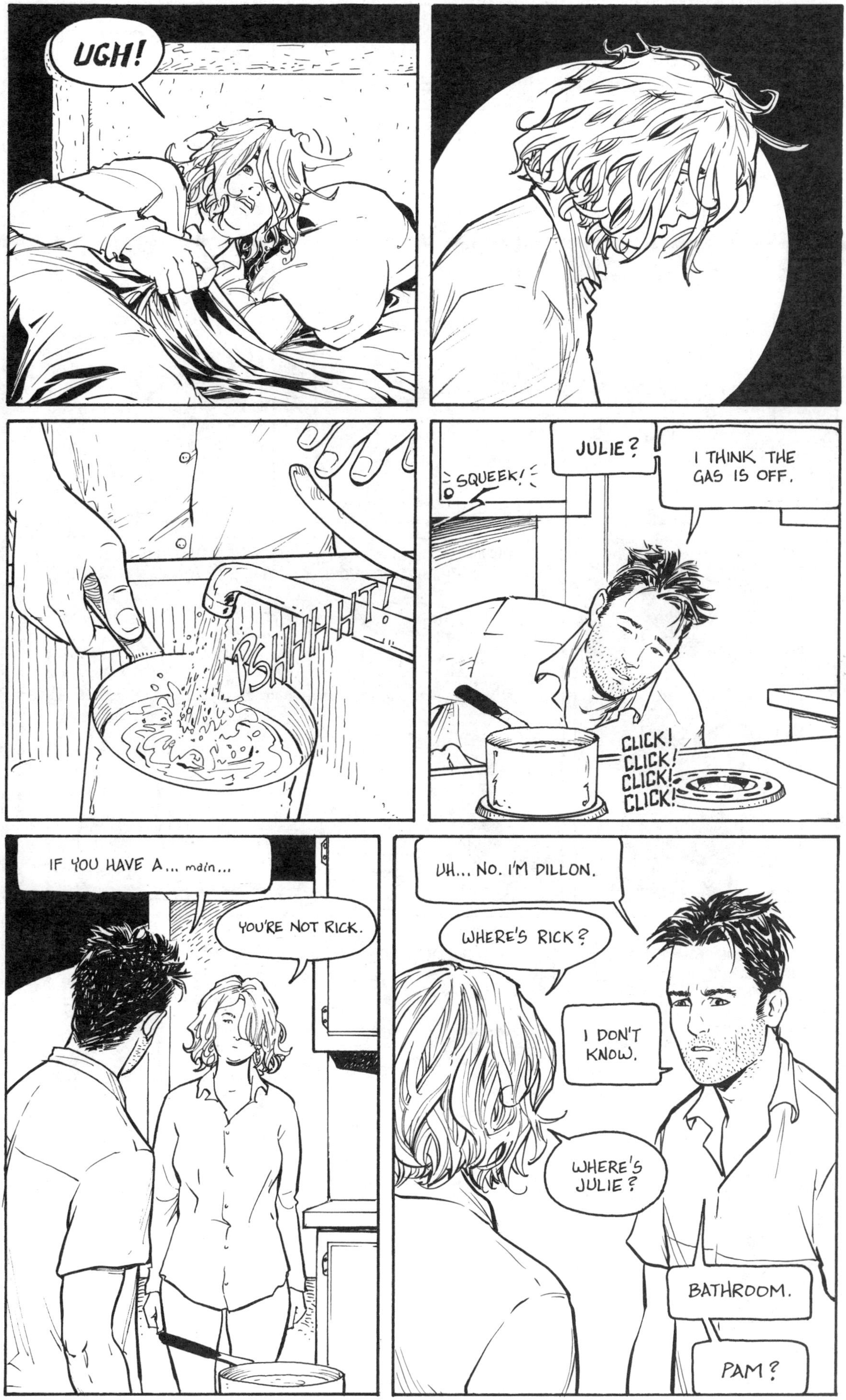
UGH!
PSHHHHHT!
SQUEEK!
JULIE?
I THINK THE GAS IS OFF.
CLICK! CLICK! CLICK! CLICK!
IF YOU HAVE A... main...
YOU'RE NOT RICK.
UH... NO. I'M DILLON.
WHERE'S RICK?
I DON'T KNOW.
WHERE'S JULIE?
BATHROOM.
PAM?

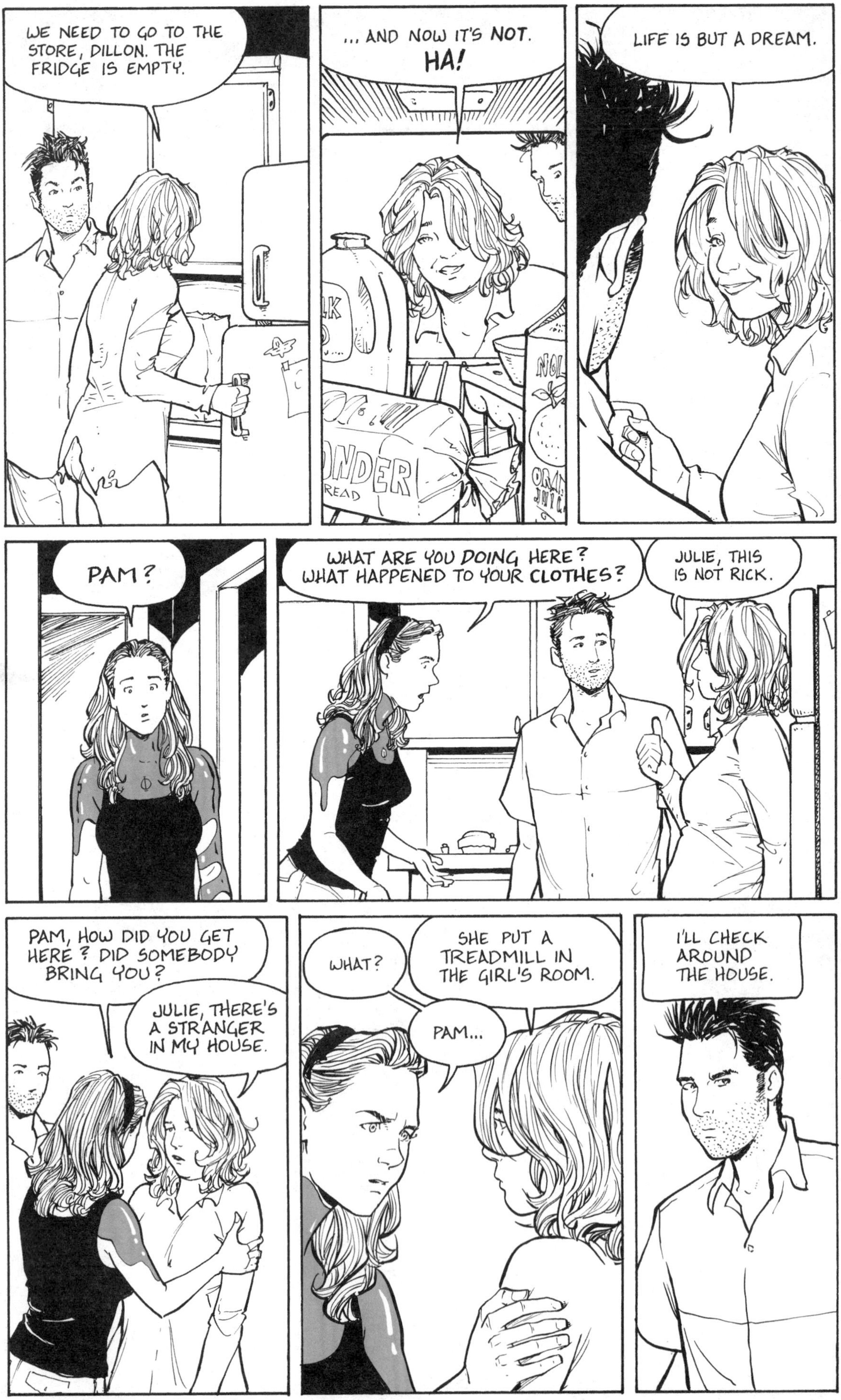
WE NEED TO GO TO THE STORE, DILLON. THE FRIDGE IS EMPTY.
... AND NOW IT'S NOT. HA!
WONDER BREAD
LIFE IS BUT A DREAM.
PAM?
WHAT ARE YOU DOING HERE? WHAT HAPPENED TO YOUR CLOTHES?
JULIE, THIS IS NOT RICK.
PAM, HOW DID YOU GET HERE? DID SOMEBODY BRING YOU?
JULIE, THERE'S A STRANGER IN MY HOUSE.
WHAT?
SHE PUT A TREADMILL IN THE GIRL'S ROOM.
PAM...
I'LL CHECK AROUND THE HOUSE.

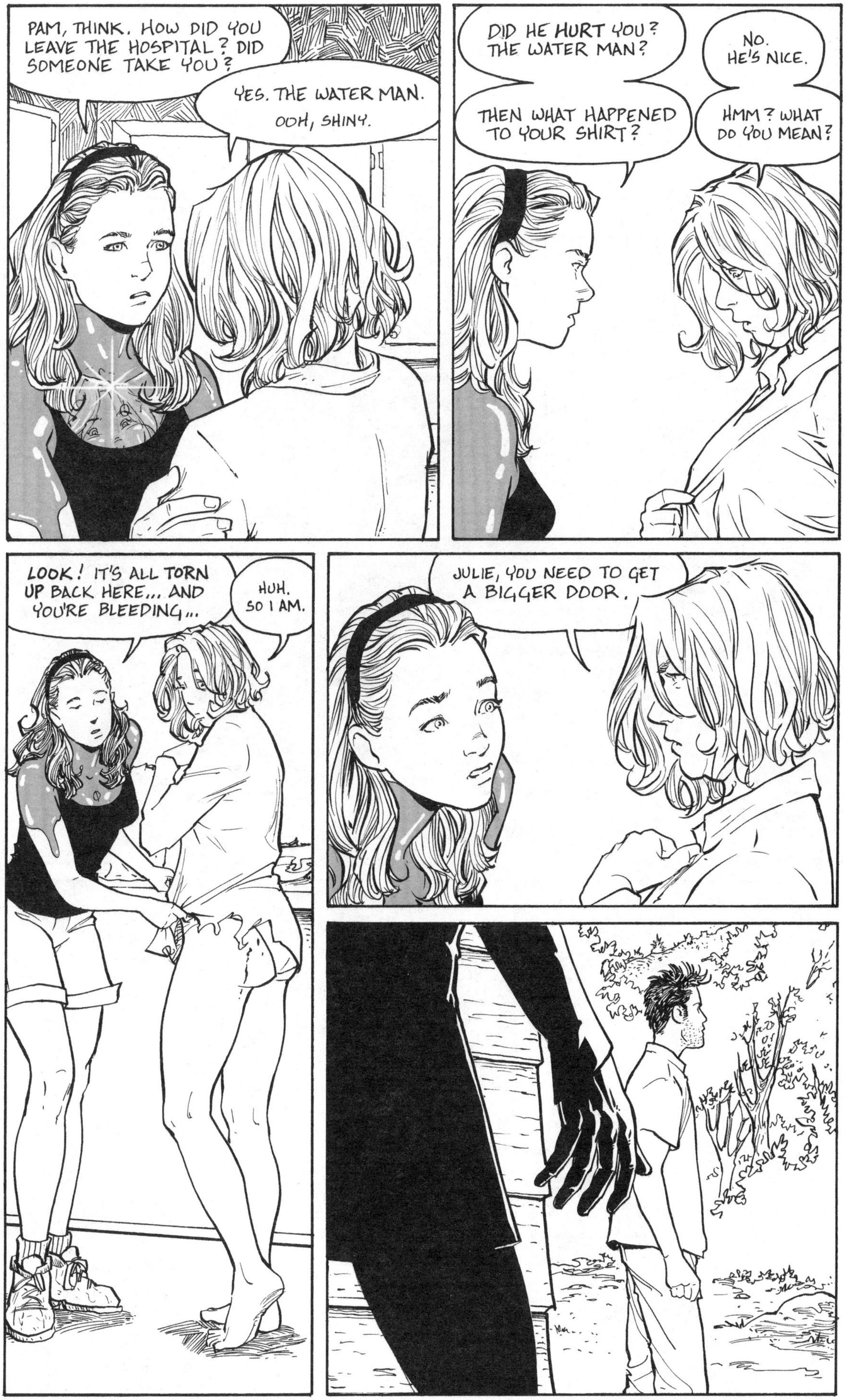
PAM, THINK. HOW DID YOU LEAVE THE HOSPITAL? DID SOMEONE TAKE YOU?
YES. THE WATER MAN.
OOH, SHINY.
DID HE HURT YOU? THE WATER MAN?
NO. HE'S NICE.
THEN WHAT HAPPENED TO YOUR SHIRT?
HMM? WHAT DO YOU MEAN?
LOOK! IT'S ALL TORN UP BACK HERE... AND YOU'RE BLEEDING...
HUH. SO I AM.
JULIE, YOU NEED TO GET A BIGGER DOOR.

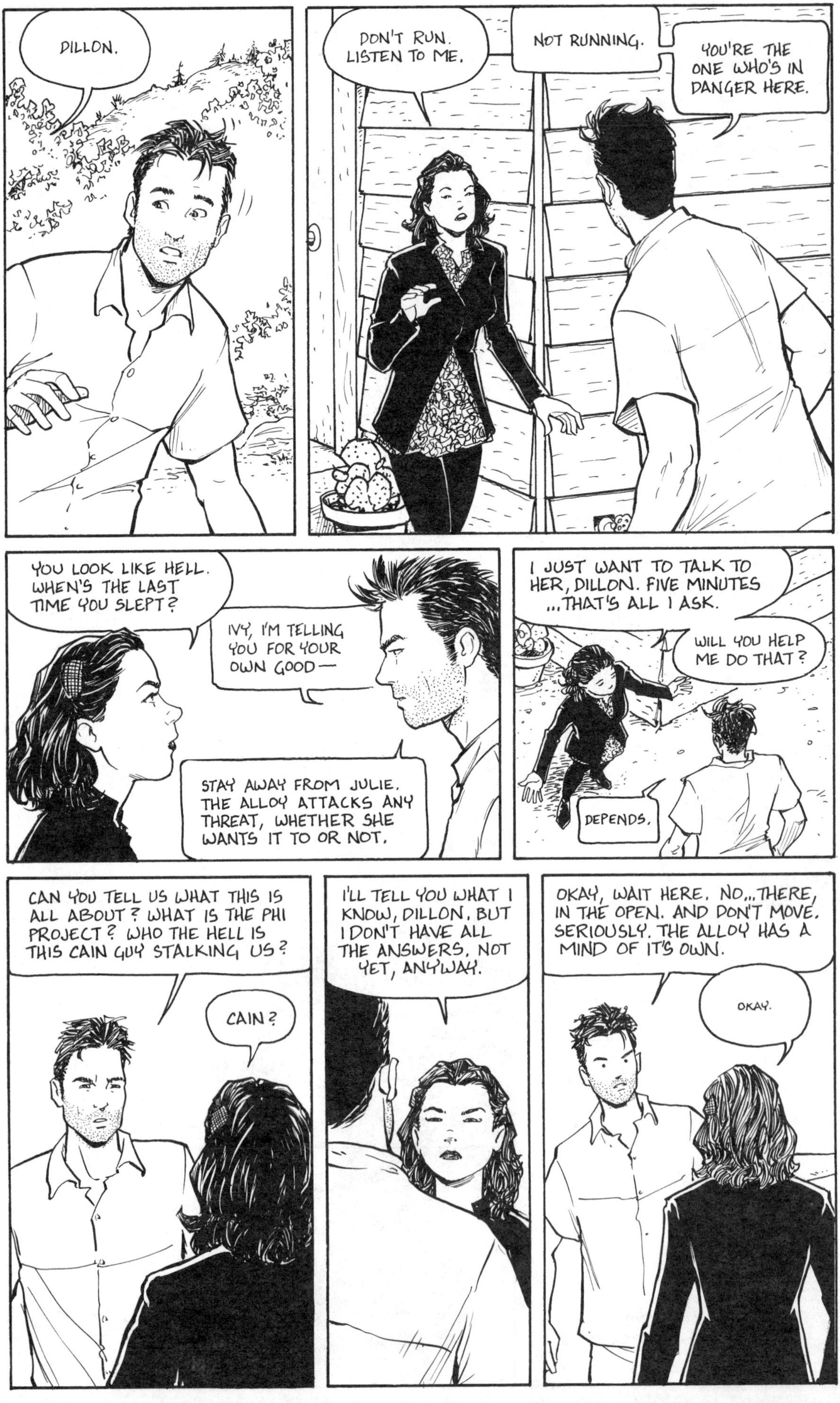
DILLON.
DON'T RUN. LISTEN TO ME.
NOT RUNNING.
YOU'RE THE ONE WHO'S IN DANGER HERE.
YOU LOOK LIKE HELL. WHEN'S THE LAST TIME YOU SLEPT?
IVY, I'M TELLING YOU FOR YOUR OWN GOOD—
STAY AWAY FROM JULIE. THE ALLOY ATTACKS ANY THREAT, WHETHER SHE WANTS IT TO OR NOT.
I JUST WANT TO TALK TO HER, DILLON. FIVE MINUTES ...THAT'S ALL I ASK.
WILL YOU HELP ME DO THAT?
DEPENDS.
CAN YOU TELL US WHAT THIS IS ALL ABOUT? WHAT IS THE PHI PROJECT? WHO THE HELL IS THIS CAIN GUY STALKING US?
CAIN?
I'LL TELL YOU WHAT I KNOW, DILLON. BUT I DON'T HAVE ALL THE ANSWERS. NOT YET, ANYWAY.
OKAY, WAIT HERE. NO... THERE, IN THE OPEN. AND DON'T MOVE. SERIOUSLY. THE ALLOY HAS A MIND OF IT'S OWN.
OKAY.

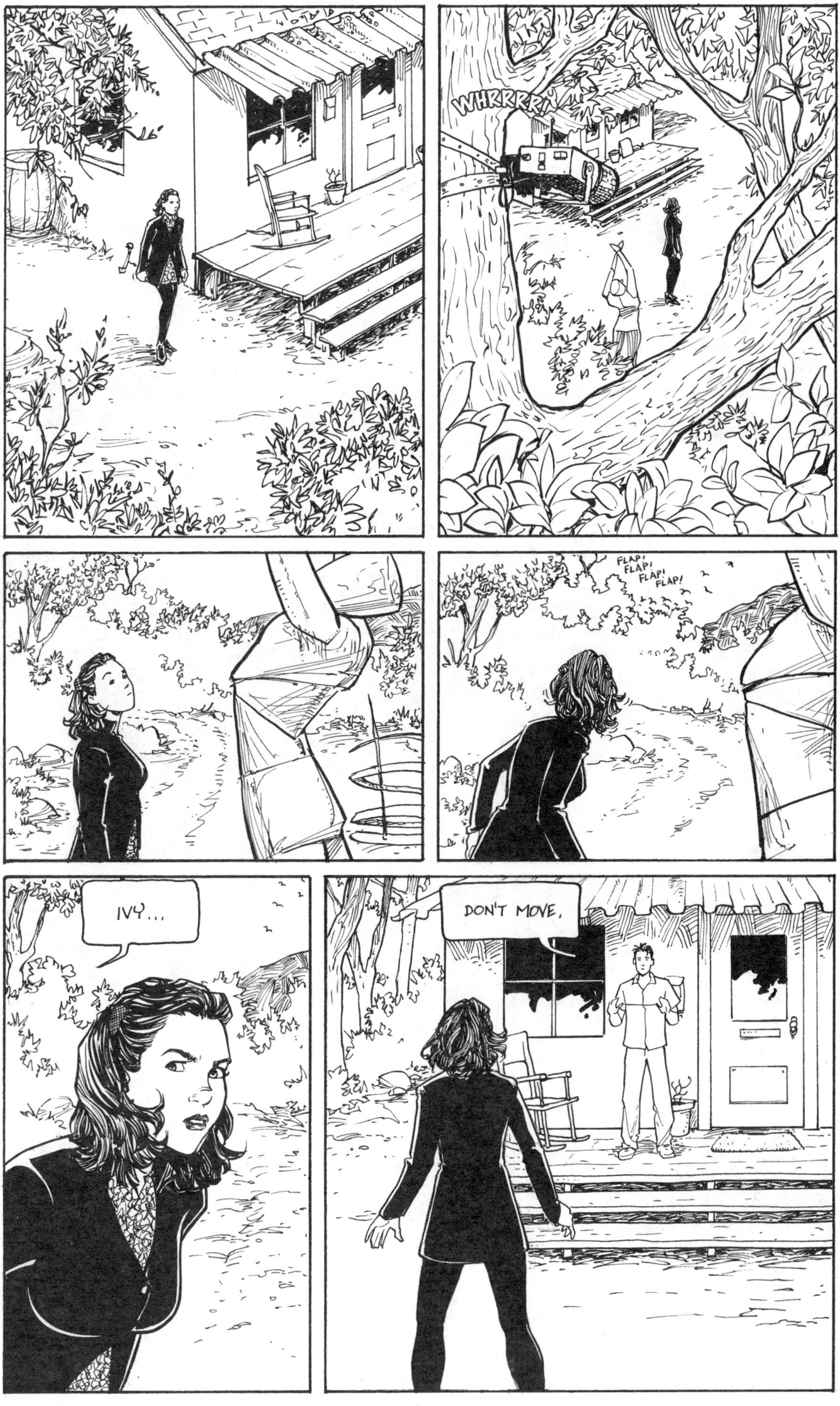
WHRRRR!
FLAP! FLAP! FLAP! FLAP!
IVY...
DON'T MOVE.

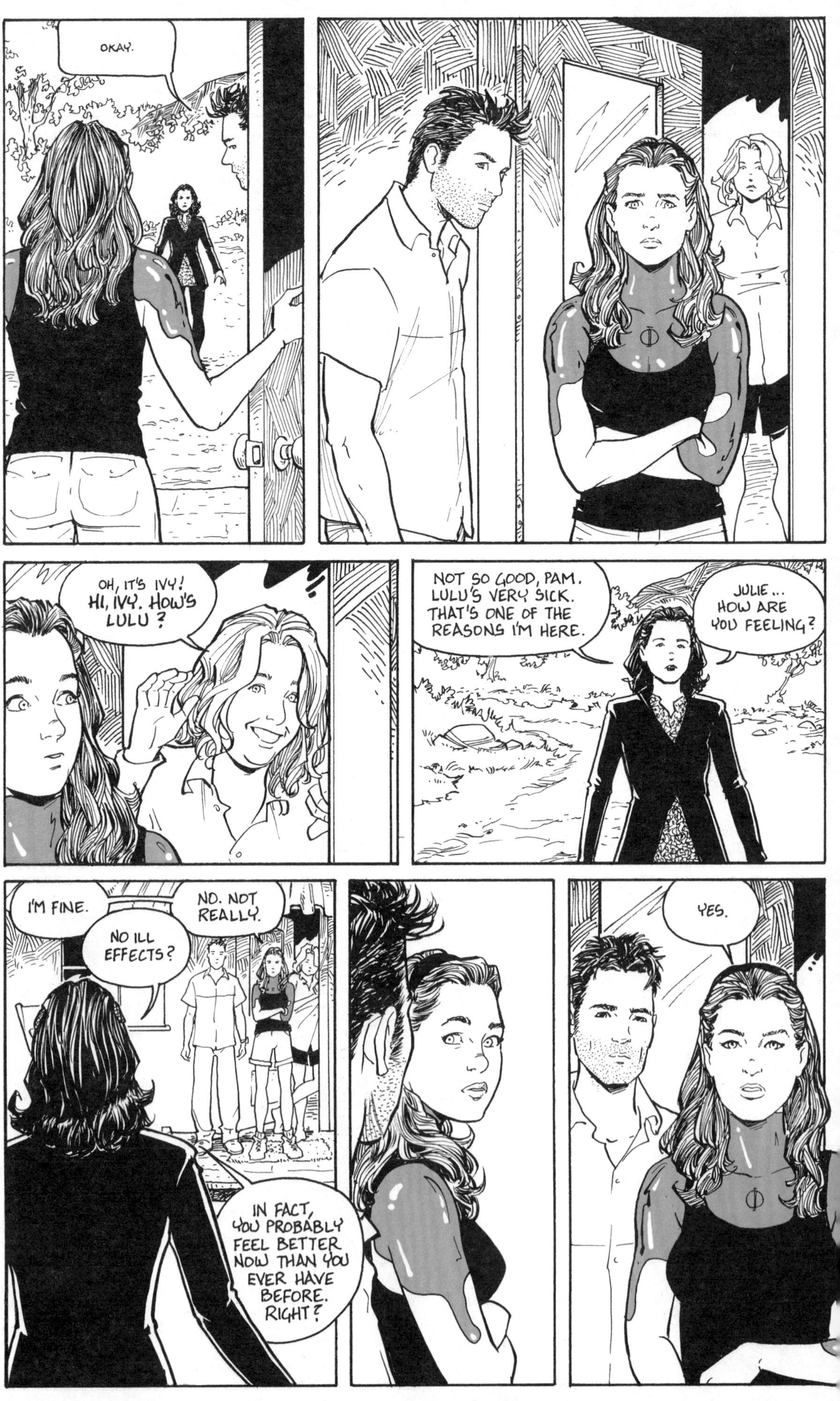
OKAY.
OH, IT'S IVY! HI, IVY. HOW'S LULU ?
NOT SO GOOD, PAM. LULU'S VERY SICK. THAT'S ONE OF THE REASONS I'M HERE.
JULIE... HOW ARE YOU FEELING?
I'M FINE.
NO ILL EFFECTS?
NO. NOT REALLY.
IN FACT, YOU PROBABLY FEEL BETTER NOW THAN YOU EVER HAVE BEFORE. RIGHT?
YES.

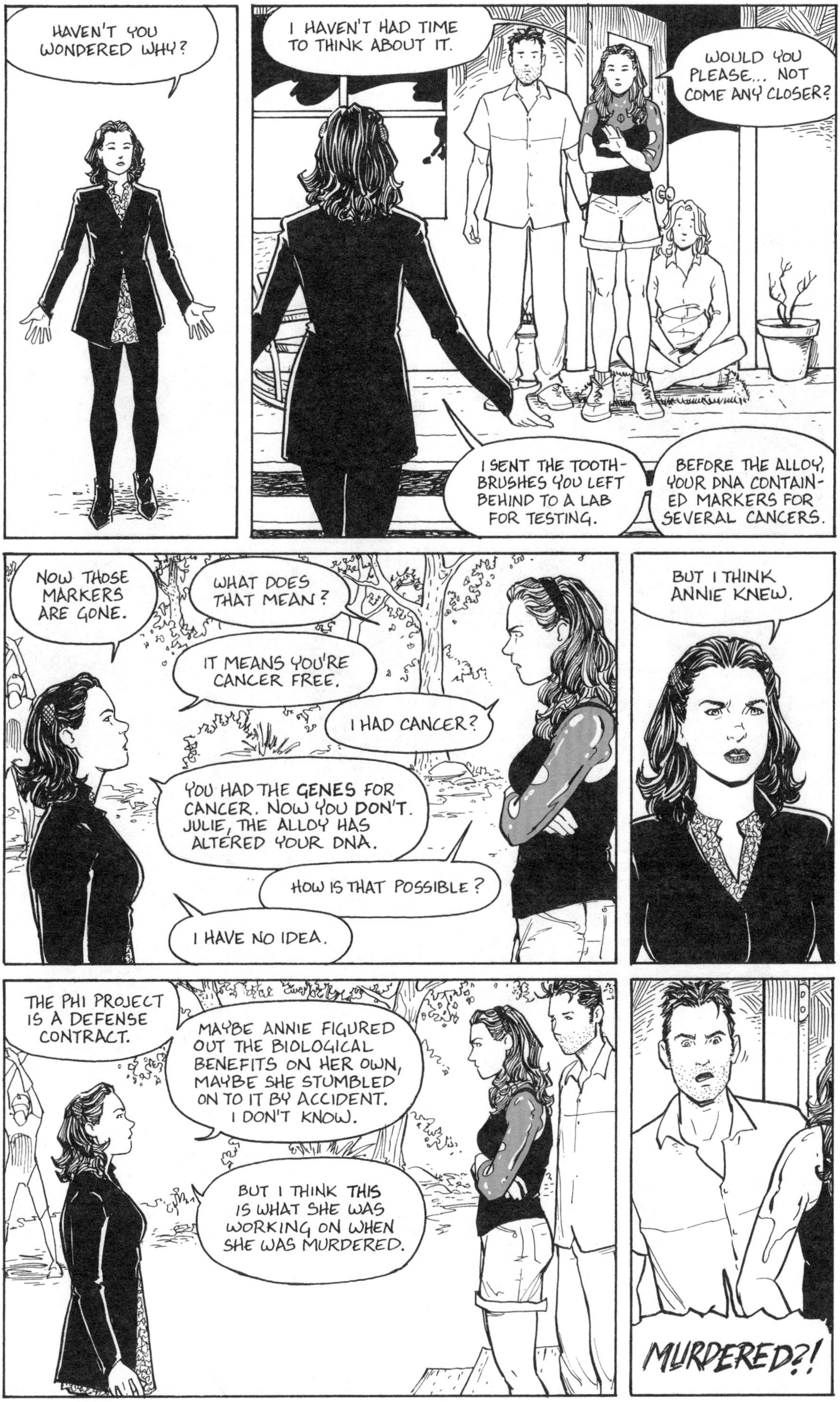
HAVEN'T YOU WONDERED WHY?
I HAVEN'T HAD TIME TO THINK ABOUT IT.
WOULD YOU PLEASE... NOT COME ANY CLOSER?
I SENT THE TOOTH-BRUSHES YOU LEFT BEHIND TO A LAB FOR TESTING.
BEFORE THE ALLOY, YOUR DNA CONTAIN-ED MARKERS FOR SEVERAL CANCERS.
NOW THOSE MARKERS ARE GONE.
WHAT DOES THAT MEAN?
IT MEANS YOU'RE CANCER FREE.
I HAD CANCER?
YOU HAD THE **GENES** FOR CANCER. NOW YOU **DON'T**. JULIE, THE ALLOY HAS ALTERED YOUR DNA.
HOW IS THAT POSSIBLE?
I HAVE NO IDEA.
BUT I THINK ANNIE KNEW.
THE PHI PROJECT IS A DEFENSE CONTRACT.
MAYBE ANNIE FIGURED OUT THE BIOLOGICAL BENEFITS ON HER OWN, MAYBE SHE STUMBLED ON TO IT BY ACCIDENT. I DON'T KNOW.
BUT I THINK **THIS** IS WHAT SHE WAS WORKING ON WHEN SHE WAS MURDERED.
MURDERED?!

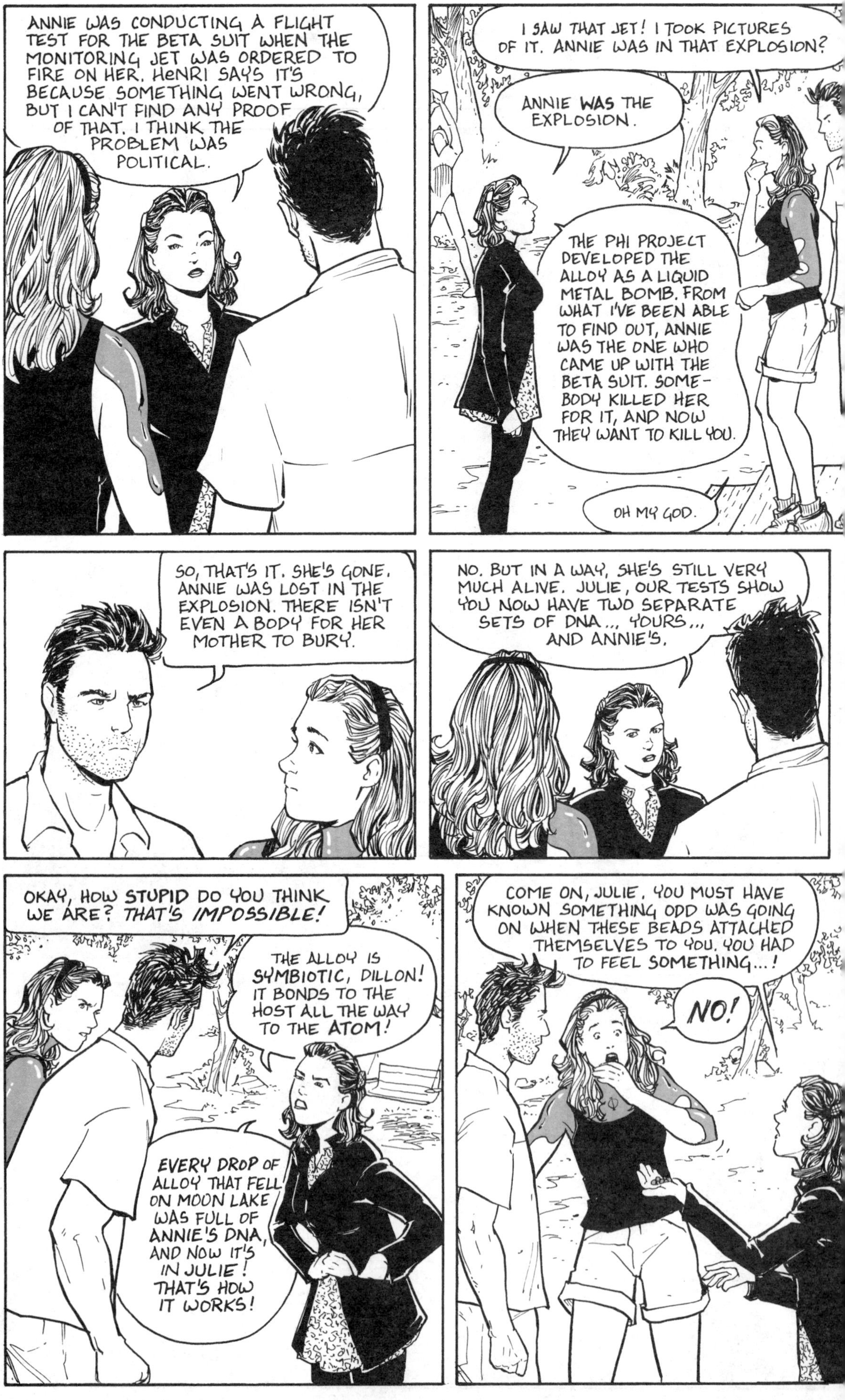
ANNIE WAS CONDUCTING A FLIGHT TEST FOR THE BETA SUIT WHEN THE MONITORING JET WAS ORDERED TO FIRE ON HER. HENRI SAYS IT'S BECAUSE SOMETHING WENT WRONG, BUT I CAN'T FIND ANY PROOF OF THAT. I THINK THE PROBLEM WAS POLITICAL.
I SAW THAT JET! I TOOK PICTURES OF IT. ANNIE WAS IN THAT EXPLOSION?
ANNIE **WAS** THE EXPLOSION.
THE PHI PROJECT DEVELOPED THE ALLOY AS A LIQUID METAL BOMB. FROM WHAT I'VE BEEN ABLE TO FIND OUT, ANNIE WAS THE ONE WHO CAME UP WITH THE BETA SUIT. SOMEBODY KILLED HER FOR IT, AND NOW THEY WANT TO KILL YOU.
OH MY GOD.
SO, THAT'S IT. SHE'S GONE. ANNIE WAS LOST IN THE EXPLOSION. THERE ISN'T EVEN A BODY FOR HER MOTHER TO BURY.
NO. BUT IN A WAY, SHE'S STILL VERY MUCH ALIVE. JULIE, OUR TESTS SHOW YOU NOW HAVE TWO SEPARATE SETS OF DNA..., YOURS..., AND ANNIE'S.
OKAY, HOW **STUPID** DO YOU THINK WE ARE? *THAT'S IMPOSSIBLE!*
THE ALLOY IS **SYMBIOTIC**, DILLON! IT BONDS TO THE HOST ALL THE WAY TO THE **ATOM**!
EVERY DROP OF ALLOY THAT FELL ON MOON LAKE WAS FULL OF **ANNIE'S DNA**, AND NOW IT'S IN **JULIE**! THAT'S HOW IT WORKS!
COME ON, JULIE. YOU MUST HAVE KNOWN SOMETHING ODD WAS GOING ON WHEN THESE BEADS ATTACHED THEMSELVES TO YOU. YOU HAD TO FEEL **SOMETHING**...!
NO!

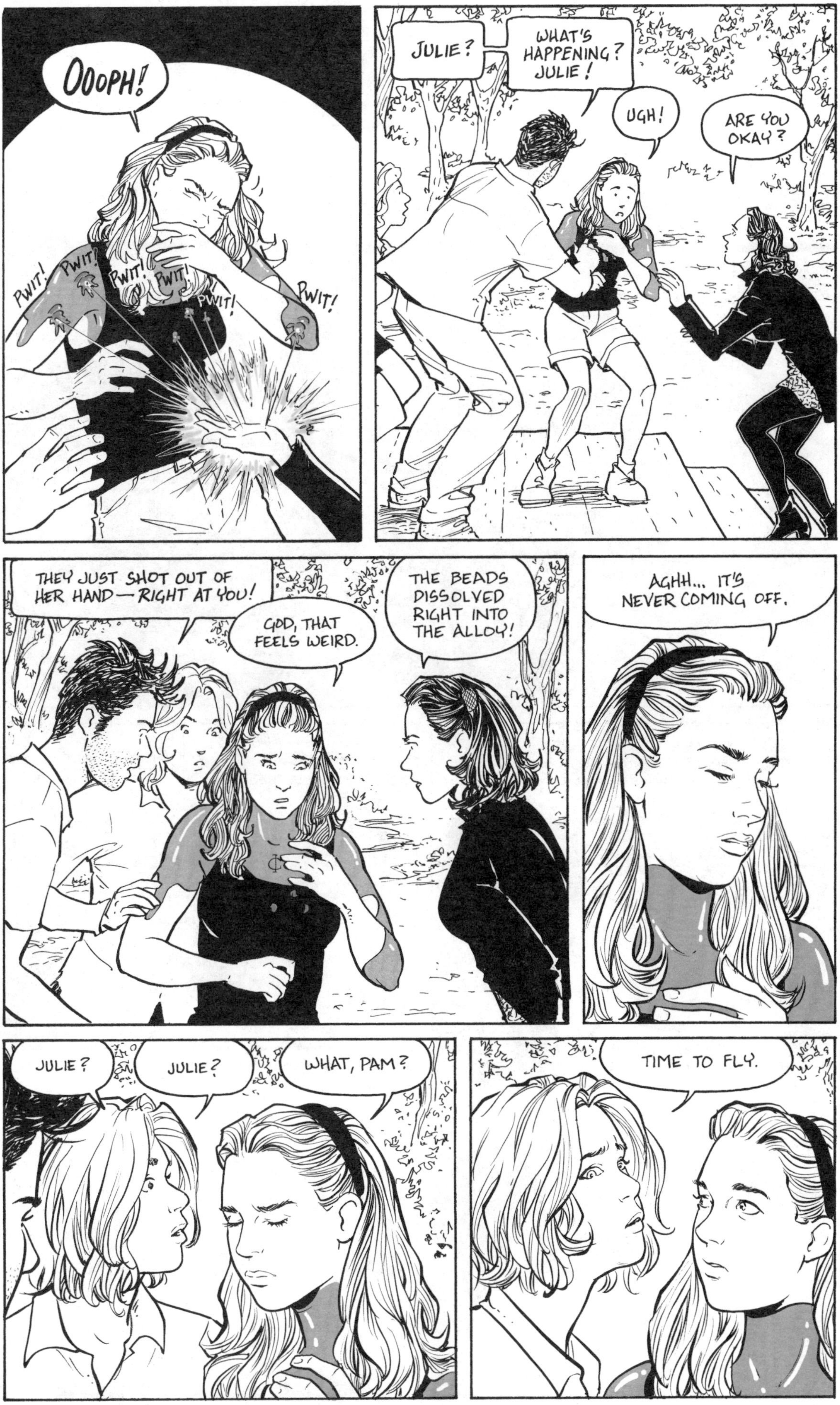
OOOPH!
PWIT! PWIT! PWIT! PWIT! PWIT! PWIT!
JULIE?
WHAT'S HAPPENING? JULIE!
UGH!
ARE YOU OKAY?
THEY JUST SHOT OUT OF HER HAND — RIGHT AT YOU!
GOD, THAT FEELS WEIRD.
THE BEADS DISSOLVED RIGHT INTO THE ALLOY!
AGHH... IT'S NEVER COMING OFF.
JULIE?
JULIE?
WHAT, PAM?
TIME TO FLY.

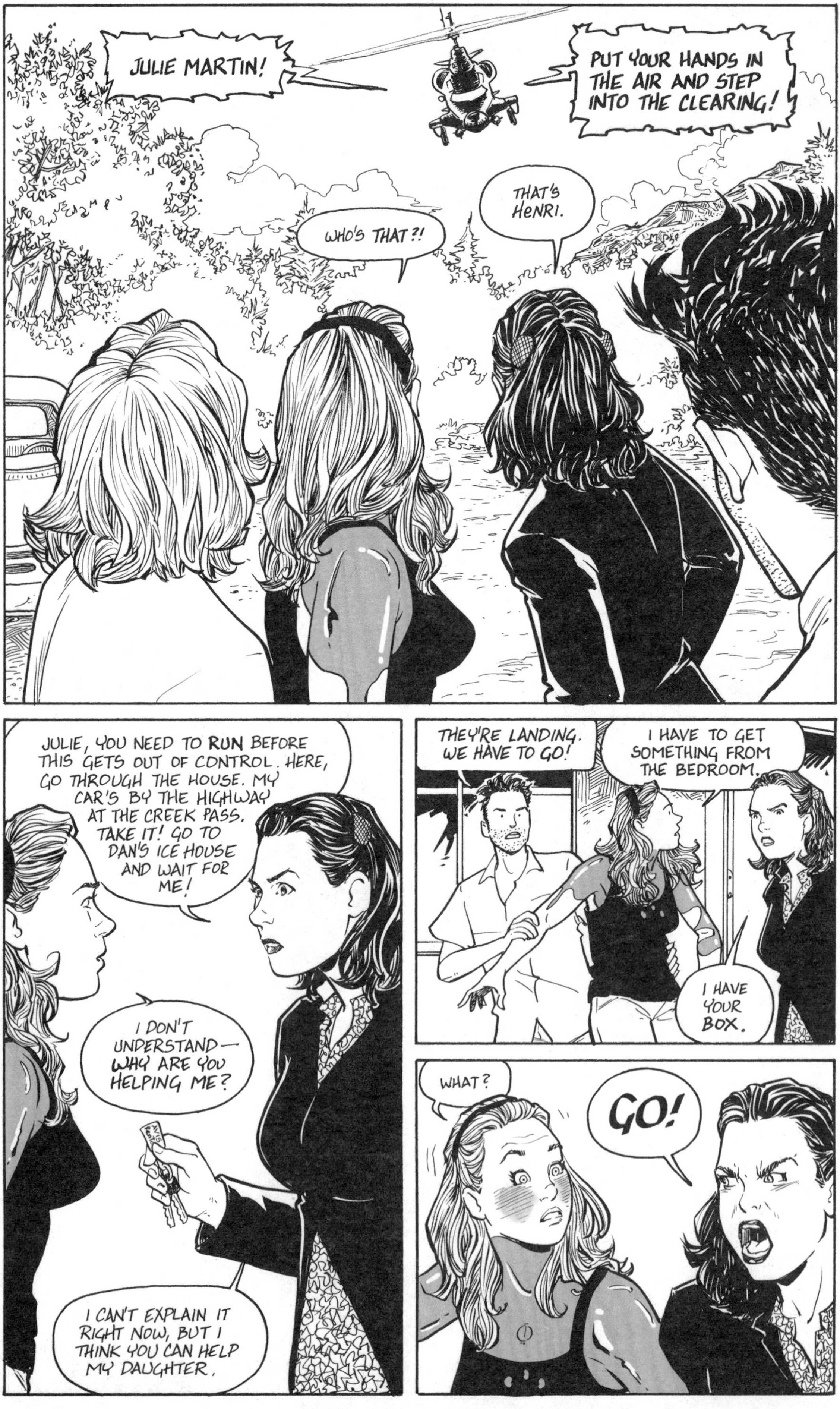
JULIE MARTIN!
PUT YOUR HANDS IN THE AIR AND STEP INTO THE CLEARING!
WHO'S THAT?!
THAT'S HENRI.
JULIE, YOU NEED TO RUN BEFORE THIS GETS OUT OF CONTROL. HERE, GO THROUGH THE HOUSE. MY CAR'S BY THE HIGHWAY AT THE CREEK PASS. TAKE IT! GO TO DAN'S ICE HOUSE AND WAIT FOR ME!
I DON'T UNDERSTAND— WHY ARE YOU HELPING ME?
I CAN'T EXPLAIN IT RIGHT NOW, BUT I THINK YOU CAN HELP MY DAUGHTER.
THEY'RE LANDING. WE HAVE TO GO!
I HAVE TO GET SOMETHING FROM THE BEDROOM.
I HAVE YOUR BOX.
WHAT?
GO!

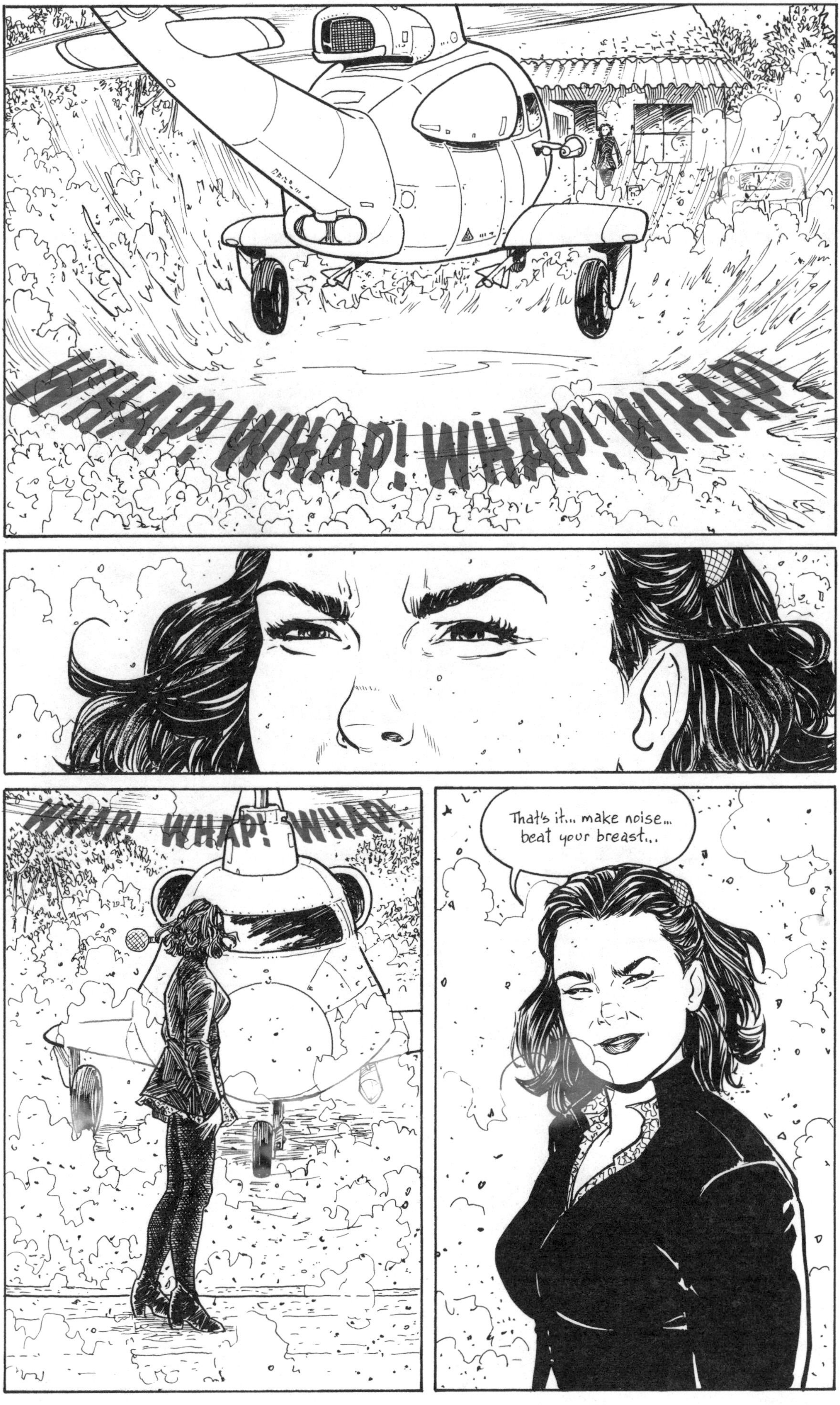
WHAP! WHAP! WHAP! WHAP!
WHAP! WHAP! WHAP!
That's it... make noise... beat your breast...

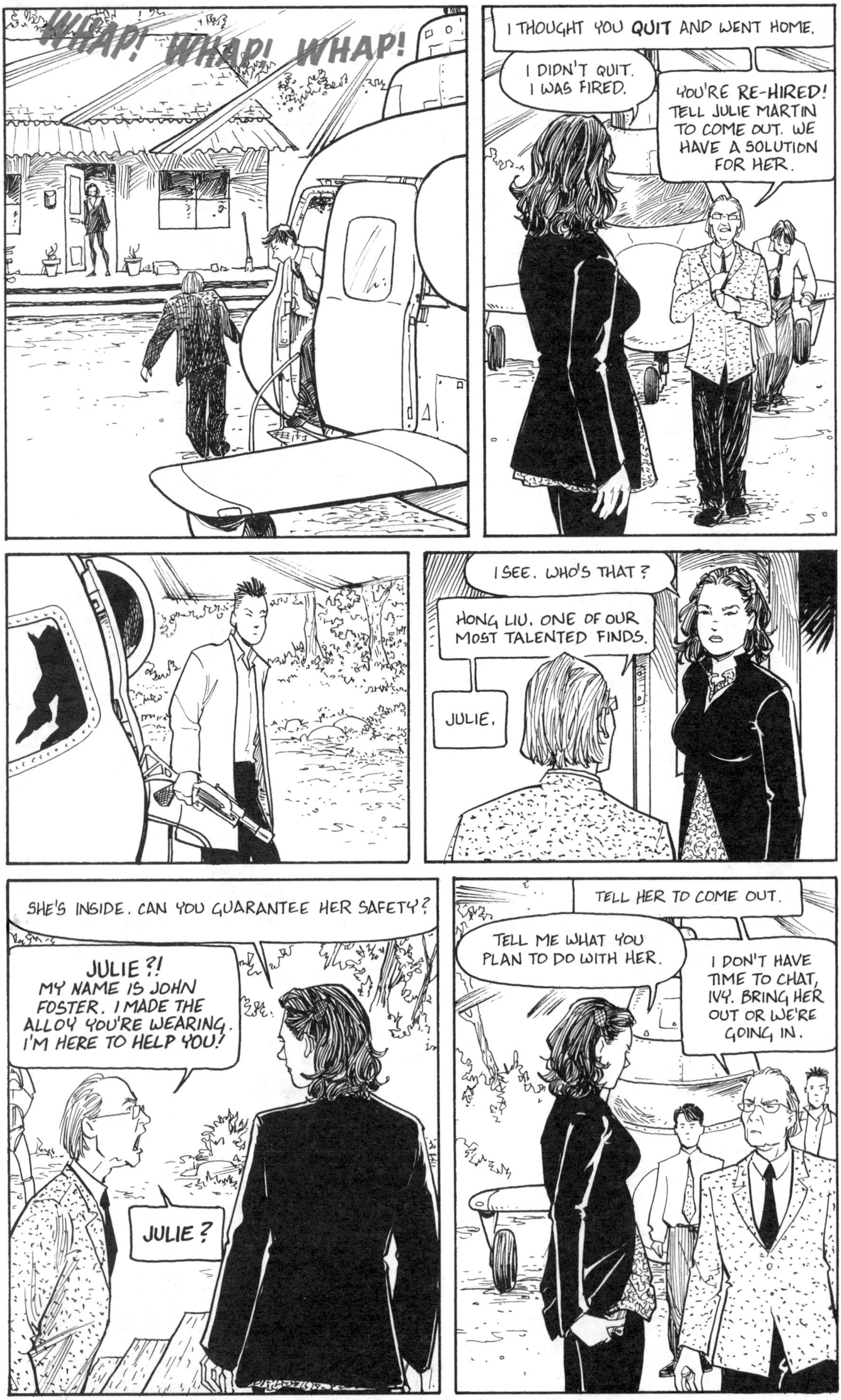
WHAP! WHAP! WHAP!
I THOUGHT YOU QUIT AND WENT HOME.
I DIDN'T QUIT. I WAS FIRED.
YOU'RE RE-HIRED! TELL JULIE MARTIN TO COME OUT. WE HAVE A SOLUTION FOR HER.
I SEE. WHO'S THAT?
HONG LIU. ONE OF OUR MOST TALENTED FINDS.
JULIE.
SHE'S INSIDE. CAN YOU GUARANTEE HER SAFETY?
JULIE?! MY NAME IS JOHN FOSTER. I MADE THE ALLOY YOU'RE WEARING. I'M HERE TO HELP YOU!
JULIE?
TELL HER TO COME OUT.
TELL ME WHAT YOU PLAN TO DO WITH HER.
I DON'T HAVE TIME TO CHAT, IVY. BRING HER OUT OR WE'RE GOING IN.

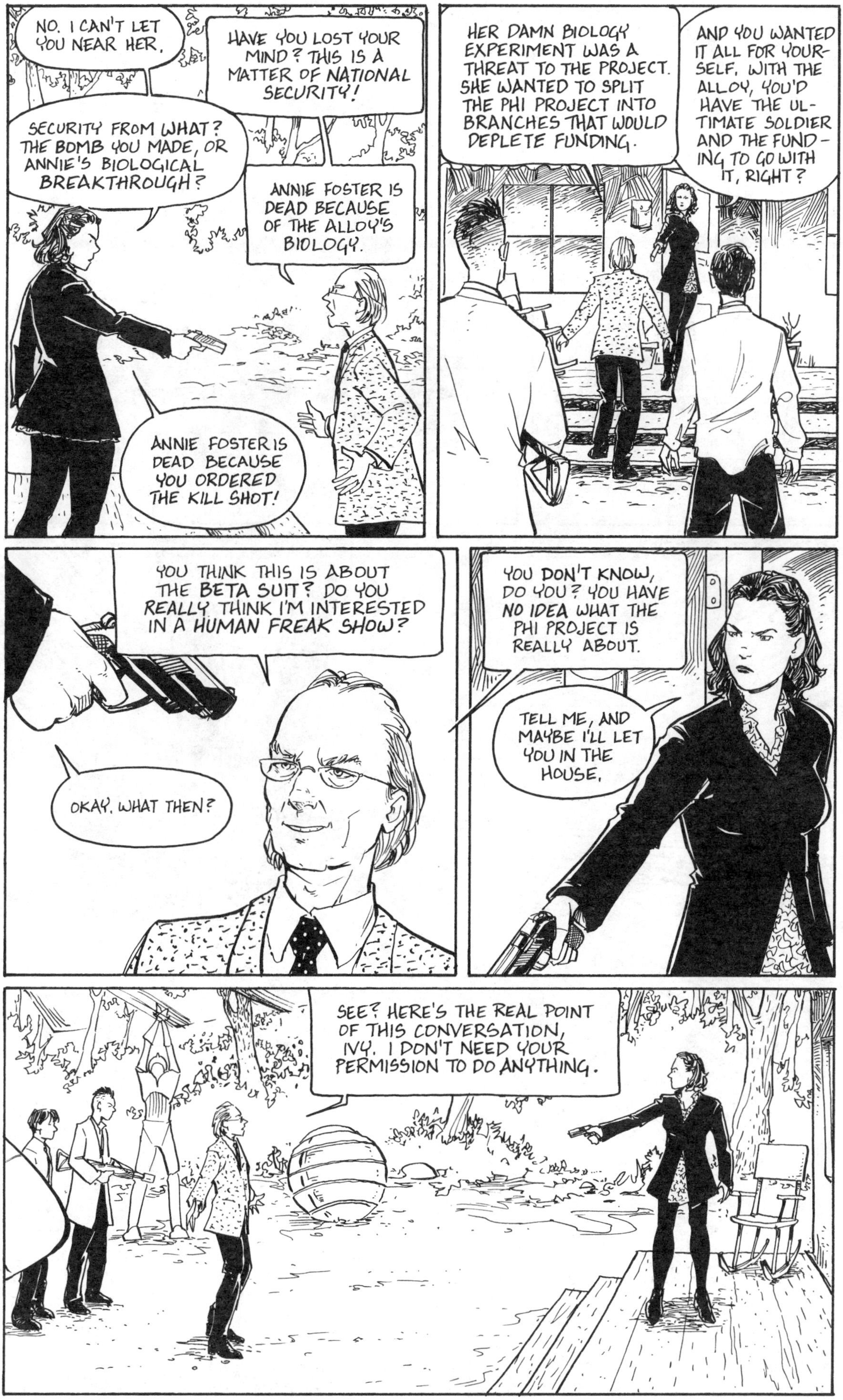
NO. I CAN'T LET YOU NEAR HER.
HAVE YOU LOST YOUR MIND? THIS IS A MATTER OF NATIONAL SECURITY!
SECURITY FROM WHAT? THE BOMB YOU MADE, OR ANNIE'S BIOLOGICAL BREAKTHROUGH?
ANNIE FOSTER IS DEAD BECAUSE OF THE ALLOY'S BIOLOGY.
ANNIE FOSTER IS DEAD BECAUSE YOU ORDERED THE KILL SHOT!
HER DAMN BIOLOGY EXPERIMENT WAS A THREAT TO THE PROJECT. SHE WANTED TO SPLIT THE PHI PROJECT INTO BRANCHES THAT WOULD DEPLETE FUNDING.
AND YOU WANTED IT ALL FOR YOURSELF. WITH THE ALLOY, YOU'D HAVE THE ULTIMATE SOLDIER AND THE FUNDING TO GO WITH IT, RIGHT?
YOU THINK THIS IS ABOUT THE BETA SUIT? DO YOU REALLY THINK I'M INTERESTED IN A HUMAN FREAK SHOW?
OKAY. WHAT THEN?
YOU DON'T KNOW, DO YOU? YOU HAVE NO IDEA WHAT THE PHI PROJECT IS REALLY ABOUT.
TELL ME, AND MAYBE I'LL LET YOU IN THE HOUSE.
SEE? HERE'S THE REAL POINT OF THIS CONVERSATION, IVY. I DON'T NEED YOUR PERMISSION TO DO ANYTHING.

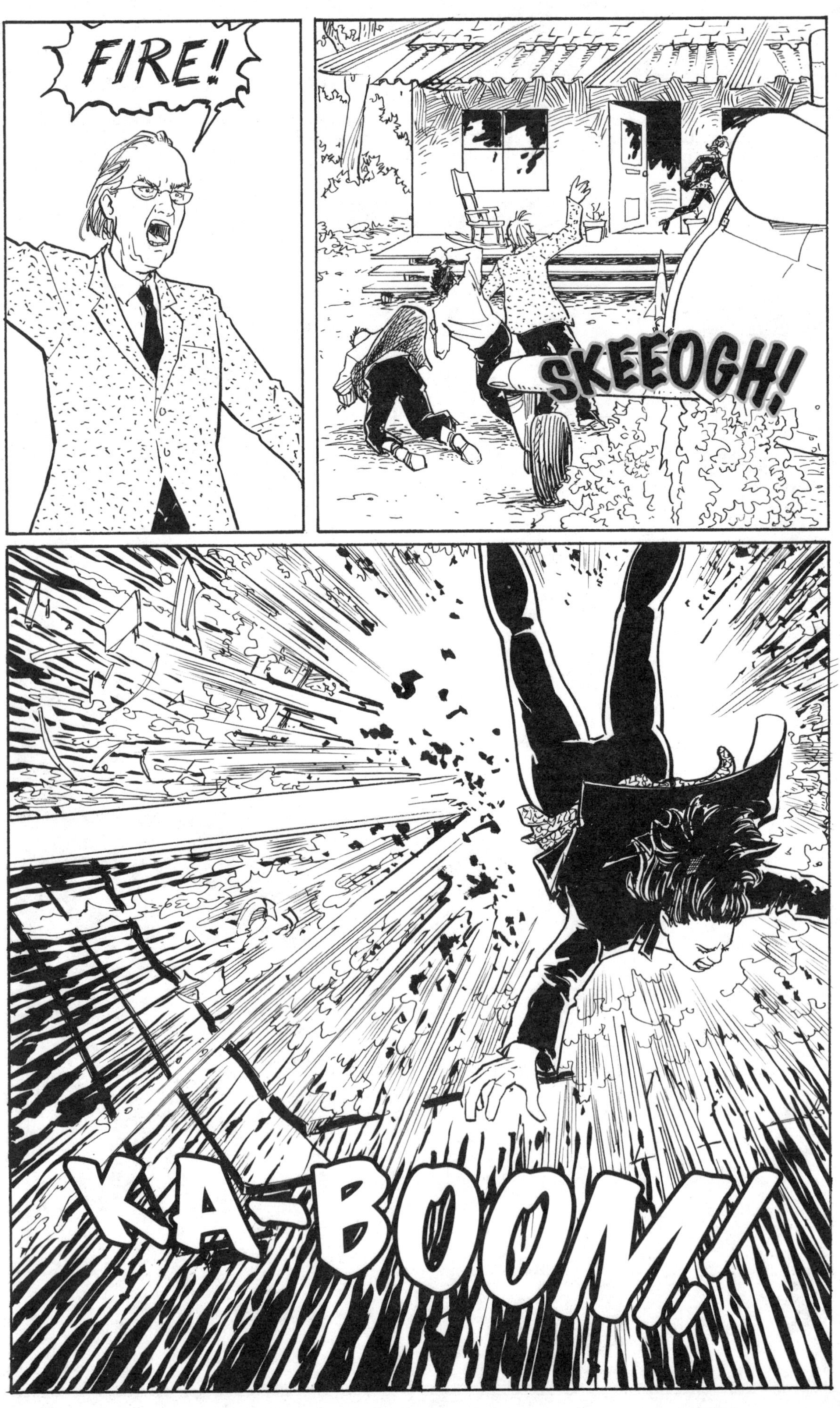
FIRE!
SKEEOGH!
KA-BOOM!!

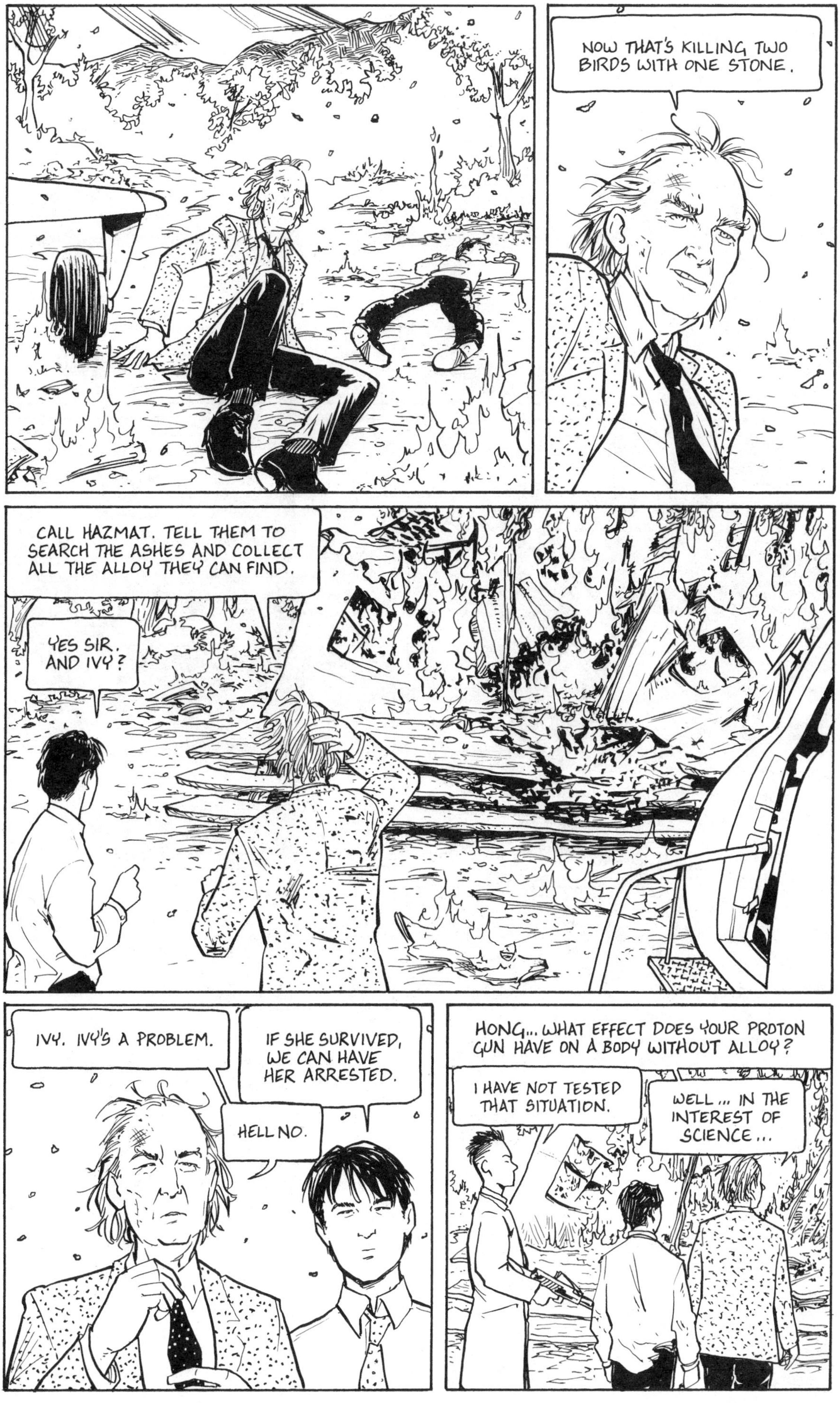
NOW THAT'S KILLING TWO BIRDS WITH ONE STONE.
CALL HAZMAT. TELL THEM TO SEARCH THE ASHES AND COLLECT ALL THE ALLOY THEY CAN FIND.
YES SIR. AND IVY?
IVY. IVY'S A PROBLEM.
IF SHE SURVIVED, WE CAN HAVE HER ARRESTED.
HELL NO.
HONG... WHAT EFFECT DOES YOUR PROTON GUN HAVE ON A BODY WITHOUT ALLOY?
I HAVE NOT TESTED THAT SITUATION.
WELL... IN THE INTEREST OF SCIENCE...

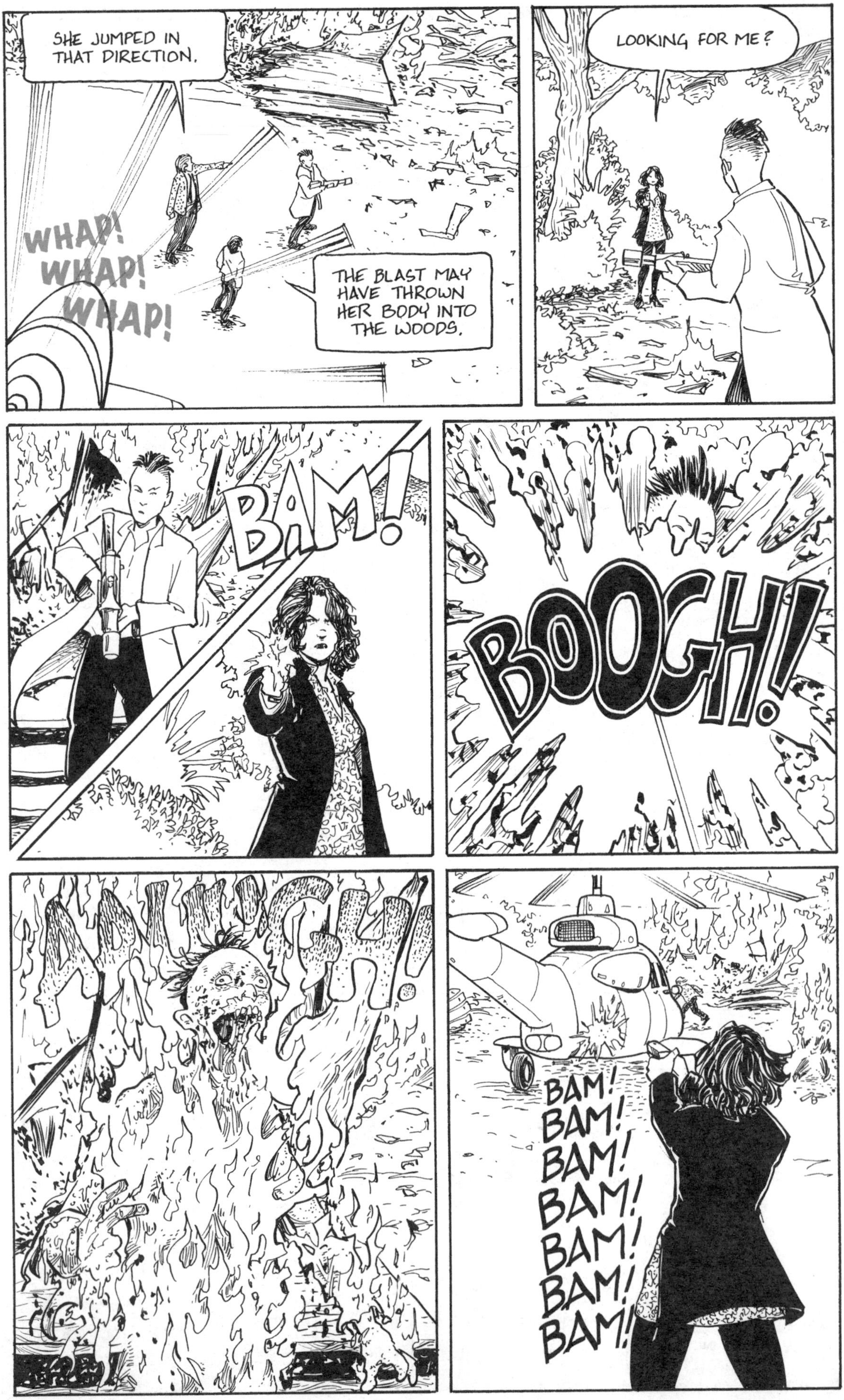
SHE JUMPED IN THAT DIRECTION.
WHAP! WHAP! WHAP!
THE BLAST MAY HAVE THROWN HER BODY INTO THE WOODS.
LOOKING FOR ME?
BAM!
BOOGH!
BAM! BAM! BAM! BAM! BAM! BAM! BAM!

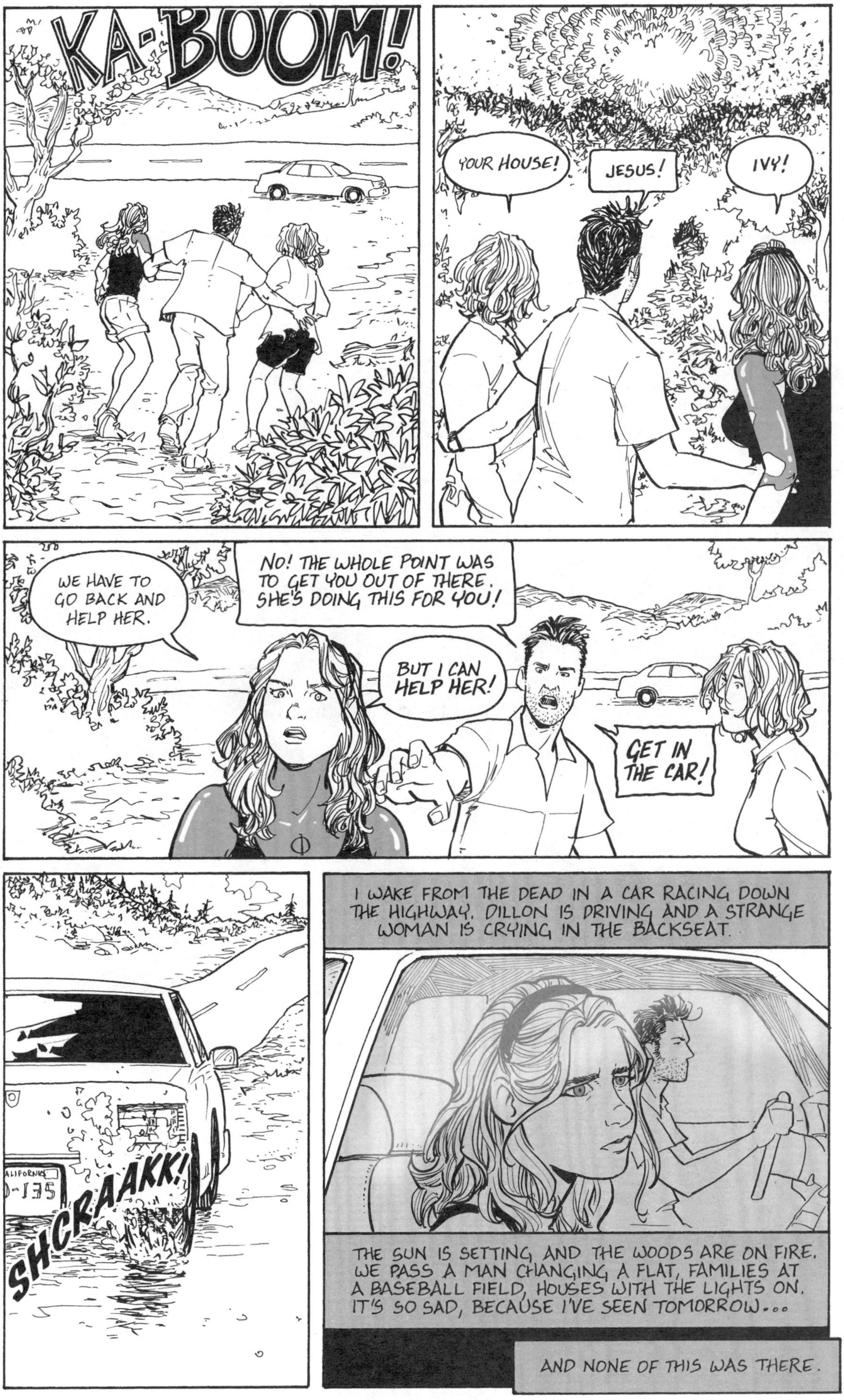
KA-BOOM!
YOUR HOUSE!
JESUS!
IVY!
WE HAVE TO GO BACK AND HELP HER.
NO! THE WHOLE POINT WAS TO GET YOU OUT OF THERE. SHE'S DOING THIS FOR YOU!
BUT I CAN HELP HER!
GET IN THE CAR!
CALIFORNIA
SHCRAAKK!
I WAKE FROM THE DEAD IN A CAR RACING DOWN THE HIGHWAY. DILLON IS DRIVING AND A STRANGE WOMAN IS CRYING IN THE BACKSEAT.
THE SUN IS SETTING AND THE WOODS ARE ON FIRE. WE PASS A MAN CHANGING A FLAT, FAMILIES AT A BASEBALL FIELD, HOUSES WITH THE LIGHTS ON. IT'S SO SAD, BECAUSE I'VE SEEN TOMORROW...
AND NONE OF THIS WAS THERE.

Books by Terry Moore

Echo: Moon Lake

Echo: Atomic Dreams

Strangers In Paradise